YOUR PERSONAL
HOROSCOPE
2020

JOSEPH POLANSKY

YOUR PERSONAL HOROSCOPE 2020

Month-by-month
forecast for every sign

Thorsons

The author is grateful to the people
of STAR ★ DATA, who truly fathered
this book and without whom it
could not have been written.

Thorsons
An imprint of HarperCollins*Publishers*
1 London Bridge Street
London SE1 9GF

www.harpercollins.co.uk

First published by Thorsons 2019

3 5 7 9 10 8 6 4

A catalogue record for this book is
available from the British Library

ISBN 978-0-00-831929-8

Printed and bound in Great Britain by
CPI Group (UK) Ltd, Croydon, CR0 4YY

MIX
Paper from
responsible sources
FSC™ C007454

FSC
www.fsc.org

Contents

Introduction

Welcome to the fascinating and intricate world of astrology!

For thousands of years the movements of the planets and other heavenly bodies have intrigued the best minds of every generation. Life holds no greater challenge or joy than this: knowledge of ourselves and the universe we live in. Astrology is one of the keys to this knowledge.

Your Personal Horoscope 2020 gives you the fruits of astrological wisdom. In addition to general guidance on your character and the basic trends of your life, it shows you how to take advantage of planetary influences so you can make the most of the year ahead.

The section on each sign includes a Personality Profile, a look at general trends for 2020, and in-depth month-by-month forecasts. The Glossary (page 5) explains some of the astrological terms you may be unfamiliar with.

One of the many helpful features of this book is the 'Best' and 'Most Stressful' days listed at the beginning of each monthly forecast. Read these sections to learn which days in each month will be good overall, good for money, and good for love. Mark them on your calendar – these will be your best days. Similarly, make a note of the days that will be most stressful for you. It is best to avoid booking important meetings or taking major decisions on these days, as well as on those days when important planets in your horoscope are retrograde (moving backwards through the zodiac).

The Major Trends section for your sign lists those days when your vitality is strong or weak, or when relationships with your co-workers or loved ones may need a bit more effort on your part. If you are going through a difficult time, take a look at the colour, metal, gem and scent listed in the 'At a Glance' section of your Personality Profile. Wearing a piece of jewellery that contains your metal and/or gem will strengthen your vitality, just as wearing clothes or decorating your room or office in the colour ruled by your sign, drinking teas made from the herbs ruled by your sign or wearing the scents associated with your sign will sustain you.

Another important virtue of this book is that it will help you to know not only yourself but those around you: your friends, co-workers, partners and/or children. Reading the Personality Profile and forecasts for their signs will provide you with an insight into their behaviour that you won't get anywhere else. You will know when to be more tolerant of them and when they are liable to be difficult or irritable.

In this edition we have included foot reflexology charts as part of the health section. So many health problems could perhaps be avoided or alleviated if we understood which organs were most vulnerable and what we could do to protect them. Though there are many natural and drug-free ways to strengthen vulnerable organs, these charts show a valid way to proceed. The vulnerable organs for the year ahead are clearly marked in the charts. It's very good to massage the whole foot on a regular basis, as the feet contain reflexes to the entire body. Try to pay special attention to the specific areas marked in the charts. If this is done diligently, health problems can be avoided. And even if they can't be completely avoided, their impact can be softened considerably.

I consider you – the reader – my personal client. By studying your Solar Horoscope I gain an awareness of what is going on in your life – what you are feeling and striving for and the challenges you face. I then do my best to address these concerns. Consider this book the next best thing to having your own personal astrologer!

It is my sincere hope that *Your Personal Horoscope 2020* will enhance the quality of your life, make things easier, illuminate the way forward, banish obscurities and make you more aware of your personal connection to the universe. Understood properly and used wisely, astrology is a great guide to knowing yourself, the people around you and the events in your life – but remember that what you do with these insights – the final result – is up to you.

A Note on the 'New Zodiac'

Recently an article was published that postulated two things: the discovery of a new constellation – Ophiuchus – making a thirteenth constellation in the heavens and thus a thirteenth sign, and the statement that because the Earth has shifted relative to the constellations in the past few thousand years, all the signs have shifted backwards by one sign. This has caused much consternation, and I have received a stream of letters, emails and phone calls from people saying things like: 'I don't want to be a Taurus, I'm happy being a Gemini', 'What's my real sign?' or 'Now that I finally understand myself, I'm not who I think I am!'

All of this is 'much ado about nothing'. The article has some partial truth to it. Yes, in two thousand years the planets have shifted relative to the constellations in the heavens. This is old news. We know this and Hindu astrologers take this into account when casting charts. This shift doesn't affect Western astrologers in North America and Europe. We use what is called a 'tropical' zodiac. This zodiac has nothing to do with the constellations in the heavens. They have the same names, but that's about it. The tropical zodiac is based on the Earth's revolution around the Sun. Imagine the circle that this orbit makes, then divide this circle by twelve and you have our zodiac. The Spring Equinox is always 0 degrees (Aries), and the Autumn Equinox is always 0 degrees Libra (180 degrees from 0 Aries). At one time a few thousand years ago, these tropical signs coincided with the actual constellations; they were pretty much interchangeable, and it didn't matter what zodiac you used. But in the course of thousands of years the planets have shifted relative to these constellations. Here in the West it doesn't affect our practice one iota. You are still the sign you always were.

In North America and Europe there is a clear distinction between an astrological sign and a constellation in the heavens. This issue is more of a problem for Hindu astrologers. Their zodiac is based on the actual constellations – this is called the 'sidereal' zodiac. And Hindu astrologers have been accounting for this shift all the time. They keep close tabs on it. In two thousand years there is a shift of 23 degrees, and they subtract this from the Western calculations. So in their system many a Gemini would be a Taurus and this is true for all the signs. This is nothing new – it is all known and accounted for, so there is no bombshell here.

The so-called thirteenth constellation, Ophiuchus, is also not a problem for the Western astrologer. As we mentioned, our zodiac has nothing to do with the constellations. It could be more of a problem for the Hindus, but my feeling is that it's not a problem for them either. What these astronomers are calling a new constellation was probably considered a part of one of the existing constellations. I don't know this as a fact, but I presume it is so intuitively. I'm sure we will soon be getting articles by Hindu astrologers explaining this.

Glossary of Astrological Terms

Ascendant

We experience day and night because the Earth rotates on its axis once every 24 hours. It is because of this rotation that the Sun, Moon and planets seem to rise and set. The zodiac is a fixed belt (imaginary, but very real in spiritual terms) around the Earth. As the Earth rotates, the different signs of the zodiac seem to the observer to rise on the horizon. During a 24-hour period every sign of the zodiac will pass this horizon point at some time or another. The sign that is at the horizon point at any given time is called the Ascendant, or rising sign. The Ascendant is the sign denoting a person's self-image, body and self-concept – the personal ego, as opposed to the spiritual ego indicated by a person's Sun sign.

Aspects

Aspects are the angular relationships between planets, the way in which one planet stimulates or influences another. If a planet makes a harmonious aspect (connection) to another, it tends to stimulate that planet in a positive and helpful way. If, however, it makes a stressful aspect to another planet, this disrupts that planet's normal influence.

Astrological Qualities

There are three astrological qualities: *cardinal, fixed* and *mutable*. Each of the 12 signs of the zodiac falls into one of these three categories.

Cardinal Signs

Aries, Cancer, Libra and Capricorn

The cardinal quality is the active, initiating principle. Those born under these four signs are good at starting new projects.

Fixed Signs

Taurus, Leo, Scorpio and Aquarius

Fixed qualities include stability, persistence, endurance and perfectionism. People born under these four signs are good at seeing things through.

Mutable Signs

Gemini, Virgo, Sagittarius and Pisces

Mutable qualities are adaptability, changeability and balance. Those born under these four signs are creative, if not always practical.

Direct Motion

When the planets move forward through the zodiac – as they normally do – they are said to be going 'direct'.

Grand Square

A Grand Square differs from a normal Square (usually two planets separated by 90 degrees) in that four or more planets are involved. When you look at the pattern in a chart you will see a whole and complete square. This, though stressful, usually denotes a new mani-festation in the life. There is much work and balancing involved in the manifestation.

Grand Trine

A Grand Trine differs from a normal Trine (where two planets are 120 degrees apart) in that three or more planets are involved. When you look at this pattern in a chart, it takes the form of a complete triangle – a Grand Trine. Usually (but not always) it occurs in one of the four elements: Fire, Earth, Air or Water. Thus the particular element in which it occurs will be highlighted. A Grand Trine in Water is not the same as a Grand Trine in Air or Fire, etc. This is a very fortunate and happy aspect, and quite rare.

Houses

There are 12 signs of the zodiac and 12 houses of experience. The 12 signs are personality types and ways in which a given planet expresses itself; the 12 houses show 'where' in your life this expression takes place. Each house has a different area of interest. A house can become potent and important – a house of power – in different ways: if it contains the Sun, the Moon or the 'ruler' of your chart; if it contains more than one planet; or if the ruler of that house is receiving unusual stimulation from other planets.

1st House
Personal Image and Sensual Delights

2nd House
Money/Finance

3rd House
Communication and Intellectual Interests

4th House
Home and Family

5th House
Children, Fun, Games, Creativity, Speculations and Love Affairs

6th House
Health and Work

7th House
Love, Marriage and Social Activities

8th House
Transformation and Regeneration

9th House
Religion, Foreign Travel, Higher Education and Philosophy

10th House
Career

11th House
Friends, Group Activities and Fondest Wishes

12th House
Spirituality

Karma

Karma is the law of cause and effect which governs all phenomena. We are all where we find ourselves because of karma – because of actions we have performed in the past. The universe is such a balanced instrument that any act immediately sets corrective forces into motion – karma.

Long-term Planets

The planets that take a long time to move through a sign show the long-term trends in a given area of life. They are important for forecasting the prolonged view of things. Because these planets stay in one sign for so long, there are periods in the year when the faster-moving (short-term) planets will join them, further activating and enhancing the importance of a given house.

Jupiter
stays in a sign for about 1 year

Saturn
2½ years

Uranus
7 years

Neptune
14 years

Pluto
15 to 30 years

Lunar

Relating to the Moon. See also 'Phases of the Moon', below.

Natal

Literally means 'birth'. In astrology this term is used to distinguish between planetary positions that occurred at the time of a person's birth (natal) and those that are current (transiting). For example, Natal Sun refers to where the Sun was when you were born; transiting Sun refers to where the Sun's position is currently at any given moment – which usually doesn't coincide with your birth, or Natal, Sun.

Out of Bounds

The planets move through the zodiac at various angles relative to the celestial equator (if you were to draw an imaginary extension of the Earth's equator out into the universe, you would have an illustration of this celestial equator). The Sun – being the most dominant and powerful influence in the Solar system – is the measure astrologers use as a standard. The Sun never goes more than approximately 23 degrees north or south of the celestial equator. At the winter solstice the Sun reaches its maximum southern angle of orbit (declination); at the summer solstice it reaches its maximum northern angle. Any time a planet exceeds this Solar boundary – and occasionally planets do – it is said to be 'out of bounds'. This means that the planet exceeds or tres-passes into strange territory – beyond the limits allowed by the Sun, the ruler of the Solar system. The planet in this condition becomes more emphasized and exceeds its authority, becoming an important influence in the forecast.

Phases of the Moon

After the full Moon, the Moon seems to shrink in size (as perceived from the Earth), gradually growing smaller until it is virtually invisible to the naked eye – at the time of the next new Moon. This is called the waning Moon phase, or the waning Moon.

After the new Moon, the Moon gradually gets bigger in size (as perceived from the Earth) until it reaches its maximum size at the time of the full Moon. This period is called the waxing Moon phase, or waxing Moon.

Retrogrades

The planets move around the Sun at different speeds. Mercury and Venus move much faster than the Earth, while Mars, Jupiter, Saturn, Uranus, Neptune and Pluto move more slowly. Thus there are times when, relative to the Earth, the planets appear to be going backwards. In reality they are always going forward, but relative to our vantage point on Earth they seem to go backwards through the zodiac for a period of time. This is called 'retrograde' motion and tends to weaken the normal influence of a given planet.

Short-term Planets

The fast-moving planets move so quickly through a sign that their effects are generally of a short-term nature. They reflect the immediate, day-to-day trends in a horoscope.

Moon
stays in a sign for only 2½ days

Mercury
20 to 30 days

Sun
30 days

Venus
approximately 1 month

Mars
approximately 2 months

T-square

A T-square differs from a Grand Square (see page 6) in that it is not a complete square. If you look at the pattern in a chart it appears as 'half a complete square', resembling the T-square tools used by architects and designers. If you cut a complete square in half, diagonally, you have a T-square. Many astrologers consider this more stressful than a Grand Square, as it creates tension that is difficult to resolve. T-squares bring learning experiences.

Transits

This term refers to the movements or motions of the planets at any given time. Astrologers use the word 'transit' to make the distinction between a birth, or Natal, planet (see 'Natal', page 9) and the planet's current movement in the heavens. For example, if at your birth Saturn was in the sign of Cancer in your 8th house, but is now moving through your 3rd house, it is said to be 'transiting' your 3rd house. Transits are one of the main tools with which astrologers forecast trends.

Aries

THE RAM

Birthdays from
21st March to
20th April

Personality Profile

ARIES AT A GLANCE

Element – Fire

Ruling Planet – Mars
  Career Planet – Saturn
  Love Planet – Venus
  Money Planet – Venus
  Planet of Fun, Entertainment, Creativity and Speculations – Sun
  Planet of Health and Work – Mercury
  Planet of Home and Family Life – Moon
  Planet of Spirituality – Neptune
  Planet of Travel, Education, Religion and Philosophy – Jupiter

Colours – carmine, red, scarlet

Colours that promote love, romance and social harmony – green, jade green

Colour that promotes earning power – green

Gem – amethyst

Metals – iron, steel

Scent – honeysuckle

Quality – cardinal (= activity)

Quality most needed for balance – caution

Strongest virtues – abundant physical energy, courage, honesty, independence, self-reliance

Deepest need – action

Characteristics to avoid – haste, impetuousness, over-aggression, rashness

Signs of greatest overall compatibility – Leo, Sagittarius

Signs of greatest overall incompatibility – Cancer, Libra, Capricorn

Sign most helpful to career – Capricorn

Sign most helpful for emotional support – Cancer

Sign most helpful financially – Taurus

Sign best for marriage and/or partnerships – Libra

Sign most helpful for creative projects – Leo

Best Sign to have fun with – Leo

Signs most helpful in spiritual matters – Sagittarius, Pisces

Best day of the week – Tuesday

Understanding an Aries

Aries is the activist *par excellence* of the zodiac. The Aries need for action is almost an addiction, and those who do not really understand the Aries personality would probably use this hard word to describe it. In reality 'action' is the essence of the Aries psychology – the more direct, blunt and to-the-point the action, the better. When you think about it, this is the ideal psychological makeup for the warrior, the pioneer, the athlete or the manager.

Aries likes to get things done, and in their passion and zeal often lose sight of the consequences for themselves and others. Yes, they often try to be diplomatic and tactful, but it is hard for them. When they do so they feel that they are being dishonest and phoney. It is hard for them even to understand the mindset of the diplomat, the consensus builder, the front office executive. These people are involved in endless meetings, discussions, talks and negotiations – all of which seem a great waste of time when there is so much work to be done, so many real achievements to be gained. An Aries can understand, once it is explained, that talk and negotiations – the social graces – lead ultimately to better, more effective actions. The interesting thing is that an Aries is rarely malicious or spiteful – even when waging war. Aries people fight without hate for their opponents. To them it is all good-natured fun, a grand adventure, a game.

When confronted with a problem many people will say, 'Well, let's think about it, let's analyse the situation.' But not an Aries. An Aries will think, 'Something must be done. Let's get on with it.' Of course neither response is the total answer. Sometimes action is called for, sometimes cool thought. But an Aries tends to err on the side of action.

Action and thought are radically different principles. Physical activity is the use of brute force. Thinking and deliberating require one not to use force – to be still. It is not good for the athlete to be deliberating the next move; this will only slow down his or her reaction time. The athlete must act instinctively and instantly. This is how Aries people tend to behave in life. They are quick, instinctive decision-makers and their decisions tend to be translated into action almost immediately. When their intuition is sharp and well tuned, their actions are powerful and successful. When their intuition is off, their actions can be disastrous.

Do not think this will scare an Aries. Just as a good warrior knows that in the course of combat he or she might acquire a few wounds, so too does an Aries realize – somewhere deep down – that in the course of being true to yourself you might get embroiled in a disaster or two. It is all part of the game. An Aries feels strong enough to weather any storm.

There are many Aries people who are intellectual. They make powerful and creative thinkers. But even in this realm they tend to be pioneers – outspoken and blunt. These types of Aries tend to elevate (or sublimate) their desire for physical combat in favour of intellectual, mental combat. And they are indeed powerful.

In general, Aries people have a faith in themselves that others could learn from. This basic, rock-solid faith carries them through the most tumultuous situations of life. Their courage and self-confidence make them natural leaders. Their leadership is more by way of example than by actually controlling others.

Finance

Aries people often excel as builders or estate agents. Money in and of itself is not as important as are other things – action, adventure, sport, etc. They are motivated by the need to support and be well-thought-of by their partners. Money as a way of attaining pleasure is another important motivation. Aries function best in their own businesses or as managers of their own departments within a large business or corporation. The fewer orders they have to take from higher up, the better. They also function better out in the field rather than behind a desk.

Aries people are hard workers with a lot of endurance; they can earn large sums of money due to the strength of their sheer physical energy.

Venus is their money planet, which means that Aries need to develop more of the social graces in order to realize their full earning potential. Just getting the job done – which is what an Aries excels at – is not enough to create financial success. The co-operation of others needs to be attained. Customers, clients and co-workers need to be made to feel comfortable; many people need to be treated properly in order for success to happen. When Aries people develop these abilities – or hire someone to do this for them – their financial potential is unlimited.

Career and Public Image

One would think that a pioneering type would want to break with the social and political conventions of society. But this is not so with the Aries-born. They are pioneers within conventional limits, in the sense that they like to start their own businesses within an established industry.

Capricorn is on the 10th house of career cusp of Aries' solar horoscope. Saturn is the planet that rules their life's work and professional aspirations. This tells us some interesting things about the Aries character. First off, it shows that, in order for Aries people to reach their full career potential, they need to develop some qualities that are a bit alien to their basic nature: they need to become better administrators and organizers; they need to be able to handle details better and to take a long-range view of their projects and their careers in general. No one can beat an Aries when it comes to achieving short-range objectives, but a career is long term, built over time. You cannot take a 'quickie' approach to it.

Some Aries people find it difficult to stick with a project until the end. Since they get bored quickly and are in constant pursuit of new adventures, they prefer to pass an old project or task on to somebody else in order to start something new. Those Aries who learn how to put off the search for something new until the old is completed will achieve great success in their careers and professional lives.

In general, Aries people like society to judge them on their own merits, on their real and actual achievements. A reputation acquired by 'hype' feels false to them.

Love and Relationships

In marriage and partnerships Aries like those who are more passive, gentle, tactful and diplomatic – people who have the social grace and skills they sometimes lack. Our partners always represent a hidden part of ourselves – a self that we cannot express personally.

An Aries tends to go after what he or she likes aggressively. The tendency is to jump into relationships and marriages. This is especially true if Venus is in Aries as well as the Sun. If an Aries likes you, he or she will have a hard time taking no for an answer; many attempts will be made to sweep you off your feet.

Though Aries can be exasperating in relationships – especially if they are not understood by their partners – they are never consciously or wilfully cruel or malicious. It is just that they are so independent and sure of themselves that they find it almost impossible to see somebody else's viewpoint or position. This is why an Aries needs as a partner someone with lots of social graces.

On the plus side, an Aries is honest, someone you can lean on, someone with whom you will always know where you stand. What he or she lacks in diplomacy is made up for in integrity.

Home and Domestic Life

An Aries is of course the ruler at home – the Boss. The male will tend to delegate domestic matters to the female. The female Aries will want to rule the roost. Both tend to be handy round the house. Both like large families and both believe in the sanctity and importance of the family. An Aries is a good family person, although he or she does not especially like being at home a lot, preferring instead to be roaming about.

Considering that they are by nature so combative and wilful, Aries people can be surprisingly soft, gentle and even vulnerable with their children and partners. The sign of Cancer, ruled by the Moon, is on the cusp of their solar 4th house of home and family. When the Moon is well aspected – under favourable influences – in the birth chart, an Aries will be tender towards the family and will want a family life that is nurturing and supportive. Aries likes to come home after a hard day on the battlefield of life to the understanding arms of their partner and the unconditional love and support of their family. An Aries feels that there is enough 'war' out in the world – and he or she enjoys participating in that. But when Aries comes home, comfort and nurturing are what's needed.

Horoscope for 2020

Major Trends

Your career has been an important focus for many, many years, and since 2018, as Saturn moved into your 10th house of career, it has become even more important. You've had to work hard and methodically. This year you will see the payoff. The career will bloom. More on this later.

Health has been an issue for the past two years as well. Your normally abundant and dynamic energy hasn't been up to scratch, and this could have made you more vulnerable to problems. This is the trend in the year ahead. The good news is that much of the health pressure will go by the end of the year – health is steadily improving in 2020. More details later.

The Eastern sector of the self is overwhelmingly dominant this year, Aries. There will be periods where there are no planets – zero, nada, nil – in the social Western sector. And even though the Western sector will strengthen as the year progresses it will never be dominant. Only short-term planets will move through there. So this is not an especially strong love year. It is a year for independence and self-reliance – something you enjoy. More on this later.

Uranus moved into your money house in March of 2019 and will be there for many years to come. This indicates many dramatic financial changes, some voluntary, some involuntary. In finance expect the unexpected. Details below.

Neptune has been in your 12th house of spirituality for many years now and will remain there for many more. This shows a focus on spirituality and great internal growth. It will be a challenge to meld this with your super-busy outer life. But you will do it.

Mars, your ruling planet, will spend an unusual amount of time in your own sign this year. Normally he is in a sign for approximately a month and a half at a time, but he will be in Aries for six months – quadruple his usual transit. This further reinforces the focus on self-absorption and independence that we mentioned earlier. It can be a benefit healthwise too – so long as you don't overdo things.

Eclipse activity is very much increased 'in the year ahead, guaranteeing a year of sudden and dramatic change. Normally there are four eclipses in a given year. This year there will be six. Normally there are two lunar eclipses in a given year, but this year there will be four. This will impact on the home, family and domestic situation. More on this later.

Your areas of greatest focus and interest this year will be the career (all year); spirituality (all year); finance (all year); and friends, groups and group activities (from March 23 to July 2 and from December 18 onwards).

Your paths of greatest fulfilment this year are the career (until December 20); friends, groups and group activities (from December 20 onwards); home and family (until May 16); and children, fun and creativity (from May 16 onwards).

Health

(Please note that this is an astrological perspective on health and not a medical one. In days of yore there was no difference, both perspectives were identical. But these days there could be quite a difference. For a medical perspective, please consult your doctor or health practitioner.)

As we mentioned above, health is an important area to watch this year. Three long-term planets are in stressful alignment with you for most of 2020. This of itself is a problem, but there will be periods where the short-term planets also join the fray and these will be your most vulnerable months. These periods are from January 1 to January 20; June 21 to July 20 (less stressful than January though); and September 22 to October 23. Make sure you take it nice and easy over those periods.

What further complicates health is the weakness in your 6th house of health. It is, for the most part, empty, with only short-term planets moving through there. So your tendency is to ignore your health or to take it for granted. This would be a mistake. You need to force yourself – even when you don't feel like it – to focus on health.

The medieval astrologers (and many modern astrologers) believed in Destiny: if something is going to happen, there is nothing we can do about it. I am not in this camp. Personal experience has taught me that our free will choices can alter, or at least soften, Destiny. Destiny can show encounters with ill health, but how we choose to meet Destiny can make all the difference.

Thus there is much that can be done to enhance the health and prevent problems from developing. Give more attention to the following – the vulnerable areas of your Horoscope (the reflex points are shown in the chart below):

- The head, face and scalp. Always important for Aries, regular scalp and face massage is a wonderful preventive. It not only strengthens the particular area, but the entire body as well through reflexes there that go to the whole body. Craniosacral therapy is also excellent for this area.
- The musculature is also always important for Aries. You don't need to be a body-builder or become muscle bound; you only need good muscle tone. Weak or flabby muscles can knock the spine and bones out of alignment and this will cause all kinds of other

Important foot reflexology points for the year ahead

Try to massage all of the foot on a regular basis – the top of the foot as well as the bottom – but pay extra attention to the points highlighted on the chart. When you massage, be aware of 'sore spots' as these need special attention. It's also a good idea to massage the ankles and below them.

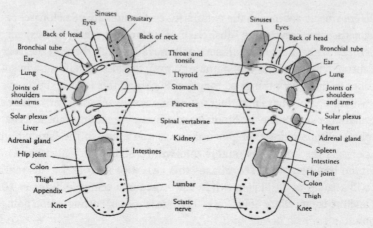

problems. So, vigorous physical exercise is important – according to your age and stage in life.

- The adrenals. The important thing here (as our regular readers know) is to avoid anger and fear – the two emotions that stress the adrenals. Meditation is a great help for this.
- The lungs, arms, shoulders, small intestine and respiratory system. Arms and shoulders should be regularly massaged. Tension tends to collect in the shoulders and needs to be released.
- The heart has only become important for Aries since Pluto's entry into Capricorn in 2008, although it has become increasingly important over the past two years. The main thing with the heart is to avoid worry and anxiety, the two emotions that stress it out. Replace worry with faith.

Since health problems, if they happen (God forbid) would most likely begin here, keeping these areas healthy and fit is sound preventive medicine.

Since your health planet Mercury is a fast-moving (and erratic) planet, there are many short-term trends in health depending on where Mercury is and the aspects he receives. These are best dealt with in the monthly reports.

Home and Family

Here we see another of the wonderful contradictions in a Horoscope. On the one hand, your 4th house of home and family is basically empty. Only short-term planets will move through there in the year ahead. This tends to the status quo and, taken by itself, it shows a contentment with things as they are. But – and this is a big 'but' – we will have, as we have mentioned, four lunar eclipses this year, twice as many as usual. Since the Moon is your family planet this indicates that there will be many changes, upheavals and crises in the family and perhaps the home. The status quo will be shaken up. Also keep in mind that two of the six eclipses this year (two solar and four lunar) will actually occur in your 4th house – the lunar eclipse of January 10 and the solar eclipse of June 21. So there is a lot of cosmic action going on.

As is the way with these things, in contrast your 10th house of career is chock-full of planets – overwhelmingly stronger than your 4th house. And this can be part of the problem. You are so focused on your career and outer objectives that you might be ignoring things at home. The eclipses will remind you – in ways you can't avoid – to give more attention to the family.

So there will be dramas – often life-changing – in the lives of family members and parents or parent figures. Moves could happen – probably not comfortable. Repairs could be needed in the home as well.

A parent or parent figure will be redefining him or herself multiple times. His or her self-concept, the way he or she thinks of him or her self, will change, and this will lead to changes in their 'presentation' to the public. This will go on all year. The marriage of parents or parent figures has been severely tested over the past two years, but things should improve this year. We will discuss this further in the monthly reports.

Siblings and sibling figures are having a quiet year. They seem satisfied with where they are and have no need to move. However, they will be making many major financial changes this year.

Parents or parent figures are experiencing dramas in their lives, as we mentioned, but they are not likely to move. However, children or children figures in your life are likely to move. Their current relationships will get tested. They have many job opportunities. Those of child-bearing age seem more fertile than usual. Grandchildren (if you have them) are having a status quo family year.

If you're planning renovations to the home, June 21 to July 22 would be a good time. If you want to improve the home in a cosmetic kind of way – or if you're buying objects of beauty for the home – August 7 to September 6 is a good time. Your aesthetic sense will be sharper and your choices will be better.

Finance and Career

Ever since Uranus entered your money house for the long term (in March 2019) this area has become a focal point in your life. It is also a very exciting and interesting area of life. Anything can happen at any time. Money, and financial opportunity, can come suddenly and out of the blue. Earnings can go sky high – beyond your imagination – but they can also dip very low. This is what makes things so interesting and exciting. Finances are a roller coaster these days.

Every person is a law unto him or herself. Every person is unique. What works for one doesn't work for another. Even the conventional wisdom – some of which is quite good – is not applicable to all people. You are not a statistic but an individual wired up in a unique way. So your job now is to learn what works for you. Forget conventional wisdom; you are learning your personal financial law. Thus you are in a period of financial experimentation. Some experiments work, some don't. But it is through experimentation that we obtain new knowledge.

Uranus is the planet of science and technology, the planet of new inventions and innovations. So all these areas are interesting on the financial level. Computers, smart phones, online activities, programming are all interesting as investments, businesses and jobs. With Uranus in your money house for years to come, you could be earning from technologies not yet invented. Uranus rules astrology too, so the insights of astrology will be important in your financial life. Astrologers have important financial information for you, and if you face some decision it is wise to consult with one.

With Uranus in your money house earnings will tend to be erratic. The highs will be ultra-high but the lows will also be ultra-low. It would be a good idea to set aside money from the good times to cover the bad times.

Uranus rules friends and friendships. This indicates that your friends, your social connections, are important in finances. They seem very helpful in this area. It would be a good idea to get more involved with groups and professional or trade organizations. This will help the bottom line too.

Fast-moving Venus is your financial planet. Thus there are many short-term trends in finance that depend on where Venus is and the aspects she receives. These are best covered in the monthly reports.

She will make one of her rare retrogrades this year – from May 13 to June 25. This only happens once every two years. So this will be a period for financial review; not a good time for making expensive purchases or important financial decisions.

Venus will spend approximately four months in the sign of Gemini – four times the length of her usual transit. This indicates earnings from sales, marketing, PR, advertising, teaching, writing and trading.

Career is really the main headline for the year, Aries. Career has been challenging over the past two years and you've had to work hard. You didn't catch the lucky breaks and you have had to earn everything through sheer merit. Many of you were dealing with demanding bosses and perhaps unreasonable customers. More was expected of you. But now, with Jupiter in your 10th career house almost all year you will see the payoff. You will start to catch the lucky breaks. Promotions come your way. Your public and professional status is elevated. If you own a business, the status of the business is elevated. But it's your hard work that is bringing the good luck. There is much career-related travel in the year ahead too.

Love and Social Life

As we mentioned earlier, the year ahead is not an especially romantic kind of year. Some years are like that. Career is much more important than the social life. Your social life will improve at the end of the year, when Jupiter moves into your 11th house of friends, but this is more about friendships and being involved with friends and groups rather than romance.

Your 7th house of love is empty this year. Only short-term planets will move through there, bringing temporary effects. More important is the fact that *all* the long-term planets are in the East this year. Your Western social sector will never be dominant. Relationships seem less important than usual. It's all about independence and creating your own conditions for happiness. The tendency for relationships will be to the status quo. Singles will tend to remain single. Those who are married will tend to stay married.

Venus is not only your financial planet but your love planet as well. This shows that for you, Aries, love and money go together. When love is going well finances are going well, and when finances are going well the love life goes well. Problems in one area impact the other too.

Venus is a fast-moving planet and usually she will move through all the signs and houses of your Horoscope in a given year. This year, because she goes retrograde, she will only move through 11 signs and houses. This is still a lot of movement, and thus there are many short-term trends in love that depend on where Venus is and the aspects she receives. These short-term trends are best dealt with in the monthly reports.

As we have mentioned, Venus will spend four months in the sign of Gemini, your 3rd house, which will be significant for singles. There will be social and romantic opportunities to be found in your neighbourhood and perhaps with neighbours. The expression 'smart is the new sexy' certainly resonates with you this year. You gravitate to intellectuals; to people with the gift of the gab; to people who are easy to talk to. Talking, good communication, is a form of foreplay. Sexual magnetism is always important in a relationship, but you need more than that – you need mental compatibility. There will be romantic opportunities at school, educational functions, seminars, lectures, literary events, even at bookshops or the library. Pursue your intellectual interests and love will find you. Venus will be in Gemini from April 3 to August 7.

Self-improvement

Career, as we have said, is the single most important area for you this year, more important than love, finance and even health. This is all well and good. There are times in life where this kind of focus is necessary. However, you should not allow this to affect your health. Real career success will happen as you learn to attain it with good health. This will mean working smarter and not harder, learning to delegate tasks and never allowing yourself to get overtired.

We see some interesting things in your spiritual life this year. Neptune in your 12th house for many years can make you mystical and dreamy. You are apt to fall into reveries. But Jupiter in Capricorn, in your 10th house, shows a more practical kind of theology. There is a feeling that God wants you to succeed; that your career is 'God's work'. This faith will be helpful to your career. People in your place of worship are also likely to be helpful in your career.

Jupiter in Capricorn favours traditional religion. However, Neptune in Pisces indicates a desire to transcend all religion, to be in a place that is 'above religion'. So these conflicting urges need to be integrated. Every person does this in their own way. In many cases you will have one foot in the mystical realms and the other foot in traditional religion. In other cases, one supports the other. There is no real conflict; all religions are merely the offshoots of the mystical experiences of their founders.

We mentioned earlier that the Eastern sector of your Horoscope is overwhelmingly dominant this year. In addition Mars, your ruling planet, will be in your own sign for more than six months – from June 28 onwards. While it is natural for you to be independent and self-willed, this year it could be too much of a good thing. The tendency will be to ignore or run roughshod over others, perhaps to demean them. It is true that your way is the best way for you these days, but others still need to be treated with love and respect. You can go your own way without offending others. It will take some spiritual work though.

Month-by-month Forecasts

January

Best Days Overall: 2, 3, 12, 20, 21, 29, 30, 31
Most Stressful Days Overall: 9, 10, 16, 22, 23
Best Days for Love: 13, 14, 16, 18, 19, 27, 28
Best Days for Money: 5, 6, 13, 14, 22, 23
Best Days for Career: 6, 14, 15, 22, 23

You begin your year in the midst of a yearly career peak. Your 10th house of career is easily the strongest in the Horoscope, with at least half and sometimes 60 per cent of the planets either there or moving through there. So the career is successful – but very demanding. You are focused on your career as you should be, but this focus can cause some problems at home. A lunar eclipse on the 10th occurs in your 4th house of family and shakes things up. This can bring dramas in the lives of family members, and in the lives of parents and parent figures (both sets), and often a need for repairs in the home. Siblings and sibling figures also seem affected by the eclipse; they are forced to make important financial changes because of some disruption or unexpected event.

This eclipse looks pretty strong, so take it nice and easy during this time. You should rest and relax more all month – especially until the 20th, but particularly during this eclipse period. The problem is that the demands of the career are very great now and it might not be so easy to 'rest and relax'. Career and home issues must be handled, but focus on the essentials. Don't sweat the small stuff, as the saying goes.

Health is an issue this month, especially until the 20th. The eclipse impacts Mercury, your health planet, so there are changes to your health regime and perhaps changes in your doctors. Sometimes there are health scares; if so make sure to get a second opinion. Later in the month – even next month – will be a better time to get these second opinions. The body is not a 'thing' but a dynamic energy system. It responds to the energy world. Tests taken when energy is not right can often show things that are not really there.

Enhance your health this month through back and knee massage until the 16th, and through calf and ankle massage afterwards. Most importantly, maintain high energy levels.

There can be job changes this month, either within your present company or with another one. There are shakeups in your career as the eclipse affects your career planet Saturn. This often manifests as shakeups in the upper management where you work, in changes of company policy, dramas in the lives of bosses and changes in your industry. Sometimes the government changes regulations that impact on your industry.

February

Best Days Overall: 8, 9, 16, 17, 26, 27
Most Stressful Days Overall: 6, 7, 12, 13, 18, 19, 20
Best Days for Love: 7, 8, 12, 13, 16, 17, 26, 27
Best Days for Money: 1, 2, 7, 8, 10, 11, 16, 17, 19, 20, 26, 27, 28, 29
Best Days for Career: 2, 11, 18, 19, 20, 29

If you got through last month with your health and sanity intact, pat yourself on the back. You did very well. Health still needs watching but it is much less stressful than last month. Enhance your health in the ways mentioned in the yearly report, but also through ankle and calf massage until the 3rd and through foot massage after that date. You respond very well to spiritual healing techniques after the 3rd, and if you feel under the weather see a spiritual healer.

The month ahead is a strong social month. Your 11th house of friends is powerful until the 19th, and on the 7th your love planet Venus enters your sign and stays there for the rest of the month. Venus in your sign is a happy transit. She bestows beauty and social grace. You look good. You have a flair for fashion. Love and romantic opportunities pursue you, rather than the other way around. You have love on your terms. Those of you who are married or in a relationship will find that the spouse, partner or current love is unusually devoted and eager to please.

Venus's move into your sign is also a wonderful financial transit. Money and financial opportunity come to you. You don't need to run after it. Often this transit indicates financial windfalls, and just as often it shows clothing or accessories coming to you.

On the 16th Mars, the ruler of your Horoscope, enters your 10th house. This shows career success, but you are earning it. You are on top, in charge. People look up to you. People aspire to be like you.

Mars's move into your career house puts all the planets in the Eastern sector of your chart – even the Moon will move to the East on the 18th. This is highly unusual. You are at the peak of your personal independence (and this lasts into next month too). You're self-reliant and in charge of your destiny. You're not much in need of others' approval. You know what's best for you and you should follow that path. Others might not agree initially, but they will come round. So make those changes that need to be made. You have a lot of personal power. You can and should have things your way.

Venus, your love and financial planet, will have her solstice from the 8th to the 10th. She pauses in the heavens and then changes direction (in latitude). So, a pause in finance and love will happen, followed by a change of direction.

March

Best Days Overall: 6, 7, 14, 15, 24, 25
Most Stressful Days Overall: 4, 5, 10, 11, 17, 18
Best Days for Love: 8, 10, 11, 17, 18, 27, 28
Best Days for Money: 1, 8, 9, 17, 18, 27, 28
Best Days for Career: 1, 9, 17, 18, 28, 29

Spirituality has been strong all year but now – since February 19 – it is even stronger. Your 12th house is very powerful. So this is a good period for spiritual practices, for meditation, the study of sacred literature and reading spiritual-type books. It is also a very creative period. You are inspired from on high, especially on the 8th and 9th. This is a period for supernatural experiences and for enhanced ESP (extra-sensory perception).

All the planets are still in the East this month – only the Moon will move through your Western social sector, from the 4th to 16th. Your own house becomes powerful, too, from the 20th onwards. Continue to make the changes that need to be made and create the conditions for your happiness. Like last month, you can and should have things your way. There is nothing wrong in following your self-interest, so long as you're not damaging others. Your self-interest is just as important as another's.

Though health still needs watching – you can't take things for granted – your health is much improved over January. Like last month, ankle and calf massage (from 4th to the 16th) and foot massage (from the 1st to the 4th and from the 16th onwards) will be beneficial. Spiritual-healing methods are still powerful for you too, from the 1st to the 4th and from the 16th onwards.

Although career is important all year, this month it is less so. Saturn leaves your career house on the 23rd and Mars will leave it on the 31st. Bosses should be less demanding now.

On the 20th the Sun moves into your sign and you begin one of your yearly personal pleasure peaks. A time for fun and for indulging the body. This is a good time to get the body in the shape that you would like. Fun and leisure opportunities will come to you and you'll probably take them. Children and children figures seem more devoted to you.

The personal appearance shines – abundant energy is the best beauty product in the world!

The month ahead will also be prosperous, with Venus entering the 2nd money house on the 5th. She is powerful in her own sign and house, and thus your earning power is strong. Her transit also brings the help of social contacts, the spouse, partner or current love and opportunities for business partnerships or joint ventures. Venus travels with Uranus from the 6th to the 9th and this can bring unexpected financial and social opportunity.

Children and children figures of the appropriate age are more sexually active this month.

April

Best Days Overall: 3, 4, 11, 12, 20, 21, 22
Most Stressful Days Overall: 1, 2, 7, 8, 13, 14, 28, 29
Best Days for Love: 7, 8, 15, 16, 17, 25, 26
Best Days for Money: 6, 7, 8, 15, 16, 17, 14, 23, 24, 25, 26
Best Days for Career: 6, 7, 13, 14, 15, 24, 25

A happy and prosperous month ahead, Aries. Enjoy! Until the 19th you remain in one of your yearly personal pleasure peaks and, like last month, a lot of fun and leisure activities will come your way. The personal appearance shines. You have charisma and star quality.

This is still very much a period of personal independence and personal power. Other people are always important, but make sure you take care of Number 1. The Western social sector of your chart becomes a little bit stronger after the 3rd as Venus moves to the West, but the Eastern sector of self is still overwhelmingly dominant.

Venus goes 'out of bounds' from the 3rd to the end of the month. Practically speaking, she spends the month 'out of bounds' – this describes both your financial and love life this month. You need to go outside your normal boundaries, socially and financially. There are no answers or opportunities in your normal circles. This can be read another way, too: your financial and social urges pull you out of your normal spheres. The spouse, partner or current love is also outside his or her normal boundaries. The money people in your life are venturing into the unknown as well.

Health is good this month – especially when compared to the past few months. Now you only have two long-term planets stressing you and you have help from the short-term planets. So your health and energy are the best they've been so far this year. You can enhance your health further through foot massage until the 11th, scalp and face massage from the 11th to the 27th and neck and throat massage from the 27th onwards. Physical exercise is always good for you, but especially between the 11th and 27th.

Mercury has his solstice from the 14th to the 16th. He pauses in the heavens and reverses direction (in latitude). So, a pause at work and in health matters will happen and then a change of direction. This is a pause that refreshes – a cosmic pause.

Jupiter travels with Pluto all month and this gives many messages. It indicates a good month to pay down debt or to borrow (depending on your need). A good month to approach outside investors for your projects. The spouse, partner or current love will have a banner financial month. You are also having a banner financial month, for on the 19th you begin a yearly financial peak. This is a good month for tax planning or for buying insurance, and if you are of the appropriate age it is good for estate planning too.

May

Best Days Overall: 1, 8, 9, 18, 19, 27, 28
Most Stressful Days Overall: 4, 5, 10, 11, 25, 26
Best Days for Love: 4, 5, 13, 14, 23, 24
Best Days for Money: 3, 4, 5, 12, 13, 14, 20, 21, 22, 23, 24
Best Days for Career: 4, 10, 11, 12, 13, 22

Planetary retrograde activity increases this month; after the 16th 40 per cent of the planets are moving backwards. While this isn't yet the maximum for the year, it is still a high percentage. The pace of life slows down a bit.

The retrograde of Venus is perhaps the most significant for you. She rules both the love and the financial life. This is a rare retrograde – it happens once every two years – that begins on May 16. So any major purchases or investments should be done before the 16th. Afterwards, avoid these things and take stock of your financial life. Give it a good review and see where improvements can be made. The same is true for the spouse, partner or current love. But for him or her this taking stock is in effect all month – and for the next few months. In spite of this, he or she will prosper this month. Earnings might come more slowly but they will come.

The love life will slow down after the 16th too. Relationships or friendships can seem to go backwards. But as with finance, don't make important love decisions during Venus's retrograde.

Venus will spend the month in your 3rd house. This shows that love and romantic opportunities can be found close to home, in the neighbourhood and perhaps with neighbours. Financial opportunities happen here too.

The retrograde of Saturn, your career planet, begins on May 11, and it coincides with strength in the lower half of your Horoscope. The upper half, the day side of the chart, is still the strongest, but the lower half is stronger than it has been all year. (Next month the lower half will be at its maximum for the year.) So, you can devote more time to the home and family. Career is still important but it is slowing down. Many issues will need time to resolve.

You are still in a yearly financial peak until the 20th, but because of Venus's retrograde, wrap up financial dealings before the 16th. This is still a good month to pay down or to make debt – especially before the 16th. Also good, like last month, for tax and estate planning (for those of you of the appropriate age).

Health is even better than last month. Your health planet, Mercury, will be 'out of bounds' this month from the 17th onwards. This would indicate that you are looking 'outside the box' in health matters.

June

Best Days Overall: 5, 6, 14, 15, 24, 30
Most Stressful Days Overall: 1, 7, 8, 21, 22
Best Days for Love: 1, 9, 10, 19, 20
Best Days for Money: 1, 8, 9, 10, 16, 17, 18, 20, 21, 27
Best Days for Career: 2, 7, 8, 9, 18, 19

Retrograde activity increases even further this month. We will have three days – the 23rd to the 25th – where 60 per cent of planets will be travelling backwards. This is the maximum for the year, although we will hit this number again in September. Retrogrades are annoying for everyone, but especially for you Aries. The pace of life slows down even more than last month. Aries, the lover of action, needs to learn patience.

Much retrograde activity is the cosmos calling us to be more perfect in all that we do. Handle the details of life perfectly. Avoid short cuts (these are an illusion this month) and make slow, methodical progress. Being perfect in what you do won't eliminate delays, but it will reduce them.

Health is an issue this month after the 21st. This is not as severe a problem as in January but still something to watch. Do your best to maintain high energy levels. Do your best to reduce your schedule around the two eclipse periods this month as well.

The lunar eclipse of June 5 occurs in your 9th house, affecting college-level students – there can be shakeups in their schools and changes in educational plans. If you're involved in a legal action it takes a dramatic turn, one way or another. With the Moon as your family planet, every lunar eclipse affects the family and family members – and this one is no different. So repairs could be needed in the home and passions at home can run high. Two other important planets in your chart – Mars and Venus – are also impacted here, so this is a powerful eclipse. The impact on Mars, the ruler of your Horoscope, can bring a need to redefine yourself and your personality. Often this comes from slanders or bad-mouthing from other people. It can bring a detox of the body too. The impact on Venus shows financial and romantic/social changes. You need to make course corrections in your financial

life. Your financial thinking hasn't been realistic. Your current relationship gets tested too.

The solar eclipse of the 21st is powerful on a worldly level – it occurs
on a cardinal point. Those of you born early in Aries (March 20 and 21)
will feel the effects most strongly, but all of you will feel it to some
degree. This too impacts on the home and family as it occurs in your
4th house. There are more dramas in the lives of family members.
Children and children figures are having life-changing kinds of experiences. A parent or parent figure is making important financial changes.
The marriage or current relationship is being tested.

July

Best Days Overall: 2, 3, 11, 12, 21, 22, 29, 30
Most Stressful Days Overall: 4, 5, 19, 20, 25, 26, 31
Best Days for Love: 6, 7, 8, 16, 17, 25, 26
Best Days for Money: 4, 5, 6, 7, 8, 14, 15, 16, 17, 23, 24, 25, 26,
     31
Best Days for Career: 4, 5, 15, 24, 31

After the two eclipses last month, we have another one this month   a
lunar eclipse on the 5th. This one occurs in your 10th house of career,
indicating changes going on there in your company, in its management
and policies, and dramas in the lives of bosses. The government can
change regulations that force changes in your industry, too. Once again
the home and family is impacted. There are more dramas at home.
There are dramas in the lives of family members and with parents or
parent figures.

This eclipse 'grazes' three planets in your chart, affecting Mercury,
Jupiter and Mars. The impact on both Mercury and Jupiter suggests
that travelling is better off delayed (if you must travel, try to schedule
your trip around this eclipse). It also affects students and there could
be changes of schools, educational plans or shakeups in the actual
school. The health regime will also change – but wait until after the
12th to make these changes.

Health still needs attention until the 22nd. Mercury, your health
planet, will spend the month in the sign of Cancer, your 4th house.

Thus, abdominal massage and correct diet will enhance the health. However, maintaining emotional harmony and harmony in the family will be more important, healthwise (and this will be a challenge because of the eclipse).

Career is becoming more important again as Saturn retrogrades back into your career house. Yet home and family is also very important, with your 4th house strong. So you will have to balance both. You go back and forth. You can't ignore either of these areas.

Retrograde activity is still strong this month; until the 12th half of the planets are retrograde, and after that date it is still 40 per cent – still a high percentage. Patience. Patience. Patience.

Love and money are good this month. Venus has been moving forward since June 15, so there is good financial clarity. She spends the month in your 3rd house and this favours sales, marketing, advertising and PR activities. Whatever it is you do, good marketing is important. People have to know about your product or service. It is also a good transit for writers, teachers and journalists. Your gift of the gab is important in finance.

Love can be found in the neighbourhood and perhaps with neighbours. There are romantic opportunities at school functions or other educational-type settings – lectures, seminars, workshops, the library or bookstore.

August

Best Days Overall: 8, 9, 17, 18, 25, 26, 27
Most Stressful Days Overall: 1, 2, 15, 16, 21, 22, 28, 29
Best Days for Love: 3, 4, 15, 16, 21, 22, 23, 24
Best Days for Money: 2, 3, 4, 10, 11, 15, 16, 20, 23, 24
Best Days for Career: 1, 2, 11, 20, 28, 29

Planetary retrograde activity is more or less the way it was last month. August starts with 40 per cent of the planets retrograde, and after the 15th, 50 per cent of them will be moving backwards, as Uranus begins to reverse.

The good news is that since July 22 you've been in a yearly personal pleasure peak. A time to enjoy life. This continues until the 22nd of this month. You may as well have some fun as nothing much is going on in the world. It's a good time to take a vacation.

Health is much improved since July 22. However, with four (and sometimes five) planets in stressful alignment with you it still needs watching. Correct diet and abdominal massage is still beneficial until the 5th. From the 5th to the 20th, chest massage will be effective, while abdominal massage and diet become important again after then.

From the 20th onwards there will be a rare Grand Trine in the Earth signs. This is good for prosperity and for handling the details of the material plane. Children and children figures will be prospering during this period too.

Your love and financial planet changes signs on the 7th, after spending the past four months in your 3rd house. So both love and financial changes are happening. Family support seems stronger than usual. You will spend more on the home and family. There will be opportunities to earn money from home. Family connections are important financially too. Be careful of being too moody about finance. Financial decisions – and major spending – should be made when you're in a calm peaceful mood, never when you're upset or depressed.

It is a similar situation in the love life. You'll be entertaining more from home and with the family. Family and family connections are playing Cupid. You're attracted to people with whom you can share feelings; emotional intimacy seems as important as physical intimacy.

Mars has been in your own sign since June 28, giving you more energy, which is in general good for health. However, it can make you impatient and, with so many retrogrades, can make you feel frustrated. Also, it can lead you to push the body further than is warranted. This is the downside healthwise.

The power in your 6th house from the 22nd onwards is good news for health. It shows that you're paying attention here. It is also good for job-seekers and for those who employ others. There are nice prospects in store. This also gives a good work ethic and superiors will take note.

September

Best Days Overall: 4, 5, 14, 15, 22, 23
Most Stressful Days Overall: 11, 12, 18, 19, 24, 25
Best Days for Love: 2, 3, 13, 14, 18, 19, 22, 23
Best Days for Money: 2, 3, 6, 7, 8, 13, 14, 16, 17, 22, 23, 24, 25
Best Days for Career: 8, 17, 24, 25

Retrograde activity once again reaches the maximum for the year. From the 9th to the 12th 60 per cent of the planets will be retrograde, and even after the 12th there will still be half of the planets going backwards. The good news is that in the coming months retrograde activity will gradually decline. Things will start moving forward again, little by little.

There are some good points to so much retrograde activity. It forces us to slow down and take stock in many areas of life. It's not so much about 'doing' but about gaining clarity on things, and as clarity is gained, plans can be formulated for the future. When the planetary momentum shifts to forward motion, you will be in a good position to make progress.

Your strong 6th house until the 22nd – showing a focus on health – will stand you in good stead for afterwards when health is less easy than usual. Until the 5th you can enhance the health through abdominal massage and diet. You also respond well to earth-based therapies (with the Grand Trine in Earth until the 22nd). So, mud packs applied to parts of the body that bother you, mud bathing or bathing in waters with high mineral content are all good. After the 5th give more attention to the kidneys and hips. Hip massage will be beneficial. Apply the methods mentioned in the yearly report. The most important thing is to maintain high energy levels. Never allow yourself to get overtired.

The month ahead is a strong social month – this month and October are probably the socially strongest in your year. The Eastern sector of self is still stronger than the social West, but the West is more pronounced than usual. Everything is relative. On the 22nd you enter a yearly love and social peak. (You've had greater love and social peaks in your life, but this is relative to this year.) Singles are going to date more. All of you, single, married or in a relationship, will be going to more parties and gatherings.

Love doesn't seem that serious though. It's all about fun and games – another form of entertainment. Venus, your love planet, will be in your 5th house of fun from the 6th onwards, while the Sun (your fun planet) will be in your 7th house of love from the 22nd. The two planets are in mutual reception, guests in each other's sign and house, which is a positive aspect. The two planets are cooperating with each other.

This is also good financially. It shows that you're earning money in happy ways. You're probably taking on more risk than usual (and that's a lot), but you seem lucky in speculations. You're spending on fun things too. The message of the Horoscope is enjoy your life, and love and finance will take care of themselves.

October

  Best Days Overall: 1, 2, 11, 12, 19, 20, 28, 29, 30
  Most Stressful Days Overall: 9, 10, 15, 16, 21, 22
  Best Days for Love: 3, 15, 16, 21, 22
  Best Days for Money: 4, 5, 13, 14, 21, 23, 31
  Best Days for Career: 5, 14, 21, 22

Last month on the 22nd the planetary power shifted from the night side of your Horoscope to the day side, from the lower to the upper half. Home, family and emotional issues are becoming less important and the focus is more on the career. Your career planet, Saturn, started to move forward on September 29 so the timing is perfect. Things in the career are moving forward. You're getting ready for a new career push.

Health still needs your attention. This is one of your vulnerable months – especially until the 23rd. So, as always, rest and relax as much as possible. Do your best to maintain high energy levels. This is a month where you respond well to detox regimes. Perhaps surgery is recommended to you, but since your health planet Mercury will go into retrograde motion on the 14th, get a second opinion. Detox should also be explored. Safe sex and sexual moderation are important. A herbal colon cleanse might be a good idea.

You're still in the midst of a yearly love and social peak, which will go on until the 23rd. However, Venus will spend most of the month in Virgo – from the 2nd to the 28th – and she is not very comfortable in this sign. In astrological lingo, she is in her 'fall' – her weakest position. The urge to socialize is there, but the social magnetism is not up to its usual standards. The important thing is to avoid destructive criticism and perfectionism. This is not going to help love. If you can avoid these pitfalls, love should go well.

Venus in Virgo is better for finance than for love. She is part of a Grand Trine in the Earth signs – a very fortunate aspect for wealth. The financial judgement will be sound. You will be a more careful shopper and get value for your money. You will tend to earn money the old-fashioned way, through work and productive service. Bosses, elders, parents and parent figures seem helpful financially.

Venus has another one of her solstices from October 29 to November 2. She pauses in the heavens (in her latitude motion) and then changes direction. This will happen in love and finance too. It is a good pause. A pause that refreshes.

On the 28th Venus enters Libra, her own sign and house. Here she is more powerful. Earning power will be stronger, although you'll work harder for it. Your social magnetism will also be stronger – but do you have the interest?

November

Best Days Overall: 7, 8, 16, 25, 26
Most Stressful Days Overall: 5, 6, 12, 18, 19
Best Days for Love: 2, 3, 12, 21, 22
Best Days for Money: 1, 2, 3, 11, 12, 19, 21, 22, 27, 28
Best Days for Career: 2, 11, 18, 19

The planetary momentum is now forward: by the 29th 90 per cent of the planets will be in forward motion. So the pace of life is quickening, just as you like things. If you've used the retrograde periods properly, you'll be in a good position to move forward.

Mars's retrograde will end on the 14th. This is an important development as Mars rules your Horoscope and he has been retrograde since September 9. You now have more confidence, more direction, more clarity about things.

Venus is still in her solstice state until the 2nd, so don't be alarmed at the natural pause in love and finance. It is a cosmic pause that will lead you in a new direction.

We have another lunar eclipse at the end of the month – the fourth one this year. It happens, technically, on the 30th but you will feel its effects earlier. Sensitive people feel an eclipse as much as two weeks before it actually happens. The good news is that this eclipse affects you relatively mildly and it does not impact powerfully on other planets (only Neptune is sideswiped). The eclipse occurs in your 3rd house, and students below college level are affected. They can change schools and educational plans. There can be disruptions at school or shakeups in the management of the school.

Siblings, sibling figures and neighbours are also affected. Siblings and sibling figures will need to redefine themselves for the next few months. This will change their mode of dress and the image they present to the world. Cars and communication equipment are likely to be temperamental – repairs or replacement might be necessary. It will be a good idea to drive more carefully over this period. Every lunar eclipse affects the home and family; this has been happening all year and this eclipse brings more of the same. There are dramas in the lives of family members, and especially of parents or parent figures. Family members are more temperamental too.

Health is much improved over last month, and it will improve even further next month. In the meantime, enhance the health in the ways mentioned in the yearly report. Until the 11th do more hip massage; after the 11th you respond well to detox regimes. Safe sex and sexual moderation are also important after the 11th.

Love seems delicate until the 21st. You and the beloved are seeing things in opposite ways and seem distant with each other. This doesn't necessarily mean a break up: there is just a need to bridge differences. Love will improve after the 21st. It becomes more erotic. Sexual magnetism seems the most important factor for singles. Even for those in a relationship, good sex will cover many sins.

December

Best Days Overall: 5, 6, 13, 14, 22, 23
Most Stressful Days Overall: 2, 3, 9, 10, 15, 16, 29, 30, 31
Best Days for Love: 2, 3, 9, 10, 11, 12, 22, 23
Best Days for Money: 2, 3, 8, 11, 12, 16, 22, 23, 24, 25, 26, 27
Best Days for Career: 8, 9, 15, 16, 17, 27

You have a very eventful month ahead, Aries, but good. Saturn moves away from his stressful aspect with you on the 18th and will start making harmonious aspects. Jupiter will do the same on the 20th. And though you will still need to keep an eye on the health after the 21st, the stresses will be nowhere near the intensity of January, June/July or September/October. Until the 21st enhance the health with thigh massage. A herbal liver cleanse might also be a good idea. After the 21st enhance health through back and knee massage.

The sixth eclipse of the year occurs on the 14th. It is a solar eclipse which occurs in your 9th house, so avoid foreign travel over that period. If you must travel, try to schedule your stay around the eclipse. This eclipse affects children, children figures and college-level students. There are changes in educational plans – sometimes they change schools, sometimes they change courses, sometimes there are shakeups in the school – in the management or the rules. If you are involved in a legal issue there will be a dramatic turn one way or another. You are closer to resolution.

Perhaps more importantly, your religious, theological and philo-sophical beliefs get tested (this will go on well into next year). The eclipse brings a crisis of faith. Some beliefs will need to be modified; some will need to be discarded. These changes will impact your whole life. They are probably not pleasant when they happen, but ultimately they are good. Neptune, your spiritual planet, is affected by this eclipse (it is a more direct impact than last month's eclipse). Thus there are spiritual changes – changes in practice, teachers and teachings. A spiritual 'course correction' is happening. A good thing. There are shakeups in charities and spiritual or altruistic organizations that you're involved with, and there will be dramas in the lives of guru figures in your life.

On the 21st you enter a yearly career peak, although it won't be as strong as your last one in January. You have probably attained many of your short-term goals. Career is still important, but now you are not so career driven in the way you have been for most of the year.

Jupiter and Saturn in your 11th house (Saturn entering on the 18th and Jupiter on the 20th) show that you are making new and significant friends, and that these friends are helpful in your career. You are mixing socially (not necessarily romantically) with important people.

Venus will be in your 8th house until the 15th. Thus you seem very involved in the finances of the spouse, partner or current love. He or she had a very good financial period last month, and it will still be good in the month ahead. There is good financial cooperation between you. This is also a good period to pay down debt or to borrow, depending your need.

In love sexual magnetism is still the prime factor. This will change after the 15th when there will be a need for more philosophical compatibility. Love and finance are good this month.

Taurus

THE BULL

Birthdays from
21st April to
20th May

Personality Profile

TAURUS AT A GLANCE

Element – Earth

Ruling Planet – Venus
   Career Planet – Uranus
   Love Planet – Pluto
   Money Planet – Mercury
   Planet of Health and Work – Venus
   Planet of Home and Family Life – Sun
   Planet of Spirituality – Mars
   Planet of Travel, Education, Religion and Philosophy – Saturn

Colours – earth tones, green, orange, yellow

Colours that promote love, romance and social harmony – red-violet, violet

Colours that promote earning power – yellow, yellow-orange

Gems – coral, emerald

Metal – copper

Scents – bitter almond, rose, vanilla, violet

Quality – fixed (= stability)

Quality most needed for balance – flexibility

Strongest virtues – endurance, loyalty, patience, stability,
    a harmonious disposition

Deepest needs – comfort, material ease, wealth

Characteristics to avoid – rigidity, stubbornness, tendency to be overly
    possessive and materialistic

Signs of greatest overall compatibility – Virgo, Capricorn

Signs of greatest overall incompatibility – Leo, Scorpio, Aquarius

Sign most helpful to career – Aquarius

Sign most helpful for emotional support – Leo

Sign most helpful financially – Gemini

Sign best for marriage and/or partnerships – Scorpio

Sign most helpful for creative projects – Virgo

Best Sign to have fun with – Virgo

Signs most helpful in spiritual matters – Aries, Capricorn

Best day of the week – Friday

Understanding a Taurus

Taurus is the most earthy of all the Earth signs. If you understand that Earth is more than just a physical element, that it is a psychological attitude as well, you will get a better understanding of the Taurus personality.

A Taurus has all the power of action that an Aries has. But Taurus is not satisfied with action for its own sake. Their actions must be productive, practical and wealth-producing. If Taurus cannot see a practical value in an action they will not bother taking it.

Taurus's forte lies in their power to make real their own or other people's ideas. They are generally not very inventive but they can take another's invention and perfect it, making it more practical and useful. The same is true for all projects. Taurus is not especially keen on starting new projects, but once they get involved they bring things to completion. Taurus carries everything through. They are finishers and will go the distance, so long as no unavoidable calamity intervenes.

Many people find Taurus too stubborn, conservative, fixed and immovable. This is understandable, because Taurus dislikes change – in the environment or in their routine. They even dislike changing their minds! On the other hand, this is their virtue. It is not good for a wheel's axle to waver. The axle must be fixed, stable and unmovable. Taurus is the axle of society and the heavens. Without their stability and so-called stubbornness, the wheels of the world (and especially the wheels of commerce) would not turn.

Taurus loves routine. A routine, if it is good, has many virtues. It is a fixed – and, ideally, perfect – way of taking care of things. Mistakes can happen when spontaneity comes into the equation, and mistakes cause discomfort and uneasiness – something almost unacceptable to a Taurus. Meddling with Taurus's comfort and security is a sure way to irritate and anger them.

While an Aries loves speed, a Taurus likes things slow. They are slow thinkers – but do not make the mistake of assuming they lack intelligence. On the contrary, Taurus people are very intelligent. It is just that they like to chew on ideas, to deliberate and weigh them up.

Only after due deliberation is an idea accepted or a decision taken. Taurus is slow to anger – but once aroused, take care!

Finance

Taurus is very money-conscious. Wealth is more important to them than to many other signs. Wealth to a Taurus means comfort and security. Wealth means stability. Where some zodiac signs feel that they are spiritually rich if they have ideas, talents or skills, Taurus only feels wealth when they can see and touch it. Taurus's way of thinking is, 'What good is a talent if it has not been translated into a home, furniture, car and holidays?'

These are all reasons why Taurus excels in estate agency and agricultural industries. Usually a Taurus will end up owning land. They love to feel their connection to the Earth. Material wealth began with agriculture, the tilling of the soil. Owning a piece of land was humanity's earliest form of wealth: Taurus still feels that primeval connection.

It is in the pursuit of wealth that Taurus develops intellectual and communication ability. Also, in this pursuit Taurus is forced to develop some flexibility. It is in the quest for wealth that they learn the practical value of the intellect and come to admire it. If it were not for the search for wealth and material things, Taurus people might not try to reach a higher intellect.

Some Taurus people are 'born lucky' – the type who win any gamble or speculation. This luck is due to other factors in their horoscope; it is not part of their essential nature. By nature they are not gamblers. They are hard workers and like to earn what they get. Taurus's innate conservatism makes them abhor unnecessary risks in finance and in other areas of their lives.

Career and Public Image

Being essentially down-to-earth people, simple and uncomplicated, Taurus tends to look up to those who are original, unconventional and inventive. Taurus people like their bosses to be creative and original – since they themselves are content to perfect their superiors' brainwaves. They admire people who have a wider social or political consciousness and they feel that someday (when they have all the comfort and security they need) they too would like to be involved in these big issues.

In business affairs Taurus can be very shrewd – and that makes them valuable to their employers. They are never lazy; they enjoy working and getting good results. Taurus does not like taking unnecessary risks and they do well in positions of authority, which makes them good managers and supervisors. Their managerial skills are reinforced by their natural talents for organization and handling details, their patience and thoroughness. As mentioned, through their connection with the earth, Taurus people also do well in farming and agriculture.

In general a Taurus will choose money and earning power over public esteem and prestige. A position that pays more – though it has less prestige – is preferred to a position with a lot of prestige but lower earnings. Many other signs do not feel this way, but a Taurus does, especially if there is nothing in his or her personal birth chart that modifies this. Taurus will pursue glory and prestige only if it can be shown that these things have a direct and immediate impact on their wallet.

Love and Relationships

In love, the Taurus-born likes to have and to hold. They are the marrying kind. They like commitment and they like the terms of a relationship to be clearly defined. More importantly, Taurus likes to be faithful to one lover, and they expect that lover to reciprocate this fidelity. When this doesn't happen, their whole world comes crashing down. When they are in love Taurus people are loyal, but they are also very possessive. They are capable of great fits of jealousy if they are hurt in love.

Taurus is satisfied with the simple things in a relationship. If you are involved romantically with a Taurus there is no need for lavish entertainments and constant courtship. Give them enough love, food and comfortable shelter and they will be quite content to stay home and enjoy your company. They will be loyal to you for life. Make a Taurus feel comfortable and – above all – secure in the relationship, and you will rarely have a problem.

In love, Taurus can sometimes make the mistake of trying to control their partners, which can cause great pain on both sides. The reasoning behind their actions is basically simple: Taurus people feel a sense of ownership over their partners and will want to make changes that will increase their own general comfort and security. This attitude is OK when it comes to inanimate, material things – but is dangerous when applied to people. Taurus needs to be careful and attentive to this possible trait within themselves.

Home and Domestic Life

Home and family are vitally important to Taurus. They like children. They also like a comfortable and perhaps glamorous home – something they can show off. They tend to buy heavy, ponderous furniture – usually of the best quality. This is because Taurus likes a feeling of substance in their environment. Their house is not only their home but their place of creativity and entertainment. The Taurus' home tends to be truly their castle. If they could choose, Taurus people would prefer living in the countryside to being city dwellers. If they cannot do so during their working lives, many Taurus individuals like to holiday in or even retire to the country, away from the city and closer to the land.

At home a Taurus is like a country squire – lord (or lady) of the manor. They love to entertain lavishly, to make others feel secure in their home and to encourage others to derive the same sense of satisfaction as they do from it. If you are invited for dinner at the home of a Taurus you can expect the best food and best entertainment. Be prepared for a tour of the house and expect to see your Taurus friend exhibit a lot of pride and satisfaction in his or her possessions.

Taurus people like children but they are usually strict with them. The reason for this is they tend to treat their children – as they do most things in life – as their possessions. The positive side to this is that their children will be well cared for and well supervised. They will get every material thing they need to grow up properly. On the down side, Taurus can get too repressive with their children. If a child dares to upset the daily routine – which Taurus loves to follow – he or she will have a problem with a Taurus parent.

Horoscope for 2020

Major Trends

There are two major headlines in your Horoscope this year. The first is the enormous power in your 9th house – three long-term planets are there for most of the year. The second is Uranus in your own sign. This began last year in March and will continue for many more to come.

The power in your 9th house is a positive thing. The 9th house is very beneficent. It is so beneficent that even maleficent planets that occupy or pass through there become kinder. So this is a year for making religious and philosophical breakthroughs. It is a year for travelling and expanding your horizons. It is especially good for students either in college or applying to college and it indicates success in their studies. Focus tends to bring success. It is a year where a deep theological discussion or the visit of a minister or guru is more interesting than a night out on the town. It is a year for going deeper into the meaning of life and your personal philosophy of life.

The Uranus transit is a mixed picture. All of you will feel it, but especially those of you with birthdays from April 21 to May 1. Uranus will range through 2 to 11 degrees of your sign this year. Life becomes exciting and unpredictable. Anything can happen at any time – things you never even imagined. It brings sudden and dramatic changes to your life. Excitement, unpredictability and change are not Taurean favourites. Taurus is adept at creating comfort and ease on the material plane. You have your comfort zone – your groove – and don't like to be taken out of there. Yet, this is what's going on. Never mind that many of the sudden changes will be good changes, it is the discomfort of being taken out of your comfort zone that is disturbing. So there are many life lessons to be learned. The primary one is to embrace change and be comfortable with it. Change is really your friend.

The love life seems much better this year than in 2019. Saturn is still near your love planet Pluto, showing caution and delays, but benevolent Jupiter will also be travelling with Pluto. This will bring serious love opportunities for singles. Marriage might not happen, but love is there. More on this later.

Health looks good this year, especially until December. At the end of the year it becomes more delicate, but there's not anything to worry about. More details later.

The career will be excellent all year, but especially from December 20 onwards. More on this later.

Your areas of greatest interest this year will be the body and image; religion, philosophy, theology and foreign travel; career (from March 23 to July 1 and from December 20 onwards); and friends, groups and group activities.

Your paths of greatest fulfilment will be intellectual pursuits and interests (until May 6); home and family (after May 6); religion, philosophy, foreign travel and theology (until December 20); and career (from December 20 onwards).

Health

(Please note that this is an astrological perspective on health and not a medical one. In days of yore there was no difference, both these perspectives were identical. But now there could be quite a difference. For a medical perspective, please consult your doctor or health practitioner.)

Health, as we have said, looks very good this year. There are no long-term planets in stressful alignment with you until December 18 – practically the whole year. They are all kind to you, which is highly unusual, and so your health and energy are abundant. You tend to be disease resistant, and if you have any pre-existing conditions they seem to be under control.

Another good health signal is your empty 6th house. Only short-term planets will move through there this year and their influence is short-lived. This shows that you don't need to pay too much attention here; you can sort of take good health for granted. Sure, there will be periods in the year where health and energy are less 'easy' than usual. These periods come from short-term planetary transits and are temporary and not trends for the year. When the difficult transit passes, your normal health and energy returns. We will cover this more fully in the monthly reports.

Good though your health is it can be made even better. Give more attention to the following - the vulnerable areas for you, Taurus (the reflex points are shown in the chart below):

- The neck and throat. Taurus rules the neck and throat and these are always important for Taureans. The neck should be regularly massaged, as tension tends to collect there and needs to be released. Craniosacral therapy is excellent for the neck.
- The kidneys and hips are also always important for Taurus. Hips should be regularly massaged. If you feel under the weather, a herbal kidney cleanse might be a good idea.
- The lungs, arms, shoulders, small intestine and respiratory system become more delicate between April 3 and August 7, when your health planet Venus spends more than four months in Gemini. During that period arm and shoulder massage will be beneficial; breathing exercises too.

Important foot reflexology points for the year ahead

Try to massage all of the foot on a regular basis - the top of the foot as well as the bottom - but pay extra attention to the points highlighted on the chart. When you massage, be aware of 'sore spots' as these need special attention. It's also a good idea to massage the ankles and below them.

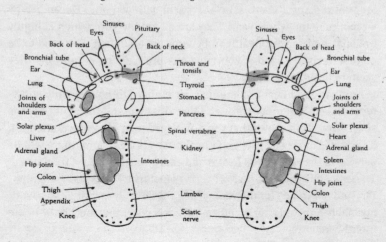

Your health planet Venus is a very fast-moving planet, as our regular readers know. This year she won't move as fast as usual as she will have one of her retrogrades. In spite of that she will move through 11 of your 12 signs and houses this year, so there are many short-term health trends that depend on where Venus is and the kinds of aspects she receives. These are best covered in the monthly reports.

Siblings and sibling figures seem more stressed this year, and could be facing surgeries. The health of parents and parent figures seems better than last year. The health of children and children figures needs more attention from March 23 to July 1, and from December 18 onwards.

Uranus in your sign for the long term indicates experimentalism with the body. You are testing its limits. Basically this is a good thing. Often our physical limitations are not what we think – we can do more than we think we can. The only way we learn is through experimentation. However, this should be done in a mindful way. Thus, exercises like yoga, tai chi or other martial arts would be good. These are safe ways to test the physical limits.

Home and Family

Though you are probably travelling more and staying in various places for longer periods than usual, a permanent move is not likely this year. There's nothing against it, but nothing that especially supports it either. Your empty 4th house (only short-term planets move through there) tends to the status quo. You seem basically satisfied with the current domestic arrangements and family situation and have no need to make major changes.

There are the usual two solar eclipses this year and, since the Sun is your family planet, these will bring some disruptions here. They will bring dramas in the lives of parents, parent figures and family members. Often unexpected repairs are needed to the home. But then the dust settles and things get back to normal.

As already mentioned, siblings and sibling figures in your life seem stressed out. Four lunar eclipses this year hit them twice as many times as usual. So, they will have personal dramas, a need to redefine themselves and create a new image for the world. This will go on all year. The two solar eclipses bring financial changes to siblings too. However, they don't seem likely to move.

These four lunar eclipses will affect the neighbourhood where you live. There might be construction work or other disruptions there. Relations with your neighbours will need work.

Parents and parent figures could move this year, although there seem to be many delays and glitches indicated. Their marriages or current relationships get tested this year too. One of the parents or parent figures seems unusually devoted to you. Children and children figures in your life are not likely to move; if they do they will probably stay in the neighbourhood. Grandchildren (if you have them) are having a quiet domestic year.

If you're planning any house renovations, July 22 to August 22 would be a good time. If you're redecorating the house in a cosmetic kind of way, or if you're buying objects of beauty for the home, September 6 to October 2 would be a good period.

Because your family planet, the Sun, is a fast-moving planet, moving through all the houses and signs of your Horoscope over the year, there are many short-term family trends that depend on where the Sun is and the aspects he receives. These are best dealt with in the monthly reports.

Finance and Career

Finance is always important to a Taurus, but for the past few years it has been less so than usual. This trend continues in the year ahead. The money house is basically empty with only short-term planets moving through there. I read this as a positive. You're broadly content with finances as they are and have little need to make major changes. A lunar eclipse at the end of the year – November 30 – will occur in your money house, and this could show a need for a financial course correction. But for most of the year, things are quiet.

Being earthy Taurus you have a natural affinity for real estate (especially rural real estate, farmland and the like), agriculture and agricultural products, copper and sugar. With Mercury as your financial planet you also have a good feeling for telecommunications, transportation, retailing, trading, advertising and PR. Whatever you are doing, good PR, advertising and good use of the media is very important.

Mercury is a fast and erratic planet. He is perhaps the most 'flexible' of all the planets (with the exception of the Moon). The message of the Horoscope is that in finance you have to be a bit 'un-Taurean' – you have to be more flexible, more nimble, less fixed in your ways.

Because Mercury is so fast moving, there are many short-term trends in finance that depend on where he is and the aspects that he receives. These short-term trends are best dealt with in the monthly reports. In addition, he will go into retrograde mode three times this year: from February 17 to March 9; June 18 to July 11; and October 14 to November 2. These are times for financial review, not times for overt action. If important financial decisions have to be made during those periods (life likes to sometimes force issues), do more homework and due diligence than usual. Resolve your doubts.

The real headline this year is the career. Your career planet, Uranus, entered your sign in March 2019 and will remain there for many more years. So we are dealing with a long-term trend. This is actually a positive long-term trend. It shows that career opportunities are seeking you out. There's nothing much that you need to do; they will find you. You have the image of someone successful, someone of status. You dress this way and project yourself this way. Others see you as successful. You have the favour of bosses, elders, parents and parent figures – the authority figures in your life. They seem devoted to you. They have a personal interest in you.

Saturn will make a foray into your 10th career house between March 23 and July 2. Then, on December 18, he will move in there for the next two and a half years. The message here is that your career success involves taking on more responsibility. The opportunities come easily, but in the end you have to perform – you have to be the best at what you do. In addition, Jupiter will move into your 10th house on December 20. This brings career elevation, promotions and overall success.

Career is good this year, but next year it will be even better. Most of this year is preparation for the next. Your career success might not bring extra earnings right away; it is more about status and prestige than actual earnings. But increased earnings will come later down the road.

Love and Social Life

The love life has been complicated for the past two years. Saturn has been travelling with your love planet Pluto, and this is not a great aspect for marriage. Often it shows a fear of serious relationships or serious commitment. If this is the case with you, it should be examined. These transits promote an excessive caution. Caution is probably a good thing. Fear is not. Saturn and Pluto are still travelling together for most of 2020, so these tendencies are still in effect. But this year Jupiter is in the picture too. Jupiter is benevolent and expansive, and is travelling with your love planet until December 20.

So, love is in the air this year. There is a serious relationship for singles happening. But the message of the Horoscope is not to rush things, to let things develop as they will – slowly and methodically. Marriage, as we have mentioned, is not likely. But one can enjoy love without getting too committed.

I can see two relationships happening, and you seem torn between the two. Both seem to be with highly educated and refined people. Both could be foreigners or people you meet in foreign countries. One seems older and more settled – a more conservative person. With the other sexual magnetism is much stronger. We see a similar scenario for those working on their second marriage too.

Pluto has been in Capricorn, your 9th house, for many, many years, and will be there for many more to come. This makes you conservative in love. You gravitate to conservative people. You like to go slow in love. You don't fall in love very quickly but like to test it and see the lie of the land. And, if you are not like that, you have been attracting these kinds of people.

Love and romantic opportunities happen in your place of worship or through the intervention of people in your place of worship. They also happen in college or university – or through college events or functions and in foreign lands. Foreigners are especially alluring these days.

While sexual magnetism is always important to you – Pluto is the generic ruler of sex – you need more than that. You like someone you can learn from, someone educated. These are the aspects of the person who falls in love with their professor, minister or worship leader. Good philosophical compatibility is probably just as important as sexual chemistry.

Self-improvement

Problems in life take many forms. They can be financial, social, psychological or health-oriented. But whatever form the problem takes, underneath it is a theological issue. Problems are really theological problems deeply disguised. This will require some meditation and reflection to understand, but it is so. Clear up the theology and the problem will tend to dissolve.

What do we mean here? Do you believe in a Higher Power (by whatever name you choose to call it)? Whatever your answer, there are psychological consequences to it. And these will impact on various sectors of life. Track down every problem in your life and underneath it is theology. Thus the current planetary power in your 9th house of religion and philosophy will help resolve a lot of these issues.

Uranus in your sign has already been discussed. The important thing is to experiment with the body – to test its limits – in safe and mindful ways: daredevil stunts can be dangerous. But this transit also shows other things. A continuous redefinition of the self, the self-concept and image is going on now. Your personal evolution is speeding up. No sooner do you settle on one image than a new and better idea comes to you. And this goes on and on. You upgrade your image the way others upgrade their software. This can be a problem in relationships. When you fell in love you were one kind of person. Now you are another kind is the love still there? It is even more perplexing for the spouse, partner or current love. He or she fell in love with person 'X' and now he or she is dealing with person 'Y' or 'Z' or beyond. It's hard to keep up with you. The good news is that you are an exciting person to be around these days. There is never a dull moment.

Spiritual Neptune has been in your 11th house for many years now, and will remain there for many more. We have no doubt discussed this in previous years' reports, but the trend is still in effect. It indicates spiritual friendships. You are attracted to spiritual groups and organizations. It is the very spirituality of these people that you find alluring. It also shows friendships with creative and inspired kinds of people –

poets, musicians, dancers, people in the film industry – high-glamour kinds of people.

Month-by-month Forecasts

January

Best Days Overall: 5, 6, 14, 22, 23
Most Stressful Days Overall: 12, 18, 19, 24, 25, 26
Best Days for Love: 6, 13, 14, 15, 18, 19, 23, 27, 28
Best Days for Money: 5, 6, 7, 8, 14, 15, 22, 23, 25, 26
Best Days for Career: 4, 5, 13, 14, 22, 24, 25, 26

You are in an amazing career period all month, but especially from the 20th onwards. A lot of success is happening. On the 11th your career planet, Uranus, starts to move forward, and on the 20th the Sun enters your 10th career house. So you are in a yearly career peak. The lower half of your Horoscope is practically devoid of planets. There is only one planet (not counting the Moon) that is below the horizon – and just barely at that! Home and family can be safely ignored as you focus your full energy on the career. Normally this can create some problems with the family, but for you not so. The family seem fully behind you, supporting you all the way. They see your success as a 'family project'. Also, this aspect (the family planet in the career house) often shows that the family as a whole is succeeding, and being elevated in status.

A lunar eclipse on the 10th – the first of four in the coming year – occurs in your 3rd house and impacts on the ruler of that house. So, cars and communication equipment will get tested. Be sure to drive more carefully. Students below college level have dramas at school and perhaps make changes in their schooling. Mercury, your financial planet, is affected too, so a financial 'course correction' may be needed.

In spite of the eclipse your finances look good. Mercury travels with Jupiter from the 1st to the 4th and this should bring a nice payday or financial opportunity. Your financial planet is in your 9th house until the 16th, which is another positive financial signal. The 9th house brings expansion and good luck. Mercury will be 'out of bounds' until the 12th, which shows that in financial matters you're going outside your normal comfort zone. Perhaps you are doing this consciously, perhaps financial duties are pulling you there. You're thinking outside the box financially, and it pays off.

On the 16th Mercury enters Aquarius, his sign of greatest 'exaltation', his most powerful position. Another good signal for finance! Mercury in your 10th career house often brings pay rises (official or unofficial) and the financial blessing of bosses, parents, parent figures and even the government. Your good career reputation is an important factor in earnings.

February

Best Days Overall: 1, 2, 10, 11, 18, 19, 20, 28, 29
Most Stressful Days Overall: 8, 9, 14, 15, 21, 22
Best Days for Love: 2, 7, 8, 11, 14, 15, 16, 17, 20, 26, 27, 29
Best Days for Money: 1, 2, 3, 4, 5, 6, 7, 10, 11, 14, 15, 19, 20, 23, 24, 25, 28, 29
Best Days for Career: 1, 9, 10, 18, 21, 22, 28

On an overall level, your health is excellent, but since January 20 it is a little less so (and this is the case until the 19th). Make sure you get enough rest. You can enhance your health in the ways mentioned in the yearly report, and also through foot massage until the 7th and through scalp and face massage after then. Physical exercise would be good after the 7th as well. Health and energy will improve after the 19th.

You remain in a yearly career peak until the 20th, so there is still success happening there. The night side of your Horoscope, like last month, is almost devoid of planets and your 4th house of home and family is basically empty. So continue to focus on the career. You still have good family support for this until the 19th.

Finances are good, but are a bit more complicated this month. Mercury moves into your 11th house on the 3rd, which is another positive for finance. The 11th house is a beneficent house and your financial intuition will be excellent. However, when Mercury starts to retrograde on the 17th your intuition will need some verification.

Mercury's retrograde, as our regular readers know, will not stop earnings, only slow things down. There will probably be financial delays, but you can minimize this by paying more attention to financial details, such as by making sure cheques are dated and signed properly, and online payments are made correctly – make sure you click in the right places. This is the problem with the online world; it is very easy to make mistakes.

The month ahead looks more active socially and romantically. Your 11th house of friendship is strong all month, and Pluto, your love planet, receives very nice aspects from the 19th onwards. Pluto stays in a sign for many years, so love trends tend to be long term in your case. You favour highly educated, refined, even religious types. Romantic opportunities occur at university or religious-type functions. Sexual magnetism is always important for you, but you also like philosophical compatibility.

Venus, the ruler of your Horoscope, will have one of her solstices from the 8th to the 10th. She pauses in the heavens (in her latitude) and then changes direction. A pause in your affairs now would be likely and benevolent.

Children and children figures in your life are having a very active and happy social month – especially after the 19th. Romance can happen this month or next. If they are not of the appropriate age for romance, they will be making friends and attending more parties and gatherings.

March

Best Days Overall: 1, 8, 9, 17, 18, 27, 28
Most Stressful Days Overall: 6, 7, 12, 13, 19, 20
Best Days for Love: 1, 8, 9, 12, 13, 17, 18, 27, 28
Best Days for Money: 1, 2, 3, 8, 9, 10, 11, 17, 18, 22, 23, 27, 28, 29, 30
Best Days for Career: 1, 8, 16, 17, 19, 20, 26, 27

Saturn crosses the Mid-heaven on the 23rd and enters your 10th house of career. This transit is basically good for the career and it indicates career-related travel. The demands of your career are strong and you must succeed by sheer merit – but you will succeed. Saturn is usually a challenging planet, but in your chart he is more benevolent. He is the ruler of your 9th house, which is always a beneficent house. You might be called on to mentor others these days and this mentoring will be helpful to you. Educational opportunities related to the career will come to you, and you should take them.

There is more good news in the career. Venus, the ruler of your Horoscope, moves into your own sign on the 5th and travels with Uranus, your career planet, from the 6th to the 9th. This indicates career opportunity and elevation. A new career opportunity can appear – and suddenly.

Health is good this month. There is only one long-term planet, Saturn, in stressful alignment with you, and only from the 23rd onwards. Indeed, most of you won't feel this too much; only those born early in the sign of Taurus (April 20–21) will feel this strongly. But you can take steps to enhance your health with scalp massage, face massage and exercise until the 5th and through neck and throat massage from the 5th onwards. Your state of health always affects your personal appearance, but after the 5th even more so. You should be looking good this period.

Your dream life seems very active this month – especially on the 8th and 9th. Pay attention to your dreams as they have important information for you.

Finances remain complicated this month until the 10th. Mercury is not only travelling backwards, but he changes signs twice. He begins the month in your 11th house, moves back into your 10th house on the 4th and then returns to your 11th house on the 16th. Financial intuition needs verification until the 4th, but after the 16th it seems very reliable. Avoid major purchases or investments until after the 10th, when your financial judgement becomes more reliable. Your financial planet in your 11th house is a positive for earnings: it is a beneficent house where fondest hopes and wishes come to pass. So this should be a prosperous month. It starts off slowly but picks up steam after the 11th. Friends seem helpful in finances. You could be buying high-tech equipment or gadgetry too. Being involved with groups and professional or trade organizations will also help the bottom line.

Love seems happy this month. Jupiter will be travelling with your love planet, Pluto, all month. This brings romantic meetings for singles – and highly erotic ones.

April

Best Days Overall: 5, 6, 13, 14, 23, 24
Most Stressful Days Overall: 3, 4, 9, 10, 15, 16, 30
Best Days for Love: 6, 7, 8, 9, 10, 14, 15, 16, 17, 24, 25, 26
Best Days for Money: 1, 2, 6, 10, 11, 14, 20, 21, 24, 25, 26, 30
Best Days for Career: 5, 13, 15, 16, 17, 23

The month ahead is happy and prosperous – enjoy. Jupiter is still travelling with your love planet all this month, indicating happiness in love. This is in spite of your 7th house being empty! All of you seem more sexually active these days, whether you are in a relationship or single. Whatever your age or stage in life, the libido is stronger than usual.

On the 19th the Sun enters your own sign. The Eastern sector of self is the strongest sector of the Horoscope this month. This means the planetary power moves towards you rather than away from you. You are in a strong period of personal independence and can have things your own way. You're less dependent on others and their opinions. Be respectful of others but do things your way. Your way is best these days.

The Sun's move into your sign initiates one of your yearly personal pleasure peaks. Give the body the pleasures it desires. It is a good time for getting the body and image into the shape that you want. Family seems very devoted to you and they are helping your career. A family member or family connection has news of a good career opportunity or advice for you – most probably between the 24th and 26th.

Finances are good. Mercury is now moving forward, and speedily – he goes through three signs and houses of your chart this month. This indicates confidence and fast financial progress. Your financial intuition is still very strong until the 27th. The dream life – still active – holds important financial information for you, as do psychics, astrologers, tarot readers and other spiritual channels. You might have to work harder for earnings from the 11th to the 27th but they will come. On the 27th Mercury crosses your Ascendant and enters your own house. This is an especially prosperous period as it brings windfalls and expensive clothing or accessories to you. Financial opportunities will seek you out. Your ruling planet Venus will move into your 2nd money house on the 3rd and will spend the rest of the month there. This shows personal involvement – personal focus – on finance and tends to prosperity. You spend on yourself and take on the image of wealth. Personal appearance and overall presentation are ultra-important financially.

Mars spends the month in your 10th house of career, along with Saturn. This shows a need for aggressiveness – a need to do battle with competitors – a need to display courage in career matters.

May

Best Days Overall: 2, 3, 10, 11, 20, 21, 29, 30
Most Stressful Days Overall: 1, 6, 7, 13, 14, 27, 28
Best Days for Love: 3, 4, 5, 6, 7, 11, 12, 13, 14, 21, 22, 23, 24
Best Days for Money: 2, 3, 12, 13, 22, 23, 24
Best Days for Career: 2, 10, 13, 14, 20

Though there are now two planets in stressful alignment with you, health is basically good. And after the 13th, as Mars leaves his stressful aspect, health will be even better. You can enhance it further in the ways described in the yearly report, and also with arm and shoulder massage. Breathing exercises are beneficial too – air has a healing influence this month. Get out on a windy day and let the wind blow all over you. Or drive out of the city with the windows open and let the in-rushing air massage you. Very invigorating.

Venus (your health and work planet as well as the ruler of your Horoscope) will spend the month 'out of bounds', thus you are venturing outside your normal sphere. This is the situation in health matters too – there are no answers in your normal circles so you need to seek outside them. Sometimes the job you're in (or the job you seek) pulls you outside your normal boundaries.

Mercury, your financial planet, will also be 'out of bounds' from the 17th onwards. So you are thinking outside the box financially too.

Financial opportunities occur outside your normal parameters. Children and children figures in your life are also going outside their normal boundaries this period.

Jupiter is still travelling with your love planet all month. Generally this is a great signal for love and romance, only Pluto has been retrograde since April 25 and Jupiter will also begin to go backwards on the 14th. So love is there, but important love decisions shouldn't be taken just now. There's no need to rush things. Let love develop as it will.

The month ahead is prosperous. Venus spends the entire month in your money house, your financial planet enters there on the 12th and the Sun moves in on the 20th and you begin a yearly financial peak. From the 20th to the 29th your money house is the strongest house in your Horoscope. The Sun in the 2nd house indicates good family support and financial opportunities that come from family connections. Mercury in the money house shows that the money people in your life are supportive and providing opportunity. Venus's presence there indicates your personal involvement and focus. It shows spending on yourself and perhaps on health gadgets and products.

The night side of your Horoscope is the strongest it will ever be this year. The day side is still stronger though, and thus the career and outer activities are still most important. But you can shift some attention to your home, family and emotional life – not a whole lot, but some.

June

Best Days Overall: 7, 8, 16, 17, 18, 26, 27
Most Stressful Days Overall: 3, 4, 9, 10, 24, 28, 29
Best Days for Love: 1, 3, 4, 8, 9, 10, 18, 19, 20, 27, 28, 29
Best Days for Money: 3, 4, 8, 11, 12, 18, 19, 20, 21, 22, 27
Best Days for Career: 7, 8, 9, 10, 16, 17, 26, 27

On one level the month ahead is very eventful. Two eclipses show change and disruption. On another level the month ahead is non-eventful as retrograde activity reaches its peak for the year. (It will reach the same peak again in September.) Overall, changes and disruptions are likely but with a delayed reaction.

The lunar eclipse of the 5th, the second of four that we will have, occurs in your 8th house and causes important financial changes for the spouse, partner or current love. It can bring encounters – generally psychological-type encounters – with death. Sometimes there are near-death kinds of experiences; sometimes there are deaths of people you know; sometimes there are dreams of death. The cosmos is urging you to confront death and get a better understanding of it. Sometimes surgery is recommended – but you seem healthy and you should get a second opinion. Siblings and sibling figures are impacted here. They can have health scares or changes in their employment. There can be dramas in the lives of neighbours too. Cars and communication equipment get tested and might need repair or replacement. It would be wise to drive more carefully, more defensively.

This eclipse is powerful because it has an impact on other planets in your chart – Mars and Venus. The effect on Venus can bring a redefinition of your self, your self-concept and the overall presentation that you make to others. This will go on for a few months. You'll dress differently, and probably change your hairstyle and your overall image. It can bring health scares (probably no more than scares) and upheavals at work or dramas in the lives of co-workers or employees. The impact of the eclipse on Mars indicates changes in your spiritual life – in your attitudes, practice, teachings and teachers. There are shake-ups in spiritual or charitable organizations that you're involved with and dramas in the lives of gurus or spiritual guides. Take it nice and easy this eclipse period. Avoid stressful activities – there's no need to tempt the fates.

The solar eclipse of the 21st occurs in your 3rd house and thus again affects siblings and sibling figures. It brings important financial changes and a need to redefine themselves – their image and presentation to the world. This can be the case with neighbours too. Students below college level are affected by both eclipses, and there are probably changes in educational plans or disruptions at school. Again, cars and communication equipment get tested, and it will be a good idea to drive carefully over this period.

July

Best Days Overall: 4, 5, 14, 15, 23, 24, 31
Most Stressful Days Overall: 1, 6, 7, 8, 21, 22, 27, 28
Best Days for Love: 1, 5, 6, 7, 8, 15, 16, 17, 24, 25, 26, 27, 28
Best Days for Money: 1, 4, 5, 9, 10, 14, 15, 16, 17, 19, 20, 23, 24, 27, 28, 31
Best Days for Career: 4, 6, 7, 8, 14, 24

Your siblings and sibling figures in your life, neighbours, cars and communication equipment can't seem to catch a break. They were pounded and tested last month and it just keeps going on. Another lunar eclipse on the 5th hits these exact same areas. This month's occurs in your 9th house. Thus it not only affects students below college level (as last month's eclipses did) but college-level students too. There are changes in educational plans and disruptions at school. If you are involved in legal issues they will take a dramatic turn one way or another – they will move forward.

Mercury, Jupiter and Mars are marginally affected by this eclipse. Thus there can be some minor financial disruption, more change in spiritual or charitable organizations you're involved with, more dramas in the lives of gurus and guru figures, and more psychological confrontations with death.

Saturn moves away from his stressful aspect with you on July 1. Health, which has been good all year, gets even better – and it will be still be good even after the 23rd when the Sun makes a stressful aspect with you. True, it is not one of your best health periods, but nothing serious seems to be happening there. You can enhance your health even further through arm and shoulder massage. Shoulder massage will also help the neck, which is always important for Taureans.

Finances are good this month. Venus will spend all month in your money house again. This shows your focus. By the spiritual law we get what we focus on. It also indicates gaining money from work. Your good work ethic is money in the bank. Your financial planet Mercury will spend the month in your 3rd house. This favours trading, retailing, buying and selling. It favours a good marketing and advertising strategy for whatever you are doing. Until the 12th your financial intuition is good; afterwards it needs some verification. The only financial complication – aside from the eclipse of the 5th – is Mercury's retrograde on the 12th. Avoid making major purchases or investments after that date: try to wrap things up before then.

You are entering the midnight hour of your year, beginning on the 23rd. But this midnight hour is different to most. You're not soundly asleep. You're still very focused on the career and outer affairs. Figuratively speaking it is as if you sleep and then wake up, sleep and then wake. You nap and then focus on your outer life. Still, as we said last month, you can shift some energy to the home and family.

August

    Best Days Overall: 1, 2, 10, 11, 19, 20, 28, 29
    Most Stressful Days Overall: 3, 4, 17, 18, 23, 24, 30, 31
    Best Days for Love: 2, 3, 4, 11, 15, 16, 20, 23, 24, 29
    Best Days for Money: 2, 8, 11, 13, 14, 17, 18, 20, 28, 29
    Best Days for Career: 1, 2, 3, 4, 10, 11, 19, 20, 28, 29, 30, 31

Planetary retrograde activity is very intense this month. From the 15th onwards half the planets are in retrograde motion. This is not quite the maximum for the year but we're close to it. Things slow down in the world. Taurus handles this slow down better than most. You are patient by nature.

The upper half of your chart – the day side – is still stronger than the lower half. But the retrograde planets are all in the upper half of your chart. Even your career planet, Uranus, is retrograde from the 15th onwards. So you may as well focus on the home, family and your emotional wellness. Career issues will need time to resolve.

Venus has been in your money house for four months now, but on the 7th she moves into your 3rd house of communication and intellectual interests. So you are more focused on these things. You're reading more, studying more, talking more and connecting more with others. It is a good transit for students below college level and for marketing people, PR people and retailers. Your mind is sharper now and the communication skills more enhanced.

Health is good overall but this is not one of your best health months. You will feel the difference after the 22nd when your health and energy return to their usual levels. In the meantime you can enhance your health and energy through arm and shoulder massage until the 7th, and through abdominal massage after that date. Diet becomes important healthwise after the 7th.

Finances are not a major interest after the 7th but still look good. Mercury is now moving speedily. You make quick progress. You have multiple paths to earnings. Until the 5th sales, marketing, PR, teaching and writing – mental activities – are profitable. Neighbours seem helpful. Until the 20th there is good financial support from the family. You are probably spending more on the home and family too. From the 5th to the end of the month you have happy money – money that is earned in happy ways and spent on happy things. Probably you spend more on the children or children figures in your life. You are more speculative than usual too. Taureans are not known as free spenders, but from the 5th to the 20th you seem to be.

Love is complicated this month – especially after the 7th. Your love planet, Pluto, is still retrograde. And Venus, your ruler, is in opposition to the love planet. So you and your current love are distant from each other. This might not be physical distance but psychological distance. You see things in opposite ways. There is a need to bridge your differences this month.

September

Best Days Overall: 6, 7, 8, 16, 17, 24, 25
Most Stressful Days Overall: 14, 15, 20, 21, 26, 27
Best Days for Love: 2, 3, 6, 7, 13, 14, 16, 17, 20, 21, 22, 23, 24, 25
Best Days for Money: 6, 7, 9, 10, 16, 17, 18, 19, 24, 25, 26, 27
Best Days for Career: 6, 7, 16, 17, 24, 25, 26, 27

Since August 20 there has been a Grand Trine in the Earth signs – your native element. This is very fortunate for you and you are comfortable with a lot of earth. Further, your financial planet was part of this Grand Trine. So there has been prosperity. Mercury moves out of this Grand

Trine on the 5th, so earnings will require more work and effort. There are more financial challenges happening. Mercury will be in your 6th house of health and work until the 27th. This indicates earnings that come from work – from employment and second jobs. It is not the aspect of a lottery winner. (Last month was better for speculations than this month.) In spite of the increased retrograde activity this month – we will be at the maximum amount for the year from the 9th to the 12th (and after the 12th we will still have half the plants moving backwards) – it doesn't seem to affect you financially. Earnings are moving forward.

The Western, social sector of your chart increased in strength last month and this month it is even stronger. It is now the dominant sector. So the social life is becoming more active and more important. Personal independence is weaker than usual. Now is a time to put the interests of others ahead of your own. Good comes to you through the good graces of others. It is time to cultivate your social skills. This is especially true in the realm of finances from the 27th onwards. Your social grace plays an important role here.

Your love planet Pluto is still retrograde, so important love decisions – one way or another – are best postponed. This is a time for social review and for attaining social clarity.

Health is good and you are more focused here after the 22nd. This is a month for focusing on your emotional health and wellbeing. Your health planet Venus enters your 4th house on the 6th and your family planet, the Sun, enters your 6th house of health on the 22nd. You might be more focused on the health of family members than on your own. Work to keep your moods positive and constructive and all will be well.

The upper half of your Horoscope has been dominant all year and this month, on the 27th, it becomes even more so. The focus is on the career. The only problem is the retrograde of your career planet, which will go on for many more months. So focus, but research and study your career moves. Resolve your doubts.

October

Best Days Overall: 4, 5, 13, 14, 21, 23, 31
Most Stressful Days Overall: 11, 12, 17, 18, 23, 24, 25
Best Days for Love: 3, 4, 5, 13, 14, 17, 18, 21, 22, 31
Best Days for Money: 4, 5, 6, 7, 9, 10, 13, 14, 17, 18, 21, 23, 26, 31
Best Days for Career: 4, 5, 13, 21, 23, 24, 25, 31

Retrograde activity is lessening this month and this will be the case for the rest of the year. Events in the world are moving forward – little by little. Mercury will go retrograde on the 14th so important purchases and investments should be made before then. There could be some financial disagreements with a parent, parent figure or boss and they will take some time to resolve. Mercury spends almost the entire month in your 7th house of love (until the 28th). So, like last month, your social grace and social connections are important in finance. Often there are opportunities for business partnerships or joint ventures under this transit, but these should be studied carefully, especially after the 14th. You seem very financially involved with the spouse, partner or current love. Your financial planet in Scorpio suggests a need for a detox of the financial life. Prosperity will come from 'getting rid' of what doesn't belong in the financial life rather than from adding to it. Taureans are accumulators by nature, but sometimes this can be a blockage. Get rid of redundant accounts or wasteful expenditures. Also get rid of possessions that you don't use or need. This will free up space for the new and better that wants to come in. Time to 'de-clutter' the financial life.

The main headline this month is the love life. There are many interesting things happening here. First, your love planet Pluto starts to move forward on the 4th after many months of retrograde motion. Secondly, your 7th house of love becomes very strong from the 23rd onwards. The timing is very nice, too. You are in a romantic mood. You have more clarity in love and socially. A lot of your socializing seems to be business- and family-related, and romantic opportunities can happen as you pursue your financial goals or with people involved in your finances. There is also more socializing with the family and at home. Family members and family connections are likely to play Cupid.

On the 2nd Venus will move into your 5th house, creating another Grand Trine in the Earth signs – a positive aspect for you personally and for love. Work will benefit to, but more caution is needed there. Venus will be making very nice aspects to Pluto – especially on the 21st and 22nd. Jupiter will be also be in close proximity to the love planet from the 25th onwards (and will be even closer next month). All of this spells romance and romantic opportunity. A wedding or engagement would not be a surprise. Those already married will be going out more and meeting new people. There will be more romance within the existing relationship.

November

Best Days Overall: 1, 10, 18, 19, 27, 28
Most Stressful Days Overall: 7, 8, 14, 15, 20, 21
Best Days for Love: 2, 3, 11, 12, 14, 15, 19, 21, 22
Best Days for Money: 2, 3, 4, 11, 19, 30
Best Days for Career: 1, 9, 10, 17, 18, 20, 21, 27

Venus is in her second solstice of the year until the 2nd. She pauses in the heavens and then changes direction (in her latitude). So a pause in your affairs would be good and then a change of direction.

Love is still active and happy this month. Jupiter is travelling with Pluto, your love planet, and it is likely to be a sexually active kind of month as well. Your 7th house of love will be strong all month. The Sun will leave your 7th house on the 21st but Venus will move in on the same day. You are still in a yearly love and social peak all month. Venus's move into your 7th house shows personal popularity. You are there for your friends and they appreciate it. You put other people's interests ahead of your own. There is less self-confidence, less personal independence, but the happy social life compensates for this.

The 4th lunar eclipse of the season occurs on the 30th; it occurs in your money house and sideswipes Neptune. So corrections are needed in your financial life, in your strategy and thinking. Things are not as you imagined them to be. But the changes you make will be good, although they may not be comfortable to make – the end result will be beneficial. The eclipse once again affects siblings, sibling figures and neighbours. Once again they need to redefine themselves. It also affects students – those at college and those below college levels. They are making changes in educational plans and dealing with disruptions at their school. They are also making changes in the spiritual life – changes in attitudes, teachings and teachers.

This is not your best health period, but health will still be OK. Overall energy is not up to its usual standards, but this is a short-term issue. The good news is that Venus will spend most of the month (until the 21st) in your 6th house of health, which indicates focus. Health can be enhanced through hip massage until the 21st. After then, safe sex and sexual moderation will be important (you are in a sexually active period, but there's no need to overdo things). You also benefit from detox regimes.

Retrograde activity is getting weaker and weaker. By the end of the month 90 per cent of the planets will be moving forward. Events move at a faster pace. Progress is swifter than it has been for many months.

December

Best Days Overall: 7, 8, 15, 16, 24, 25, 26
Most Stressful Days Overall: 5, 6, 11, 12, 17, 18
Best Days for Love: 2, 3, 8, 11, 12, 16, 22, 23, 25, 26
Best Days for Money: 1, 5, 6, 8, 13, 14, 16, 24, 27, 28
Best Days for Career: 7, 15, 17, 18, 24, 25

A very eventful month that portends changes not only for this immediate period but for all of next year as well. First off, two long-term planets change signs this month. Saturn will leave your 9th house, after two years there, and enter your 10th on the 18th, and Jupiter will move into your 10th house on the 20th, and will spend practically all of 2021 in your career house. Secondly, we will have our final eclipse of the year on December 14. This will be a solar eclipse that occurs in your 8th house. The shift of a long-term planet is always a headline. Likewise an eclipse.

With Jupiter in your 10th house, career is going to be very successful going into next year. Yes, you will earn it, but success will happen. There are also likely to be surgery or near-death kinds of experiences in the lives of bosses, parents or parent figures. There will be much dealing with death and issues to do with death in the coming year.

The solar eclipse of the 14th can bring confrontations with death, although usually on the psychological level. The cosmos wants you to have a better understanding of it. It brings dramatic financial changes to the spouse, partner or current love. Financial corrections are necessary. A parent or parent figure in your life has personal dramas – perhaps a near-death experience or surgery (another type of near-death experience). He or she will need to redefine his or her image and presentation to the world. There can be repairs needed to the home too.

This eclipse impacts on Neptune, your planet of friends. So there are dramas in the lives of friends. Friendships often get tested. High-tech equipment becomes more temperamental and often needs repair or replacement. Make sure your passwords are strong and that your anti-hacking, anti-virus software is up to date. Back up important files.

Your financial planet Mercury will be 'out of bounds' from the 13th onwards. Thus you are outside your normal sphere in financial matters. Perhaps there are no financial solutions to be found in the usual places and you have to search elsewhere. Perhaps money-making opportunities come to you from 'outside' your sphere. Mercury will be in your 8th house until the 21st so bear in mind our previous discussions about de-cluttering and detoxing the financial life. You prosper by cutting away what doesn't belong there.

When Jupiter and Saturn move into Aquarius, health will become more delicate in the coming year and will need more attention. This month, though, health is good. With the exception of Jupiter and Saturn (and that is only later in the month) the other planets are in harmonious aspect or are leaving you alone.

Gemini

Ⅱ

THE TWINS

Birthdays from
21st May to
20th June

Personality Profile

GEMINI AT A GLANCE

Element – Air

Ruling Planet – Mercury
   Career Planet – Neptune
   Love Planet – Jupiter
   Money Planet – Moon
   Planet of Health and Work – Pluto
   Planet of Home and Family Life – Mercury

Colours – blue, yellow, yellow-orange

Colour that promotes love, romance and social harmony – sky blue

Colours that promote earning power – grey, silver

Gems – agate, aquamarine

Metal – quicksilver

Scents – lavender, lilac, lily of the valley, storax

Quality – mutable (= flexibility)

Quality most needed for balance – thought that is deep rather than superficial

Strongest virtues – great communication skills, quickness and agility of thought, ability to learn quickly

Deepest need – communication

Characteristics to avoid – gossiping, hurting others with harsh speech, superficiality, using words to mislead or misinform

Signs of greatest overall compatibility – Libra, Aquarius

Signs of greatest overall incompatibility – Virgo, Sagittarius, Pisces

Sign most helpful to career – Pisces

Sign most helpful for emotional support – Virgo

Sign most helpful financially – Cancer

Sign best for marriage and/or partnerships – Sagittarius

Sign most helpful for creative projects – Libra

Best Sign to have fun with – Libra

Signs most helpful in spiritual matters – Taurus, Aquarius

Best day of the week – Wednesday

Understanding a Gemini

Gemini is to society what the nervous system is to the body. It does not introduce any new information but is a vital transmitter of impulses from the senses to the brain and vice versa. The nervous system does not judge or weigh these impulses – it only conveys information. And it does so perfectly.

This analogy should give you an indication of a Gemini's role in society. Geminis are the communicators and conveyors of information. To Geminis the truth or falsehood of information is irrelevant, they only transmit what they see, hear or read about. Thus they are capable of spreading the most outrageous rumours as well as conveying truth and light. Geminis sometimes tend to be unscrupulous in their communications and can do both great good or great evil with their power. This is why the sign of Gemini is symbolized by twins: Geminis have a dual nature.

Their ability to convey a message – to communicate with such ease – makes Geminis ideal teachers, writers and media and marketing people. This is helped by the fact that Mercury, the ruling planet of Gemini, also rules these activities.

Geminis have the gift of the gab. And what a gift this is! They can make conversation about anything, anywhere, at any time. There is almost nothing that is more fun to Geminis than a good conversation – especially if they can learn something new as well. They love to learn and they love to teach. To deprive a Gemini of conversation, or of books and magazines, is cruel and unusual punishment.

Geminis are almost always excellent students and take well to education. Their minds are generally stocked with all kinds of information, trivia, anecdotes, stories, news items, rarities, facts and statistics. Thus they can support any intellectual position that they care to take. They are awesome debaters and, if involved in politics, make good orators. Geminis are so verbally smooth that even if they do not know what they are talking about, they can make you think that they do. They will always dazzle you with their brilliance.

Finance

Geminis tend to be more concerned with the wealth of learning and ideas than with actual material wealth. As mentioned, they excel in professions that involve writing, teaching, sales and journalism – and not all of these professions pay very well. But to sacrifice intellectual needs merely for money is unthinkable to a Gemini. Geminis strive to combine the two. Cancer is on Gemini's solar 2nd house of money cusp, which indicates that Geminis can earn extra income (in a harmonious and natural way) from investments in residential property, restaurants and hotels. Given their verbal skills, Geminis love to bargain and negotiate in any situation, and especially when it has to do with money.

The Moon rules Gemini's 2nd solar house. The Moon is not only the fastest-moving planet in the zodiac but actually moves through every sign and house every 28 days. No other heavenly body matches the Moon for swiftness or the ability to change quickly. An analysis of the Moon – and lunar phenomena in general – describes Gemini's financial attitudes very well. Geminis are financially versatile and flexible; they can earn money in many different ways. Their financial attitudes and needs seem to change daily. Their feelings about money change also: sometimes they are very enthusiastic about it, at other times they could not care less.

For a Gemini, financial goals and money are often seen only as means of supporting a family; these things have little meaning otherwise.

The Moon, as Gemini's money planet, has another important message for Gemini financially: in order for Geminis to realize their financial potential they need to develop more of an understanding of the emotional side of life. They need to combine their awesome powers of logic with an understanding of human psychology. Feelings have their own logic; Geminis need to learn this and apply it to financial matters.

Career and Public Image

Geminis know that they have been given the gift of communication for a reason, that it is a power that can achieve great good or cause unthinkable distress. They long to put this power at the service of the highest and most transcendental truths. This is their primary goal, to communicate the eternal verities and prove them logically. They look up to people who can transcend the intellect – to poets, artists, musicians and mystics. They may be awed by stories of religious saints and martyrs. A Gemini's highest achievement is to teach the truth, whether it is scientific, inspirational or historical. Those who can transcend the intellect are Gemini's natural superiors – and a Gemini realizes this.

The sign of Pisces is in Gemini's solar 10th house of career. Neptune, the planet of spirituality and altruism, is Gemini's career planet. If Geminis are to realize their highest career potential they need to develop their transcendental – their spiritual and altruistic – side. They need to understand the larger cosmic picture, the vast flow of human evolution – where it came from and where it is heading. Only then can a Gemini's intellectual powers take their true position and he or she can become the 'messenger of the gods'. Geminis need to cultivate a facility for 'inspiration', which is something that does not originate in the intellect but which comes through the intellect. This will further enrich and empower a Gemini's mind.

Love and Relationships

Geminis bring their natural garrulousness and brilliance into their love life and social life as well. A good talk or a verbal joust is an interesting prelude to romance. Their only problem in love is that their intellect is too cool and passionless to incite ardour in others. Emotions sometimes disturb them, and their partners tend to complain about this. If you are in love with a Gemini you must understand why this is so. Geminis avoid deep passions because these would interfere with their ability to think and communicate. If they are cool towards you, understand that this is their nature.

Nevertheless, Geminis must understand that it is one thing to talk about love and another actually to love – to feel it and radiate it. Talking about love glibly will get them nowhere. They need to feel it and act on it. Love is not of the intellect but of the heart. If you want to know how a Gemini feels about love you should not listen to what he or she says, but rather, observe what he or she does. Geminis can be quite generous to those they love.

Geminis like their partners to be refined, well educated and well travelled. If their partners are more wealthy than they, that is all the better. If you are in love with a Gemini you had better be a good listener as well.

The ideal relationship for the Gemini is a relationship of the mind. They enjoy the physical and emotional aspects, of course, but if the intellectual communion is not there they will suffer.

Home and Domestic Life

At home the Gemini can be uncharacteristically neat and meticulous. They tend to want their children and partner to live up to their idealistic standards. When these standards are not met they moan and criticize. However, Geminis are good family people and like to serve their families in practical and useful ways.

The Gemini home is comfortable and pleasant. They like to invite people over and they make great hosts. Geminis are also good at repairs and improvements around the house – all fuelled by their need to stay active and occupied with something they like to do. Geminis have many hobbies and interests that keep them busy when they are home alone.

Geminis understand and get along well with their children, mainly because they are very youthful people themselves. As great communicators, Geminis know how to explain things to children; in this way they gain their children's love and respect. Geminis also encourage children to be creative and talkative, just like they are.

Horoscope for 2020

Major Trends

The major planetary power this year is in your 8th house, Gemini. Your 8th house has been strong for the past two years, but this year it is even more powerful. Thus, the year ahead is about personal transformation. This will happen through crisis, near-death kinds of experiences and encounters with death. Generally, this doesn't indicate actual physical death – it is usually on the psychological level. This is a year where you can give birth to the person you desire to be, the person you are capable of being. The stresses you feel are birth pangs.

The power in your 8th house shows a sexually active kind of year – especially when compared to the past two years. Whatever your age or stage in life, the libido is stronger than usual.

Neptune has been in your 10th house of career for many years now and will be there for many more. Thus the career is a major focus – that and spirituality. More on this later.

The spiritual life is even more pronounced now that Uranus is in your 12th house of spirituality. He entered last year and will be there for many more years. There is great change happening here and much spiritual experimentation. More details later.

Saturn will make a foray into your 9th house from March 23 to July 1, before moving back to your 8th house until December 18. This shows a testing of your religious and philosophical beliefs – they get 'reality therapy'. Some will have to be amended, some will be discarded. This will become a long-term trend from December onwards.

Jupiter spends most of the year in your 8th house. This too shows enhanced libido. Love is expressed physically – sexually. More on this later. Often this transit shows inheritance, but it can also indicate profiting from estates or being named to an administrative position in an estate. Hopefully no one has to actually die.

Jupiter's move into your 9th house at the end of the year (on December 20) is a wonderful aspect for college-level students and for those applying to college. There will be good fortune here.

Your most important areas of interest this year will be sex, personal transformation and occult studies; religion, philosophy, theology, higher learning and foreign travel (from March 23 to July 1 and from December 18 onwards); friends, groups and group activities (from June 28 onwards); career; and spirituality.

Your paths of greatest fulfilment this year are finance (until May 6); communication and intellectual interests (from May 6 onwards); sex, personal transformation and occult studies (until December 20); and religion, philosophy, theology, higher learning and foreign travel (from December 20 onwards).

Health

(Please note that this is an astrological perspective on health and not a medical one. In days of yore there was no difference, both these perspectives were identical. But now there could be quite a difference. For a medical perspective, please consult your doctor or health practitioner.)

Health should be good this year, and will get even better as the year progresses. The end of the year should see you with higher energy and better health than when you began. There is only one long-term planet in stressful alignment with you – Neptune. All the others are leaving you alone, and by the end of the year two (Saturn and Jupiter) will be making harmonious aspects with you.

Your empty 6th house – only short-term planets move through there this year, and their impact is temporary – is another good health signal. You don't need to pay too much attention here as your health is good.

Pluto, your health planet, travels with both Saturn and Jupiter this year. Thus there can be surgery (or it might be recommended to you), but it doesn't seem serious and the end result looks good. Pluto is the generic ruler of surgery and he has been in your 8th house of transformation for many years now, so you tend to see surgery as a 'quick fix' to a health problem. But these same aspects favour detox regimes too, and this option should be explored as well. You get good results from this and often it will do the same thing as surgery (only it usually takes longer and involves more discipline).

The spouse, partner or current love could also be having surgery. He or she should also explore detoxing options.

Good though your health is you can make it even better. Give more attention to the following – the vulnerable areas of your Horoscope (the reflex points are shown in the chart below):

- The colon, bladder and sexual organs. These are always important for Gemini as your health planet Pluto rules these areas. As always, safe sex and sexual moderation are ultra-important. A herbal colon cleanse every now and then would be a good idea.
- The spine, knees, teeth, skin and overall skeletal alignment have become important areas since 2008, when Pluto moved into Capricorn (and they will be important for many more years too). So, regular back and knee massage would be good, as would regular visits to a chiropractor or osteopath. Therapies such as Alexander Technique, Rolfing or Feldenkrais would be good. Give the knees more support when exercising. Regular dental check-ups are advisable.

Important foot reflexology points for the year ahead

Try to massage all of the foot on a regular basis – the top of the foot as well as the bottom – but pay extra attention to the points highlighted on the chart. When you massage, be aware of 'sore spots' as these need special attention. It's also a good idea to massage the ankles, and especially below them.

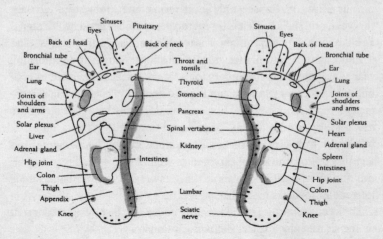

- The lungs, arms, shoulders and respiratory system. These are
  always important for Gemini and the reflexes are shown
  above. Arms and shoulders should be regularly massaged as
  tension tends to collect in the shoulders and needs to be
  released.

Though your health is good this year there will be periods when it is
less good than usual. These come from the stresses of the short-term
planets, which are temporary and not trends for the year. When they
pass your normally good health and energy return.

These vulnerable periods will be from February 19 to March 20;
August 23 to September 22; and November 22 to December 21. Make
sure to get more rest during those periods. We will discuss this in
more detail in the monthly reports.

Home and Family

Mercury, the ruler of your Horoscope is also your family planet, showing that home and family are always important for you. You tend to be
a family-oriented person. However, this year, *all* the long-term planets
are in the upper half of your chart – the day sector, the sector of career
and outer activities. And though the night sector will strengthen a bit
as the year progresses, it will never be dominant. Additionally, your 4th
family house is basically empty (only short-term planets will move
through there), thus this area is not as pronounced as usual. Career is
much more important this year than home and family issues. The
empty 4th house, as our regular readers know, tends to the status quo.
It can be read as a good thing too. You seem satisfied with your home
life and have no need to make major changes. You sort of take the
domestic situation for granted. The home front is relatively quiet this
year.

Your family planet is a very fast and often erratic planet. Sometimes
he moves very quickly (through three signs and houses in a given
month); sometimes he moves slowly (staying in one sign for a whole
month). Three times a year he goes backwards. So your family life
tends to reflect this. It can be erratic. However, you are used to this and
by now know how to handle it.

Because Mercury moves so quickly there are many short-term family trends that depend on where Mercury is and the aspects he receives. These are best discussed in the monthly reports.

Parents and parent figures in your life are also having a quiet kind of family year. One of them seems very spiritual and involved in charities and altruistic kinds of causes. The other seems more involved in having fun and enjoying life.

Siblings and Sibling figures could move this year, but it seems very complicated and could involve many delays. If they are of childbearing age they are more fertile than usual. Their marriage or current relationship will get tested. It can survive.

Children and children figures are likely to move. Here too the move seems complicated, with many glitches and delays involved. If they are of childbearing age they seem more fertile. Grandchildren (if you have them), or people who play this role in your life, can have multiple moves this year – this is a trend over many more years too. Their domestic life seems unstable. They too are more fertile than usual (if they are of the appropriate age).

If you're planning renovations in the home, August 22 to September 22 would be a good time. If you're planning to decorate and beautify the home in a cosmetic kind of way, or to buy art objects for the home, October 2 to October 28 would be a good time.

Finance and Career

Your money house is not a house of power this year. Only short-term planets will move through there and their effects will be short term. Generally this is a good thing. It shows a basic contentment in your finances. You have no need to make major changes or to overly focus here. But this year is different. Your financial planet, the Moon, will get eclipsed four times this year – double the usual number. Not only that, there will be two eclipses – one solar and one lunar – that occur in your money house. This guarantees many important and dramatic financial changes. You will have to make important course corrections. Your financial thinking and outlook are probably not realistic – as the events of the eclipse will show.

The Moon is the fastest and most erratic of all the planets. Where the other fast-moving planets (the Sun, Mercury and Venus) take a year to move through the zodiac, the Moon does so every month. So there are many short-term financial trends that depend on where the Moon is and the aspects she receives. These are best dealt with in the monthly reports. In general (and this will be discussed) your financial power is strongest on the New and Full Moon and when the Moon is waxing (growing larger). It is also strongest when the Moon is at her perigee (her closest distance to earth). When the Moon is waning (getting smaller) is a good time to use spare cash to pay down debt.

There is much power in your 8th house this year – it is easily the strongest in your Horoscope. Thus this is a year for either taking on or paying down debt depending on your need. It is a year for good tax and estate planning (if you are of appropriate age). Money can come from insurance claims or tax refunds. Inheritance often happens when the 8th house is strong, but as we've said, hopefully no one has to actually die. You can be named in someone's will or to some administrative position in an estate. Since the 8th house is about other people's money, this is a year for focusing on the prosperity of others. Others' financial interest comes before your own (although you shouldn't neglect your own interest). The spouse, partner or current love will have a very strong financial year. He or she will be earning it – no question – but there is prosperity for the beloved. He or she will pick up the slack in your personal earnings.

Career has been important for many years now, but this year even more so. It's not just that your 10th house of career is strong; it is also because, as was mentioned, the upper half – the day side – of your Horoscope will be dominant all year. This makes you even more ambitious than usual.

You were born with a sense of mission. You always had high ideals for what you wanted to accomplish in life, and now that Neptune is in your career house this sense of mission has intensified (and will continue to intensify in the coming years). Many of you have got into spiritual or charitable-type careers. Others are pursuing a worldly career but are very much involved in these activities. Just making money and being successful is not enough for you. You need to be doing something that is meaningful – something that uplifts humanity.

If you are not already involved in these things, the doors will open – this year or in the coming years.

Love and Social Life

Love is complicated this year. (Isn't it always? But some years more so than others.) Your love planet Jupiter spends almost all year in conservative Capricorn, your 8th house. Not only that, but Jupiter will be travelling with both Saturn and Pluto this year. So we have many messages here.

First of all, Jupiter is not very strong in the sign of Capricorn. Astrologers say that Jupiter is in his 'fall' – his weakest position. So the social magnetism is not up to its usual standard. Secondly, it would show less socializing than usual. Singles will still date and attend parties, but not as much as usual. There is a need now to focus on quality rather than quantity. Fewer dates, fewer social events, but good ones are better than hosts of lukewarm ones. A marriage is not likely this year and probably not advisable. Next year will be a lot better for that. You are attracted to older people, serious people, people more settled than you. The danger here is getting involved in a relationship based on convenience rather than real love. You will have opportunities for these kinds of relationships. These aspects also show that you are slow to fall in love these days. You take things nice and slow. Anyone involved romantically with a Gemini needs to understand this.

Jupiter in the 8th house and travelling with the ruler of the 8th house, Saturn, suggests that sexual magnetism is the main romantic appeal these days. (Jupiter is also travelling with Pluto, the generic ruler of sex, and this reinforces what we're saying.) There's nothing wrong with good sexual magnetism, but a solid relationship needs more than that.

The love planet in the 8th house shows that you are attracted to money people – the good earners. Wealth is a romantic turn on. Jupiter travelling with the ruler of the 6th house would show an allurement for people in the health professions or people personally involved in your health. Often this shows an office romance. But none of these things leads to marriage – not this year anyway.

For those working on their second marriage the prospects brighten after December 20, but marriage seems delayed. There is love in 2021. Those working on their third marriage have a quiet year. Those who are married will probably stay married, and singles will stay single.

For those of you already in a relationship, the relationship gets some stress testing this year. Your challenge will be to keep the spark of romance alive. Things look too practical, too down-to-earth. Everyone does what they are supposed to do – everyone does their duty – but the passion seems lacking.

Self-improvement

Neptune, the most spiritual and most idealistic of the planets, has been in your career house for many years, and will be there for many more as we have mentioned. This is leading you to a spiritual-type career – a career that is meaningful to you. But there is another way to read this, and this will be true for many of you: it shows that your spiritual practice and spiritual growth is the real career, the real mission these days. Most of you are on a spiritual path already. But this is deepening and becoming more dynamic.

Neptune, the generic spiritual planet, is in mystical Pisces. This would favour a mystical path wherein logic and reason are often seen as the enemy: it is the feeling that matters. While such a path – love, devotion and emotional exaltation – is certainly powerful, with Uranus now in your 12th house of spirituality you need some science and rationality to back you up. You are by nature a rational person. An intellectual. To ignore your mind will set up a conflict in your nature. The mind need not be the enemy. It can be an aid and ally on your path. It is the impurities in the mind that are the enemy.

Uranus rules science and technology. So many of you will be applying technology to your spiritual practice, using Virtual Reality or streaming lectures and meditations. There are all kinds of high-tech gadgets that aid meditation and you seem enamoured by these things. Uranus rules astrology too. Thus esoteric astrology, the philosophical side of astrology, is a viable spiritual path for many of you.*

---

* For more knowledge of this you can read my blog at www.spiritual-stories.com.

There is something magical and mystical about the 8th house. On the deeper levels the 8th house is about 'resurrection' – re-vivification. Making what was dead, live again. We all have things in our lives in need of resurrection. Perhaps it is a relationship, a financial project, or an artistic goal. There it lies, dormant, or perhaps even dead. How can it be resurrected? This year, the 8th house will reveal its secrets to you. Most likely the mind is cluttered with too many side issues that need pruning. Perhaps your home, your material life is also too cluttered. It's time to de-clutter and get down to bare essentials. Perhaps the emotional life is clogged with unresolved issues – again, time to de-clutter. When you do this, you suddenly find that you have more energy to resurrect your pet projects.

Month-by-month Forecasts

January

Best Days Overall: 7, 8, 16, 24, 25, 26
Most Stressful Days Overall: 1, 14, 20, 21, 27, 28
Best Days for Love: 5, 6, 13, 14, 18, 19, 20, 21, 22, 23, 27, 28
Best Days for Money: 5, 6, 9, 10, 14, 15, 22, 23, 24, 25
Best Days for Career: 1, 9, 10, 18, 19, 27, 28

You begin your year with the Western, social sector of your chart dominant. Even the ruler of your Horoscope, Mercury, is in the West. So this is not a time for too much independence. Others and their needs come first. This doesn't make you especially saintly, it's just the astrological cycle you are in. Your good comes to you through the grace of others and not so much from your personal initiative. If circumstances irk you, make a note of them and when the planets shift Eastwards, which they will, you will be able to make the changes needed.

The day side of your Horoscope is overwhelmingly dominant. By the 2nd *all* the planets (with the exception of the Moon) will be on the day side – the upper half of your Horoscope. So this is a time to focus on your career and the outward affairs of life. You serve your family best – and probably derive much emotional satisfaction – from succeeding at your career, rather than by being overly attentive to the family.

Your 8th house will be strong all year, but it is especially strong this month: 60 per cent of the planets are either there or moving through there. So this is a month for detoxing, de-cluttering and practising the science/art of resurrection and personal transformation. Things can't transform when we are weighed down with all kinds of non-useful matter – possessions or mental and emotional patterns. Clear them out and you can start to bloom. This is a very good month for in-depth psychology.

The spouse, partner or current love is having a banner financial month. He or she is very personally involved in this but also has much support (especially from you). Love is erotic these days.

A lunar eclipse on the 10th – the first of four we will have this year – occurs in your 2nd money house. (Keep in mind that the Moon, the eclipsed planet, is also your financial planet – so this eclipse seems powerful financially.) So this is a month for making corrections in the financial life. Things are not as you thought, as the events of the eclipse will show, and changes – dramatic ones – need to be made. There will also be life-changing dramas in the lives of the money people you are involved with. This eclipse also affects three other planets – so it is strong. It reveals that the spouse, partner or current love also needs to make financial changes. If you employ people there could be some staff turnover now. There can be job changes too, or changes in the conditions of work. If there is a health scare, it is most likely no more than that – your health looks good.

February

Best Days Overall: 3, 4, 5, 12, 13, 21, 22
Most Stressful Days Overall: 10, 11, 16, 17, 23, 24, 25
Best Days for Love: 1, 2, 7, 8, 10, 11, 16, 17, 19, 20, 26, 27, 28, 29
Best Days for Money: 1, 2, 3, 4, 6, 7, 10, 11, 12, 13, 19, 20, 23, 24, 28, 29
Best Days for Career: 6, 7, 14, 15, 23, 24, 25

You are in an unusually strong career period now. All the planets (with the exception of the Moon from the 3rd to the 15th) are above the horizon and your career house becomes very strong from the 19th onwards; the whole cosmic thrust is towards your outer goals. Even your family is supportive of your career. And they seem more success-ful too. Succeeding in your outer affairs is the best thing you can do for your family these days. Your success lifts up the family and vice versa.

This month your 8th and 10th houses – transformation and career – vie for power and prominence. Both seem equally powerful. The 8th house was powerful last month too and much of what we said last month applies in the month ahead. The spouse, partner or current love is very focused on finance and seems successful. He or she is earning it to be sure, but prosperity is happening. This is a great period for projects involving personal transformation and reinvention. The libido is stronger than usual. It is a good time for in-depth research and psychology. Detox regimes will work well too. Probably there is more dealing with death and death issues – usually on the psychological level.

Your money house is empty this month, with only the Moon passing through there on the 6th and 7th. Your success in your career will translate to increased earnings eventually, but not right away. In general, earning power will be strongest from the 1st to the 9th and from the 23rd to the 28th as the Moon waxes. The Full Moon of the 9th should be an especially good financial day as this occurs with the Moon at her perigee (her closest distance to earth). The waxing Moon period is good for making investments or for saving, for things that you want to see grow. The waning Moon period (from the 9th to the 23rd) is good for paying down debt or reducing expenses. It is good for things that you want to shrink.

The empty money house shows a quiet, stable financial month. I read it as positive. It shows contentment with things as they are. You don't need to pay too much attention here.

Health needs watching this month, from the 19th onwards. On an overall level your health is good, but this is not one of your best peri-ods. Your energy is not up to its usual standards. So enhance the health in the ways mentioned in the yearly report and, more impor-tantly, make sure to get enough rest. Do your best to maintain high energy levels.

March

Best Days Overall: 2, 3, 10, 11, 19, 20, 29, 30
Most Stressful Days Overall: 8, 9, 14, 15, 22, 23
Best Days for Love: 1, 8, 9, 14, 15, 17, 18, 27, 28
Best Days for Money: 1, 4, 5, 8, 9, 12, 13, 17, 18, 24, 25, 27, 28
Best Days for Career: 4, 5, 12, 13, 22, 23

Mercury, the ruler of your Horoscope, has been in your 10th house of career since February 3. He will be there until March 3 and then from the 16th onwards. Your ruling planet at the top of your chart shows success. It is not just about your professional achievements, but about your appearance, demeanour and style. People look up to you these days. The only complication is Mercury's retrograde. This began on February 17 and continues until the 10th. You are successful but seem to lack direction. It might seem that you are going backwards in your career from the 4th to the 10th, but this is not really the case. You're still in a yearly career peak until the 20th. And on the 16th you are back on top of your world. The 8th and 9th are good days to talk to superiors as they seem receptive to your ideas. You will also have good career ideas during this period.

Health still needs attention until the 20th. Review our discussion of this from last month. A detox regime is always good for you, but this month thigh massage and a liver cleanse might also be beneficial. It is also important to have good social health. Problems with the beloved or with friends can impact on your physical health. The good news is that you will see a dramatic improvement in health and energy after the 20th.

The love life is very interesting – and happy – this month. Jupiter, your love planet, travels with Pluto all month, indicating enhanced eroticism and sexual activity. It shows that sexual magnetism is the primary allurement in love. It also shows an allurement with health professionals and with people involved in your health. Love is intense and tempestuous these days. Passions run high – both positively and negatively.

Your money house is still empty this month, with only the Moon moving through there on the 4th and 5th. This shows a stable financial situation. Earning power (and your enthusiasm) is stronger from the 1st to the 9th and from the 24th onwards, as the Moon waxes. Another Full Moon with the Moon near perigee on the 9th should be an especially good financial day.

Saturn moves into your 9th house on the 23rd. Thus college-level students need to knuckle down to their studies. They need to discipline themselves.

April

Best Days Overall: 7, 8, 15, 16, 17, 25, 26
Most Stressful Days Overall: 5, 6, 11, 12, 18, 19
Best Days for Love: 6, 7, 8, 11, 12, 14, 15, 16, 17, 24, 25, 26
Best Days for Money: 1, 2, 3, 4, 6, 12, 14, 23, 24, 28, 29
Best Days for Career: 1, 2, 9, 10, 18, 19, 28, 29

Saturn will remain in your 9th house of religion, philosophy and education until July 1. This will affect college-level students, as we mentioned, but it also brings testing – reality therapy – to your philosophical, religious and theological beliefs. This will be a long-term process. These things don't get changed right away but over time. Much of what you believe will get modified. Some will get discarded. This is a good thing and has powerful implications as to how you live your life and how you feel about things.

Health is excellent this month. Overall energy seems abundant. If you have pre-existing conditions they seem in abeyance now. Good social health is still very important. Venus's move into your own sign on the 3rd enhances the physical appearance and lends glamour to the image. It shows a more fun-loving spirit too. You will enter a yearly personal pleasure peak next month, but you're experiencing the beginnings of it even now. Children and children figures in your life seem devoted to you. Opportunities for fun and leisure come to you.

Though your yearly career peak is over with (for now), there is career success on the 3rd and 4th. You also seem in harmony with bosses, elders, parents and parent figures. Your dream life will be hyper-active those days, and revelatory. Pay attention.

The Eastern sector of self gained dominance last month, bringing a period of personal independence. Other people are always important, but you are not in need of their favour or good graces now. Your happiness is up to you. Personal initiative matters. Take responsibility for your own happiness. Make any changes in your life that need to be made.

Mercury will have his solstice from the 14th to the 16th. He pauses in the heavens and then changes direction (in latitude). So a pause in your affairs is likely, but nothing to be alarmed about. It is a pause that refreshes and takes you in a new direction.

The month ahead is a spiritual kind of month – especially from the 19th onwards. It is a good month for meditation, spiritual practice and the study of sacred literature. It is a time for making spiritual breakthroughs.

The Sun travels with Uranus from the 24th to the 26th, bringing innovative and original ideas. Perhaps new technology or communication equipment comes to you.

Love is still good this month. The trends that we wrote of last month are still in effect.

May

Best Days Overall: 4, 5, 13, 14, 23, 24
Most Stressful Days Overall: 2, 3, 8, 9, 15, 16, 29, 30
Best Days for Love: 3, 4, 5, 8, 9, 12, 13, 14, 22, 23, 24
Best Days for Money: 2, 3, 11, 12, 22, 23, 25, 26
Best Days for Career: 6, 7, 15, 16, 25, 26

Planetary retrograde activity increases this month, and 40 per cent of the planets – a high percentage – will be moving backwards from the 14th onwards. Pluto, your health and work planet, went retrograde late last month (on April 25) and will be retrograde for many more months. Job seekers need to analyse job opportunities more closely. Things are not what they seem. It will not be a good idea to make major health changes now either – study things more. Children and children figures in your life need to be more careful in financial matters. More due diligence is necessary.

Your love planet Jupiter will begin to go backwards on the 14th and will also spend many months in retrograde motion. The love life slows down – as it should. There is love in your chart but there's no need to rush anything. Let love develop as it will.

The Eastern sector of self became strong in your chart last month, but is even stronger in the month ahead. On the 13th Mars moves from the West to the East and thus 60 per cent of the planets (and sometimes it's 70 per cent) are in the East. In addition, your 1st house of self becomes very strong after the 20th. From the 20th the planetary power is in its maximum Eastern position. The Eastern sector of self will never be stronger than it is now, so it is time to have things your way. You have the support of the planetary powers. Your happiness is important to the cosmos. If you are happy there is that much less misery in the world. Love and social issues will need time to resolve; look after number one now.

Mercury will be 'out of bounds' from the 17th onwards. Thus, you are operating outside your normal sphere. This is true of family members too. There are no solutions to be found in your usual environment and you must look elsewhere.

With your 1st house strong, this is a good month to get the body and image into right shape. It is also good to give the body the pleasures it craves (so long as you don't overdo it).

Your money house becomes strong after the 29th, and will be even stronger next month. Prosperity is increasing. Earnings should be stronger from the 1st to the 7th and from the 22nd onwards. The Full Moon of the 6th looks like an especially strong financial day – it is a 'Super Moon' when the Moon will be at her closest distance to earth. The 23rd also looks like an unusually strong financial day. Financial windfalls or opportunities come.

June

Best Days Overall: 1, 9, 10, 19, 20
Most Stressful Days Overall: 5, 6, 11, 12, 13, 26, 27, 30
Best Days for Love: 1, 5, 6, 8, 9, 10, 18, 19, 20, 27, 30
Best Days for Money: 1, 8, 9, 10, 18, 20, 21, 22, 27
Best Days for Career: 3, 4, 11, 12, 21, 22, 28, 29

Venus has been in your sign since April and will remain there all this month too. So your social grace is unusually strong. Your aesthetic sense is also enhanced. This is a good month (especially after the 25th) to buy clothing or accessories – to beautify the body and image. Love might be stalled, but it is not because of your attractiveness. You are still in a yearly personal pleasure peak, pretty much all month, so indulge the body now (but don't overdo it). Give the body the pleasures it craves. A little pampering is good now.

We have two eclipses this month and this is the main headline. Both of the eclipses impact on the financial life and show that financial corrections are necessary. The events caused by the eclipses will show that your financial thinking and strategy have not been realistic, so you are forced to make changes.

The lunar eclipse of the 5th occurs in your 7th house of love. Thus love is being tested. Usually repressed grievances surface for resolution. If they are handled properly, and the relationship is basically sound, the relationship survives and gets better; but if the relationship is fundamentally flawed, it will be in danger. However, with your love planet still retrograde, don't make important love decisions this month. This is a time to gain clarity on love. The money people in your life could be having health dramas, thanks to the eclipse. And since this eclipse also impacts on Mars and Venus, friendships are getting tested too. There can be dramas in the lives of friends. Children and children figures are also affected. They should be kept out of harm's way during this period. You will feel this eclipse strongly, so relax and reduce your schedule over the eclipse period. You will get unmistakable signals as to when you need to slow down.

The solar eclipse of the 21st occurs in the money house, affecting siblings, sibling figures and neighbours. They will be forced to make spiritual changes – changes in their practice, attitudes, teachings and teachers. Students are affected too, and there can be disruptions at school or changes of educational plans. The spouse, partner or current love could have dreams of death, or other psychological encounters with death.

Retrograde activity among the planets will hit a yearly high this month (there will be another high in September). So much of what we write about here can have a delayed reaction.

July

Best Days Overall: 6, 7, 8, 16, 17, 25, 26
Most Stressful Days Overall: 2, 3, 9, 10, 23, 24, 29, 30
Best Days for Love: 1, 2, 3, 6, 7, 8, 9, 10, 16, 17, 19, 20, 25, 26, 27, 28, 29, 30
Best Days for Money: 1, 4, 5, 9, 10, 14, 15, 19, 20, 21, 22, 23, 24, 29, 31
Best Days for Career: 1, 9, 10, 19, 20, 27, 28

Though you have been in a yearly financial peak since June 21, another lunar eclipse this month shakes the finances once again. The financial thinking is still not what it should be and you're making the corrections necessary. This eclipse occurs on the 5th in your 8th house, and also affects the income of the spouse, partner or current love. Both of you need to make dramatic financial changes. This eclipse can bring psychological encounters with death – sometimes through dreams, sometimes through close calls, sometimes because you hear about grisly crimes, and sometimes because someone you know has died or has had a near-death kind of experience.

Three other planets are sideswiped by this eclipse – Mercury, Jupiter and Mars. They are affected but not directly. The impact on Mercury affects you and family members. Loved ones can be more temperamental this period. Repairs might be needed in the home. You will need to redefine yourself and your image: image changes are likely in the coming months. The impact on Jupiter affects the spouse, partner or current love and tests your current relationship. The impact on Mars affects friends. Friendships can be tested and there are dramas in the lives of friends. High-tech equipment can behave erratically during this period and sometimes repair or replacement is necessary.

Love is complicated this month. For a start, the spouse, partner or current love is affected by the eclipse. Secondly, Jupiter, your love planet, is still retrograde. Thirdly, your ruling planet Mercury is retrograde until the 12th. So none of you are clear about things. And, to top it off, you and the beloved are at opposite ends of the Horoscope – the furthest away from each other. This shows that you see things in opposite ways. Your challenge will be to bridge your differences. Not so easy this month. Love will be much easier next month.

It is very fortunate that your money house is powerful this month (it has been that way since June 21). Your focus is needed here. In spite of all the drama, you should end the month in better financial shape than when you began. Mercury in the money house is a good sign. It not only shows focus but best-case scenarios in finance. You don the image of wealth. People see you as prosperous. You spend on yourself too. Personal appearance and overall demeanour – your personal style – play a big role in earnings.

On the 22nd the Sun enters your 3rd house of communication and intellectual activities – Gemini's favourite house. You are even more Gemini than usual. Your already awesome communication and mental faculties are even stronger than usual.

August

Best Days Overall: 3, 4, 13, 14, 21, 22, 30, 31
Most Stressful Days Overall: 5, 6, 19, 20, 25, 26, 27
Best Days for Love: 2, 3, 4, 11, 15, 16, 20, 23, 24, 25, 26, 27, 29
Best Days for Money: 2, 8, 9, 11, 15, 16, 18, 19, 20, 21, 28, 29
Best Days for Career: 5, 6, 15, 16, 23, 24

The upper half of your Horoscope – the day side – the sector that emphasizes outer activities and the career has been dominant all year, and will continue to be so. However, the bottom half, the sector of home, family and emotional issues, is now at its strongest that it will be this year. So though career is paramount, it is good to shift a little bit of attention to the home, family and emotional wellness. This is especially so from the 22nd onwards, when your 4th house becomes strong.

Venus has been in your sign since April and will still be there until the 7th. This has been good for the personal appearance, the spiritual life and your relationships with children and children figures. Now, on the 7th, Venus moves into your money house – a positive financial transit. It shows a good financial intuition. Financial guidance will come in dreams and through hunches, and often through astrologers, tarot readers, psychics and other spiritual channels. The invisible universe cares about your prosperity and is actively involved here. This transit indicates happy money, money that is earned in enjoyable ways – perhaps while you're having fun, on the sports field, or at a party or place of entertainment. You might have a tendency to speculate after the 7th, but this isn't advisable. Children and children figures seem active in your financial life. Much depends on their age and stage in life. Young ones inspire and motivate you. Often they have profitable ideas. Older ones can be financially supportive in more direct ways.

Earning power will be strongest from the 1st to the 3rd and from the 19th to the 31st as the Moon waxes. The 21st will be a good financial day (though you will probably work hard for it) as the Moon is at her perigee. From the 19th to the 31st use spare cash to reduce debt. This is also a good period to reduce expenses.

You're still in Gemini heaven until the 22nd. You inhale information like the breath. You communicate even better than usual. Writers, marketers, teachers and students are having a great month.

The love life will improve from the 20th onwards when Mercury and Jupiter will be in harmonious relationship. But keep in mind that Jupiter, your love planet, is still retrograde. So go slow in love. This is especially important for singles.

September

    Best Days Overall: 9, 10, 18, 19, 26, 27
    Most Stressful Days Overall: 1, 2, 3, 16, 17, 22, 23, 29, 30
    Best Days for Love: 2, 3, 6, 7, 13, 14, 16, 17, 22, 23, 24, 25
    Best Days for Money: 6, 7, 11, 12, 16, 17, 24, 25, 26
    Best Days for Career: 1, 2, 3, 11, 12, 20, 21, 29, 30

Retrograde activity reaches a crescendo this month. From the 9th to the 12th 60 per cent of the planets are in retrograde motion, while it is 50 per cent for the rest of the month. Don't be downcast about the slowness of life or the various delays that happen. It's very natural. It's the cosmic weather. You're not a bad person and the cosmos doesn't hate you. You can minimize delays and glitches by being perfect in all that you do. Slow down and make sure every detail is perfect.

Retrogrades have other positive things about them. They force us to review different areas of life and see where improvements can be made. Then when the planets start moving forward again (and they will in the coming months) we are in a good position to move forward with them.

Love is gradually improving. On the 5th Mercury moves into romantic Libra, putting you more in the mood for romance. And Jupiter, your love planet, will start moving forward on the 13th. So there is more clarity in love now – on both sides of the equation.

You have been having fun for many months now – especially from April 3 to August 7 with Venus in your own sign. And the month ahead – from the 5th onwards – brings more fun, more leisure, more creativity. On the 22nd you will enter one of your yearly personal pleasure peaks. With all this slow down on the worldly level, you might as well enjoy yourself.

Health hasn't been up to its usual standard since August 22, and it remains so until the 22nd. This is nothing serious, just the impact of short-term planets on you. However, if you let yourself get overtired, you can become vulnerable to things. So make sure you get enough rest. You will see a big improvement after from the 22nd. In the meantime, enhance the health in the ways mentioned in the yearly report.

Mars, the ruler of your 11th house, goes retrograde on the 9th and will remain so until November 11. So this is not a good time to be buying high-tech gadgetry or equipment. It's great for researching these things, but make the purchase (if possible) when Mars starts moving forward again. High-tech equipment and gadgets can be temperamental from the 9th onwards.

After the 6th when Venus moves out of your money house, that house will be empty (except for the Moon's visit on the 11th and 12th). This is good. It shows contentment with things as they are. It tends to the status quo. Earning power will be strongest from on the 1st and 2nd and from the 17th onwards as the Moon waxes. The New Moon of the 17th seems an especially good financial day as it is a 'Super New Moon' – it occurs with the Moon at her closest distance to earth.

October

Best Days Overall: 6, 7, 15, 16, 23, 24, 25
Most Stressful Days Overall: 13, 14, 19, 20, 26, 27
Best Days for Love: 3, 4, 5, 13, 14, 19, 20, 21, 22, 31
Best Days for Money: 1, 4, 5, 6, 7, 9, 10, 13, 14, 15, 16, 21, 23, 25, 31
Best Days for Career: 9, 10, 17, 18, 26, 27

A happy and healthy month, Gemini. Enjoy!

Your 5th house of fun, children and creativity is still very strong until the 23rd and you are still in the midst of a yearly personal pleasure peak. It is good every now and then to just enjoy life. A lot of problems are there because of our attachment to them. When you let go they often dissolve under their own weight. Sometimes, the solutions come as well.

Your 6th house of health and work becomes strong just as Pluto, the ruler of that house, starts moving forward again on the 4th. So the job situation is better clarified. Changes in the health regime will go more smoothly. Job seekers will have good opportunities too (especially until the 14th and from the 23rd onwards).

The month ahead should be prosperous in spite of your empty money house. We will have two Full Moons this month – both strong financial days. Usually there is only one Full Moon, so you get an extra financial jolt this month. The New Moon (always a good financial time for you) of the 16th is also stronger than usual. It is a 'Super New Moon' that occurs with the Moon at her perigee (her closest distance to earth). In general, earning power will be stronger on the 1st and from the 16th to the 31st. The Full Moon of the 31st occurs right on Uranus, the ruler of your 9th house and thus a very fortunate planet for you. This shows 'unexpected' money.

Mercury, the ruler of your Horoscope, goes retrograde on the 14th. There is a need to review your personal goals. Perhaps your self-esteem and self-confidence are temporarily weakened, but this too seems fortunate. The Western social sector of your chart becomes dominant on the 2nd. You are thus in a more social period and there's no need for too much self-confidence and self-esteem. Let others have their way (so long as it isn't destructive) and put others first. It's time to cultivate your social skills.

Venus will move into your family 4th house on the 2nd and stay there for most of the month ahead. This is a good time to buy objects of beauty for the home or to redecorate. Family members (especially children and children figures in your life) seem more spiritual, more idealistic this period.

Mars is still retrograde all month, so be patient with high-tech equipment and gadgets. If you must replace them, do your homework.

November

Best Days Overall: 2, 3, 4, 12, 20, 21, 30
Most Stressful Days Overall: 10, 16, 22, 23
Best Days for Love: 2, 3, 11, 12, 16, 19, 21, 22
Best Days for Money: 2, 5, 6, 11, 14, 15, 19, 24, 25
Best Days for Career: 5, 6, 14, 15, 22, 23

There's no need for any Gemini to be unemployed this month; at least three wonderful job opportunities are coming. Your work planet Pluto is moving forward and your 6th house of work is strong. Jupiter is also travelling with Pluto, showing that the job opportunities are good ones. Social contacts are likely to bring employment opportunities and you're in the mood for work. Employers pick up on this. Even those of you already employed can have new and better opportunities, and you are probably taking on second jobs or working overtime.

Health too is good. You are focused here – hopefully on healthy life-styles. With your health good this month too much focus can lead to hypochondria. Be careful of magnifying little things into big things. A detox is always good for you, but this month especially so. Good health for you means a healthy love and sex life. And these seem good. Another positive for health.

The Western social sector of your chart is overwhelmingly dominant this month. So this is a month where you put other people's interests ahead of your own. In addition, on the 21st, the Sun will enter your 7th house of love and you begin a yearly love and social peak. Singles have many romantic opportunities. Some come in the neighbourhood or with neighbours. Some come at school or educational functions – lectures, seminars, the library or bookstore. People at your place of worship like to play Cupid too. Your love planet is travelling very close to Pluto this month and thus there are social and romantic opportunities at the workplace, with health professionals and with people involved in your health. A trip to the doctor's or gym can turn out to be more than that.

On the 30th we have the fourth lunar eclipse of the year, and it occurs in your own sign so it is powerful. Take it nice and easy over this period. Do what needs to be done, but anything else should be rescheduled. Once again there is a need for financial corrections – the fourth time this year. If you haven't been careful in dietary matters this eclipse can trigger a detox of the body. You will be redefining yourself in the coming months – redefining, fine tuning, your personality and image. Usually this leads to wardrobe changes and changes in hairstyles, etc.

December

    Best Days Overall: 1, 9, 10, 17, 18, 27, 28
    Most Stressful Days Overall: 7, 8, 13, 14, 19, 20, 21
    Best Days for Love: 2, 3, 8, 11, 12, 13, 14, 16, 22, 23, 27
    Best Days for Money: 2, 3, 5, 6, 8, 13, 14, 16, 24, 27, 29, 30, 31
    Best Days for Career: 2, 3, 11, 12, 19, 20, 21, 29, 30, 31

The 6th and final eclipse of the year is a solar eclipse that occurs on the 14th. (Next year we will be back to the more normal two solar and two lunar eclipses.) It happens in your 7th house of love, testing love and especially a current relationship. This is the 2nd eclipse of the year in your 7th house. Love has been good lately; now it is time to see how good it *really* is. Good relationships will survive this testing but the flawed ones are in danger. Students – both at and below college level – are also affected here. There are disruptions at their schools. There are changes in educational plans and perhaps changes of establishments. Siblings, sibling figures and neighbours have personal dramas. Cars and communication equipment are temperamental. Often repairs are needed. Be sure to drive carefully during this period.

Aside from the eclipse there are other changes happening in love – these are good ones. Your love planet Jupiter will move into Aquarius, your 9th house, on the 20th, bringing a whole new ball game in love. For the past year love has been erotic. But by now you have seen the limits of this and yearn for something more. You want philosophical compatibility. You want a person who is not only satisfying in the bedroom but from whom you can learn and look up to. The past year, you've been pretty conservative in love. You were cautious, slow to fall in love. But now you become more experimental. Finally, from the astrological perspective, Jupiter is much stronger in Aquarius than he is in Capricorn. So social magnetism will become much stronger. You will be more attracted to foreigners too. These trends will continue for almost all of next year.

By the 15th, as Venus moves from the lower, night side of your Horoscope to the upper day side, we return to a condition that prevailed at the beginning of the year. Highly unusually, *all* the planets will be on the day side – the upper half of the Horoscope. So you are back to focusing on your career and outer objectives. You serve your family best by succeeding in the world. You might miss some of the children's soccer matches or school plays but you will give them the wherewithal for a better life. Outer success puts you in emotional harmony and not vice versa.

Your money house is empty this month. Only the Moon will visit on the 2nd and 3rd, and from the 29th onwards, so finance is not a big deal right now. You seem content with things as they are. However the month ahead looks prosperous. The Moon will spend double her usual time in the money house – five days instead of two. Earning power should be stronger – you have more enthusiasm for it – from the 14th to the 30th as the Moon waxes. The Moon's perigee on the 12th should also be a good financial day, though there will be challenges involved.

Cancer

THE CRAB

Birthdays from
21st June to
20th July

Personality Profile

CANCER AT A GLANCE

Element – Water

Ruling Planet – Moon
  Career Planet – Mars
  Love Planet – Saturn
  Money Planet – Sun
  Planet of Fun and Games – Pluto
  Planet of Good Fortune – Neptune
  Planet of Health and Work – Jupiter
  Planet of Home and Family Life – Venus
  Planet of Spirituality – Mercury

Colours – blue, puce, silver

Colours that promote love, romance and social harmony – black, indigo

Colours that promote earning power – gold, orange

Gems – moonstone, pearl

Metal – silver

TiA 7/21/96   USING MERCURY TABLE FOR 1996

Scents – jasmine, sandalwood

Quality – cardinal (= activity)

Quality most needed for balance – mood control

Strongest virtues – emotional sensitivity, tenacity, the urge to nurture

Deepest need – a harmonious home and family life

Characteristics to avoid – over-sensitivity, negative moods

Signs of greatest overall compatibility – Scorpio, Pisces

Signs of greatest overall incompatibility – Aries, Libra, Capricorn

Sign most helpful to career – Aries

Sign most helpful for emotional support – Libra

Sign most helpful financially – Leo

Sign best for marriage and/or partnerships – Capricorn

Sign most helpful for creative projects – Scorpio

Best Sign to have fun with – Scorpio

Signs most helpful in spiritual matters – Gemini, Pisces

Best day of the week – Monday

Understanding a Cancer

In the sign of Cancer the heavens are developing the feeling side of things. This is what a true Cancerian is all about – feelings. Where Aries will tend to err on the side of action, Taurus on the side of inaction and Gemini on the side of thought, Cancer will tend to err on the side of feeling.

Cancerians tend to mistrust logic. Perhaps rightfully so. For them it is not enough for an argument or a project to be logical – it must feel right as well. If it does not feel right a Cancerian will reject it or chafe against it. The phrase 'follow your heart' could have been coined by a Cancerian, because it describes exactly the Cancerian attitude to life.

The power to feel is a more direct – more immediate – method of knowing than thinking is. Thinking is indirect. Thinking about a thing never touches the thing itself. Feeling is a faculty that touches directly the thing or issue in question. We actually experience it. Emotional feeling is almost like another sense which humans possess – a psychic sense. Since the realities that we come in contact with during our lifetime are often painful and even destructive, it is not surprising that the Cancerian chooses to erect barriers – a shell – to protect his or her vulnerable, sensitive nature. To a Cancerian this is only common sense.

If Cancerians are in the presence of people they do not know, or find themselves in a hostile environment, up goes the shell and they feel protected. Other people often complain about this, but one must question these people's motives. Why does this shell disturb them? Is it perhaps because they would like to sting, and feel frustrated that they cannot? If your intentions are honourable and you are patient, have no fear. The shell will open up and you will be accepted as part of the Cancerian's circle of family and friends.

Thought-processes are generally analytic and dissociating. In order to think clearly we must make distinctions, comparisons and the like. But feeling is unifying and integrative.

To think clearly about something you have to distance yourself from it. To feel something you must get close to it. Once a Cancerian has accepted you as a friend he or she will hang on to you. You have to be really bad to lose the friendship of a Cancerian. If you are related to Cancerians they will never let you go no matter what you do. They will always try to maintain some kind of connection even in the most extreme circumstances.

Finance

The Cancer-born has a deep sense of what other people feel about things and why they feel as they do. This faculty is a great asset in the workplace and in the business world. Of course it is also indispensable in raising a family and building a home, but it has its uses in business. Cancerians often attain great wealth in a family business. Even if the business is not a family operation, they will treat it as one. If the Cancerian works for somebody else, then the boss is the parental figure and the co-workers are brothers and sisters. If a Cancerian is the boss, then all the workers are his or her children. Cancerians like the feeling of being providers for others. They enjoy knowing that others derive their sustenance because of what they do. It is another form of nurturing.

With Leo on their solar 2nd money house cusp, Cancerians are often lucky speculators, especially with residential property or hotels and restaurants. Resort hotels and nightclubs are also profitable for the Cancerian. Waterside properties attract them. Though they are basically conventional people, they sometimes like to earn their livelihood in glamorous ways.

The Sun, Cancer's money planet, represents an important financial message: in financial matters Cancerians need to be less moody, more stable and fixed. They cannot allow their moods – which are here today and gone tomorrow – to get in the way of their business lives. They need to develop their self-esteem and feelings of self-worth if they are to realize their greatest financial potential.

Career and Public Image

Aries rules the 10th solar career house cusp of Cancer, which indicates that Cancerians long to start their own business, to be more active publicly and politically and to be more independent. Family responsibilities and a fear of hurting other people's feelings – or getting hurt themselves – often inhibit them from attaining these goals. However, this is what they want and long to do.

Cancerians like their bosses and leaders to act freely and to be a bit self-willed. They can deal with that in a superior. They expect their leaders to be fierce on their behalf. When the Cancerian is in the position of boss or superior he or she behaves very much like a 'warlord'. Of course the wars they wage are not egocentric but in defence of those under their care. If they lack some of this fighting instinct – independence and pioneering spirit – Cancerians will have extreme difficulty in attaining their highest career goals. They will be hampered in their attempts to lead others.

Since they are so parental, Cancerians like to work with children and make great educators and teachers.

Love and Relationships

Like Taurus, Cancer likes committed relationships. Cancerians function best when the relationship is clearly defined and everyone knows his or her role. When they marry it is usually for life. They are extremely loyal to their beloved. But there is a deep little secret that most Cancerians will never admit to: commitment or partnership is really a chore and a duty to them. They enter into it because they know of no other way to create the family that they desire. Union is just a way – a means to an end – rather than an end in itself. The family is the ultimate end for them.

If you are in love with a Cancerian you must tread lightly on his or her feelings. It will take you a good deal of time to realize how deep and sensitive Cancerians can be. The smallest negativity upsets them. Your tone of voice, your irritation, a look in your eye or an expression on your face can cause great distress for the Cancerian. Your slightest gesture is registered by them and reacted to. This can be hard to get used to, but stick by your love – Cancerians make great partners once you learn how to deal with them. Your Cancerian lover will react not so much to what you say but to the way you are actually feeling at the moment.

Home and Domestic Life

This is where Cancerians really excel. The home environment and the family are their personal works of art. They strive to make things of beauty that will outlast them. Very often they succeed.

Cancerians feel very close to their family, their relatives and especially their mothers. These bonds last throughout their lives and mature as they grow older. They are very fond of those members of their family who become successful, and they are also quite attached to family heirlooms and mementos. Cancerians also love children and like to provide them with all the things they need and want. With their nurturing, feeling nature, Cancerians make very good parents – especially the Cancerian woman, who is the mother *par excellence* of the zodiac.

As a parent the Cancerian's attitude is 'my children right or wrong'. Unconditional devotion is the order of the day. No matter what a family member does, the Cancerian will eventually forgive him or her, because 'you are, after all, family'. The preservation of the institution – the tradition – of the family is one of the Cancerian's main reasons for living. They have many lessons to teach others about this.

Being so family-orientated, the Cancerian's home is always clean, orderly and comfortable. They like old-fashioned furnishings but they also like to have all the modern comforts. Cancerians love to have family and friends over, to organize parties and to entertain at home – they make great hosts.

Horoscope for 2020

Major Trends

A very interesting and turbulent year ahead, with much change happening in your life.

There will be six eclipses this coming year, all of which impact on you. (This is 50 per cent more than usual; generally there are only four eclipses a year.) Not only that, but we will have twice as many lunar eclipses than usual – four rather than two. This guarantees change and disruption, and since the Moon is your ruling planet these eclipses have a special bearing on you. Keep in mind that eclipses often bring good things, but even those are disruptive.

Almost all the long-term planets will be in the Western, social sector of your chart this year. The Eastern sector of self will strengthen as the year proceeds but it will never dominate. Further, your 7th house of love and social activities is easily the strongest in your Horoscope. So the year ahead is very social. It's about other people. It's about cultivating the social graces and gaining the cooperation of others. More on this later.

Health will need more attention this year. Health has been delicate the past two years and is even more so in the year ahead. More on this later.

Uranus is now in your 11th house and will remain there for the next seven or so years. So there are dramas in the lives of friends – life-changing events – and friendships will get tested. By the time Uranus is finished with you, you will be in a completely new social circle.

Mars will spend an unusual amount of time in your 10th house of career this year. He will be there from June 28 onwards. This shows heightened career activity. You get very busy and aggressive here. More on this later.

The areas of greatest interest this year will be love, romance and social activities; sex, personal transformation and occult studies (March 23 to July 1 and December 18 onwards); religion, philosophy, theology and foreign travel; and friends, groups and group activities.

Your paths of greatest fulfilment this year will be the body and image (until May 6); finance (from May 6 onwards); love, romance and social activities (until December 20); and sex, personal transformation and occult studies (after December 20).

Health

(Please note that this is an astrological perspective on health and not a medical one. In days of yore there was no difference, both these perspectives were identical. But now there could be quite a difference. For a medical perspective, please consult your doctor or health practitioner.)

Health, as we mentioned, needs more attention this year. There are three (and sometimes four) long-term planets in stressful alignment with you. This is challenging enough, but when the short-term planets join the gang it can be even more challenging. What is of concern here is that your 6th house of health is empty this year, with only short-term planets moving through there. This can make you take health for granted and you might not give it the attention it deserves. You will need to force yourself – even when you don't feel like it – to make health a priority.

Health needs particular attention from January 1 to January 20; March 20 to April 19; and September 23 to October 22. Be sure to rest and relax more these periods, and spend time at a health spa if you can, or schedule in massages or health treatments. You need to boost your energy.

So it is good to give special attention to the following areas – the vulnerable areas of your Horoscope (the reflex points are shown in the chart below). This will often prevent problems from developing and, even if they can't be totally prevented, soften them:

Important foot reflexology points for the year ahead

Try to massage all of the foot on a regular basis – the top of the foot as well as the bottom – but pay extra attention to the points highlighted on the chart. When you massage, be aware of 'sore spots' as these need special attention. It's also a good idea to massage the ankles particularly, and below them.

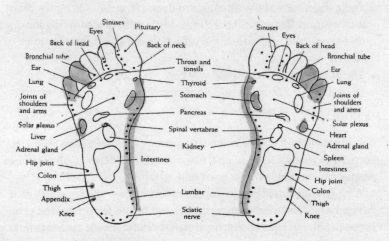

- The Heart. The reflex is shown above. The important thing with the heart, according to a consensus of spiritual healers, is to avoid worry and anxiety – the two emotions that stress it out. Worry is lack of faith. Cultivate more faith.
- The stomach and breasts are always important for Cancerians and the reflexes are shown above. Good also to massage the upper part of the foot (not shown here). Diet is always an issue for you and this should be checked with a professional. Often simple dietary changes can remove health problems. Also *how* you eat is important; work to elevate the act of eating from mere animal appetite to an act of praise and thanksgiving. This will not only elevate the energy vibrations of the food, but of the digestive system as well. Food will digest better.
- The liver and thighs. These are also always important for the Cancerian. Regular thigh massage should be part of your health regime. It will not only strengthen the liver and thighs but also the lower back – an important area this year.
- The spine, knees, teeth, skin and overall skeletal alignment became important last December, and are important until December 20 of this year. Thus this year back and knee massage will be beneficial. You might want to see a chiropractor or osteopath on a regular basis. Don't neglect your dental check-ups and make sure you pay attention to dental hygiene. Therapies such as Alexander Technique, Rolfing and Feldenkrais would be good. Good posture is important this year. Give the knees more support when exercising.
- The ankles and calves. These will become important after December 20 as your health planet moves into Aquarius. Regular ankle and calf massage will be good.

Good emotional health is always important for Cancerians. Work to keep your moods upbeat and positive. Avoid depression like the plague. Meditation will be a great help here.

With your health planet Jupiter spending almost all the year in your 7th house of love, the message is that good health for you means good social health – a healthy marriage and love life. Problems here could actually impact on your physical health. So if, God forbid, problems arise, restore harmony here as quickly as possible.

You're very 'other oriented' this year, as we have mentioned. Jupiter in the 7th house could show that you are more concerned with the health of others – the spouse, partner, current love or friends – than you are for yourself. You seem very involved in their health these days.

Home and Family

Family is always important for you, Cancer. We could say that you see this as your mission in life, the reason for your existence. There is nothing more important than family. And even financial lives – which tend to be good   are motivated by family concerns. But life is an ebb and flow. This year home and family is less important than usual, and this has been the case for the past few years. Your 4th house of home and family is basically empty – only short-term planets move through there. I read this as a good thing. You're basically content with the way things are. The home and family don't need additional focus and you don't need to make any major changes. Your marriage, your body and image seem greater priorities this year than the family. A move is not likely. There is nothing against it, but nothing especially supporting it either. You have free will here, but perhaps lack interest.

This is a much stronger social and career year than a family year. (Perhaps these are the ways that you serve your family best.) However, there will be four lunar eclipses this year and the Moon is the generic ruler of the family. So there are likely to be crises and upheavals here – and twice as much as usual. You will need more patience with family members during those periods. Passions are high. They are more temperamental.

A parent or parent figure could move this year, but it looks very complicated and fraught with delays. He or she could be doing major renovations in the home too. He or she seems emotionally stressed out.

Siblings or sibling figures are not likely to move. If they are of appropriate age they seem more fertile than usual, but pregnancy seems complicated. Children and children figures in your life are more likely to move next year, but again there are delays and complications.

If you're planning major home renovations, September 22 to October 23 seems best. If you're planning cosmetic work on the home or to buy objects of beauty for the home, October 28 to November 21 is best.

Because your family planet Venus is such a fast-moving planet there are many short-term trends here that depend on where she is and the aspects she receives. These are best dealt with in the monthly reports. However, Venus makes one of her rare retrogrades this year. (She only does this once every two years.) This happens from May 13 to June 25. This will not be a good time to make important family decisions. It is a time for review.

Your family planet will spend an unusual amount of time in Gemini, your 12th house, this year. She will be there from April 3 to August 7, approximately four times longer than her usual transit. This would tend to show that family members are more spiritual and idealistic during that period. Perhaps the home is being used for charitable or spiritual kinds of events.

Finance and Career

Though they are not known for this, Cancerians have strong financial gifts and abilities. They tend to focus on it and tend to succeed. But family – the need to be the good provider – is what motivates them. So finance tends always to be important. But as we saw with family, it is less important this year than usual. The money house is basically empty. Only short-term planets will move through there this year and their effects will be short term. This I read is a good thing. You seem content with finances as they are and have no need to give it too much attention or to make too many changes. It tends to the status quo.

If financial problems happen it could be that you haven't given the area enough attention and will need to focus more on it.

In spite of this the year ahead seems prosperous. The Moon's North Node will move into the money house on May 6 and stay there for the rest of the year. The North Node is not a planet but an 'abstract point'. The Hindus consider it a 'shadow planet' and give much weight to it. Here in the West we give it less emphasis. However, it does show a sense of 'excess'. Excess is a kind of imbalance and is generally not good, but in finance it could be a positive: it can show excess money

– not a bad problem to have. In the West we interpret the position of the North Node to denote an area of great fulfilment. So, this is another signal for a prosperous year.

The Sun is your financial planet – a good one to have. The usual two solar eclipses this year will bring opportunities for 'course corrections' in your financial life. Often these happen due to some financial disturbance – some extra expense or some unforeseen development. Once the corrections are made the financial life gets back on track. These eclipses are usually not pleasant while they're happening but the end result is good. Since they regularly happen twice a year, you know how to handle these things by now.

The Sun is a fast-moving planet, moving through all the signs and houses of your Horoscope over the year. Thus there are many short-term financial trends that depend on where the Sun is and the aspects he receives. These are best dealt with in the monthly reports.

Though your 10th house of career is empty for the first half of the year, the year ahead looks like a strong career year. The upper, day side of your Horoscope – the sector that emphasizes outer goals and activities – is overwhelmingly strong. All the long-term planets are in the upper half of the chart. The lower half, the night side, the sector of inner, subjective activities – home, family and the emotional life – will get stronger as the year progresses, but it never dominates the upper half of the chart. The focus this year is on outer activities. Your 10th house will be powerful from February 7 to March 5; March 20 to April 19; and from June 28 onwards. These will be the optimum career periods. As we have mentioned, Mars, your career planet, will spend over six months in your 10th house – an unusually long transit. Thus you will have to work hard, fight off competitors and become more warlike in the career.

Love and Social Life

Your 7th house of love and social activities is, as we said, the strongest in your Horoscope this year. Three long-term planets occupy this house for most of the year, and there will be times when 50 to 60 per cent of the planets will be in that house. So love is in the air, but it is very complicated.

The Moon's South Node (also not a planet but an abstract point) will also be in your 7th house until May 6. Where the North Node denotes excess, the South Node denotes a feeling of lack – a sense of deficiency. You feel something is missing in love. Yet, your house of love is chock-full of planets!

One way to read this is that the feeling of lack is causing overcompensation. It makes you date more, search more, etc. Indeed, singles have multiple relationships this year and multiple opportunities for romance. Another way to read it is that there are more love partners this year (or potential partners) yet, there is still a feeling of lack – something feels missing. Happily, this feeling is only temporary. The Moon's South Node will leave the 7th house early in May and love should become more fulfilling after that.

With so many planets in your 7th house you are getting along and socializing with many different kinds of people. Pluto's presence in your 7th house for many years now indicates fun and games kinds of relationships. Love affairs. Saturn in your 7th house for the past two years shows opportunities for a more serious kind of relationship – something more committed. A relationship with someone older and more settled than you: a business or corporate-type person. Someone who gives you a sense of security. Jupiter in your 7th house indicates an affinity for highly educated or religious-type people. Perhaps someone from your place of worship or someone you meet in school or a school function. It would show an attraction for health professionals or people involved in your health. Romantic meetings could happen in foreign countries too.

Singles have marriage opportunities this year. The main problem is choosing whom to marry. Sometimes too much of a good thing is not so good – it is confusing. But this is a good problem to have.

Those of you already involved in relationships will be socializing more too. You are attending more weddings, parties and gatherings – you are making new friends. Often business-type partnerships happen under these aspects.

Those working on their second marriage have love in their lives. It looks like someone spiritual or artistic. Those in or working on their third marriage have much romantic instability to deal with. The marriage or current relationship is getting tested.

Self-improvement

When we look at religion superficially it seems little more than a collection of arbitrary rules, regulations and superstitions which have little to do with rationality. But if you go deeper into it you find good spiritual reasons for many of these rules, regulations and practices. It is true that much error and superstition has entered in over the centuries, but underneath all that there is something real. This is a lesson you have been learning these days, now that Neptune is in your 9th house for the long term. Every religion is little more than the shadow – the side effect – of the mystical experiences of its founder. So your religious life is becoming more spiritualized, more real and more dynamic. You are in a cycle for major religious and philosophical breakthroughs. You are seeing 'why' the rules are what they are.

Venus, as we have mentioned, spends a lot of time (more than four months) in your spiritual 12th house. This favours the Bhakti spiritual path – the path of love and devotion. When you are in a state of love, you feel close to the divine. But there are other messages here too. Venus rules your 11th house of friends. Thus you are meeting spiritual-type friends during this period (from April 3 to August 7). It favours love and devotion, but it also favours the esoteric side of Astrology – a valid spiritual path. Your knowledge of astrology, science and technology is increasing this year (and this will be a long-term trend). Love and devotion is a powerful spiritual path, but while Venus is in your 12th house you might want to balance this with a more scientific and rational approach. There is another message here too. Your spiritual understanding will enable you to handle family members and family situations much better. During this period, if a family problem comes up don't try to solve it by overt action. Meditate first for spiritual guidance. Then you can act.

Uranus in your 11th house of friends (and for years to come) destabilizes friendships. Friends come and they go. New friends can come into the picture unexpectedly while old friends can drop out of it. Often this is not the fault of the relationship but because of the events happening in their lives. Learning to deal with social instability is the major spiritual lesson for years to come.

Your 8th house will become strong from March 23 to July 1 and from December 18 onwards. This favours personal transformation – giving birth to the person you want to be, giving birth to your ideal self. This will be important during 2021 as well. These kinds of projects require the removal of distractions and things that waste energy. Simplify the life. De-clutter it on all levels – materially, emotionally and mentally. Get rid of the effete and the spiritual power will transform what needs to be transformed.

Month-by-month Forecasts

January

Best Days Overall: 1, 9, 10, 18, 19, 27, 28
Most Stressful Days Overall: 2, 3, 16, 22, 23, 29, 30, 31
Best Days for Love: 6, 13, 14, 15, 18, 19, 22, 23, 27, 28
Best Days for Money: 5, 6, 12, 14, 15, 22, 23, 24, 25
Best Days for Career: 1, 2, 3, 12, 20, 21, 29, 30, 31

Health is a major issue this month, with five, sometimes six, planets in stressful alignment with you. Not only that, but there will be a strong lunar eclipse on the 10th in your own sign. This will not help matters. So, make sure you get enough rest, and enhance the health in the ways mentioned in the yearly report.

You begin your year in a love and social peak. Your 7th house of love and social activities is easily the strongest in the Horoscope. It is chock-full of planets. It is the kind of month where you get along with all kinds of different people – money people, intellectuals, health professionals, spiritual and artistic types. Singles have many romantic opportunities these days.

The lunar eclipse of the 10th affects you powerfully, so take it easy that period. Do what needs to be done but reschedule anything else you can. This eclipse brings a redefinition of the personality and self-image. A detox of the body could also happen – especially if you haven't been careful in dietary matters. This eclipse impacts on three other planets (adding to its strength): Saturn, your love planet; Pluto, your ruler of children, fun and creativity; and Mercury, your spiritual and communication planet. So many areas of life are getting disrupted. Your current relationship will get tested. There will be dramas in the life of the spouse, partner or current love. Children and children figures are affected and should be kept out of harm's way. Cars and communication equipment will get tested – probably they will behave erratically. There are shakeups in spiritual or charitable organizations you're involved with, and guru figures in your life have personal dramas.

The good news is that health and energy will improve after the 20th. It will still need attention, but the severity and stress is lessened.

The planetary power is almost all in the West (the social sector) this month; 80 per cent (and sometimes 90 per cent) of the planets are in the West. So the month ahead is about other people and their needs. Personal independence and initiative are not factors in success; your social grace – your ability to get on with others – is the main factor. This applies financially too. Your job this month is to prosper others. As you do this, your own financial supply will come quite naturally.

February

Best Days Overall: 6, 7, 14, 15, 23, 24, 25
Most Stressful Days Overall: 12, 13, 18, 19, 20, 26, 27
Best Days for Love: 7, 8, 11, 16, 17, 18, 19, 20, 26, 27, 29
Best Days for Money: 1, 2, 3, 4, 8, 9, 10, 11, 12, 13, 19, 20, 23, 24, 28, 29
Best Days for Career: 8, 9, 17, 18, 26, 27, 28, 29

Health is improved compared with last month, but it still needs watching in the month ahead – especially after the 16th. After that date four long-term planets make discordant aspects to you. So make sure to rest and relax wherever possible.

There are two major areas of interest this month. One is the love and social life, which seems very hectic. The other is your religious and philosophical life. The 9th house also rules foreign travel, and so foreign lands call to you. Power in the 9th house is excellent for college-level students – it indicates focus and success in their studies. They will earn their success – it's not a smooth ride – but it will happen. This is a month for philosophical and religious breakthroughs.

Finances should be good this month. Until the 19th it will be a good period to get rid of possessions that you don't need or use. Sell them, or give them to charity. Use is the primary factor in what you keep or get rid of. Financially, when you clear the decks – declutter the financial life – new and better things will come to you. The financial arteries have been clogged up. Until the 19th the Sun, your money planet, is in your 8th house. You are very much involved in the finances of the spouse, partner or current love. This is a great time to repay loans and debts, for tax planning and (if you are of appropriate age) estate planning.

Your money house is empty this month – only the Moon will move through there on the 8th and 9th. This is basically a good thing. Finances are good and you have no need to pay particular attention here. The Super Full Moon on the 9th will be a strong financial day. The Moon will be at perigee – her closest distance to earth – and is in your money house.

On the 19th the Sun moves into your 9th house – a fortunate position. Planets in the 9th house tend to expand and grow. So earning power is stronger than usual. Your financial intuition is also good. Investors would be attracted to foreign companies – especially in the oil, natural gas and water sectors. You have a good feeling for these sectors.

Two sectors of your chart are immensely powerful this month: the Western, social sector and the upper half – the day side – of your chart. Until the 7th at least 80 per cent of the planets are in the West – a huge percentage. So it is a very social kind of month. It's not a time to have things your way. Let others have their way so long as it isn't destructive. Your social grace will not only help you financially but in your career as well.

March

Best Days Overall: 4, 5, 12, 13, 22, 23
Most Stressful Days Overall: 10, 11, 17, 18, 24, 25
Best Days for Love: 1, 8, 9, 17, 18, 27, 28, 29
Best Days for Money: 1, 4, 5, 6, 7, 8, 9, 12, 13, 17, 18, 24, 25, 27, 28
Best Days for Career: 1, 8, 9, 17, 18, 24, 25, 27, 28

Health is still stressful this month, but the degree of stress is nowhere near what you had in January. Everything is relative. Make sure you're getting enough rest and enhance the health in the ways mentioned in the yearly report.

The upper half of the Horoscope – the day side – contains all the planets this month. Only the Moon will move through your night side, the lower half, between the 4th and the 16th. This is a lot of power. Career will go well. You are very motivated.

Finances look good this month too. Though your money house is empty, your financial planet gets a lot of stimulus. Its move through your 9th house is a very positive financial signal. The financial intuition will be good – especially on the 8th and 9th. Pay attention to your dreams and hunches over those days. On the 20th the Sun crosses the Mid-heaven and enters your 10th house. Often this indicates pay rises (official or unofficial) and the financial favour of bosses, elders, parents and parent figures. Even the government can be favourably disposed to you. Make sure you maintain your good career reputation as this is a source of income – it brings referrals and the like. The Sun in Aries from the 20th onward can make you too quick to jump into deals and too quick to spend. It is a speculative position. So try to slow things down a bit. On the other hand, this transit indicates quick financial progress.

The family is supporting your career these days. Thus you don't have the conflict between home and career that so many have. Venus, your family planet, is travelling with Uranus from the 6th to the 9th. This can bring disruptions in the home or dramas in the lives of parents or parent figures. They should reduce their schedules during that time.

Saturn, your love planet, makes a major move on the 23rd from your 7th house to your 8th. This brings changes in attitudes. Love is more erotic. Sexual magnetism seems paramount. Good sex will cover many sins in a relationship. The spouse, partner or current love is focused on finance these days. Focus tends to bring success.

Jupiter is travelling with Pluto all month. This indicates happy work and happy job opportunities. There is a tendency to speculate. There are opportunities for love affairs.

April

Best Days Overall: 1, 2, 9, 10, 18, 19, 28, 29
Most Stressful Days Overall: 7, 8, 13, 14, 20, 21, 22
Best Days for Love: 6, 7, 8, 13, 14, 15, 16, 17, 24, 25, 26
Best Days for Money: 3, 4, 6, 12, 14, 23, 24, 30
Best Days for Career: 7, 8, 15, 16, 20, 21, 22, 25, 26

Career is still the main focus this month – until the 19th. Not only is your 10th house strong, but the upper half of your Horoscope contains all the planets – like last month. You should have no qualms about focusing on the career.

The Western social sector of your chart is still stronger than the Eastern sector, but not as much as it has been in previous months. Day by day you are becoming more independent. You're not completely there yet, you still need other people, but you are more independent than you have been in previous months. The month ahead is about balancing your interests with those of others. You can't go too far in either direction.

You remain in a yearly career peak until the 19th, so the month ahead is successful.

Your financial planet remains in Aries until the 19th – a very speculative and risk-taking transit, but this should be avoided now (or reduced). Like last month, guard your career reputation as it is a source of earnings. On the 19th the Sun moves into more conservative Taurus. But finances are still unstable. The 24th to the 27th seems like a good financial period (good but complicated) as the Sun travels with Uranus. This can bring sudden money – unexpected money – or a sudden, unplanned expense. If it is an expense the money will come for it.

Your 8th house is strong all month. Moreover, the ruler of this house, Uranus, is highly stimulated this month. So this is a good time to pay down debt or to take on loans, depending on your need. It should be a good financial month for the spouse, partner or current love. The New Moon of the 23rd looks like a powerful financial day. It occurs right on Uranus – again showing sudden money.

Venus spends almost all month, from the 3rd onwards, 'out of bounds'. Family members are going outside their usual boundaries. Friends too. There are no answers for them in their normal spheres so they have to search elsewhere.

Your financial planet in your 11th house from the 19th onwards is a positive for finance. You will probably spend more on technology, but you also earn from it. Your social connections are very helpful. Being involved with groups, group activities and professional organizations will be beneficial: it will be the bottom line. Fondest financial hopes and wishes – at least short-term ones – come to pass.

May

Best Days Overall: 6, 7, 15, 16, 25, 26
Most Stressful Days Overall: 4, 5, 10, 11, 18, 19
Best Days for Love: 4, 5, 10, 11, 12, 13, 14, 22, 23, 24
Best Days for Money: 1, 2, 3, 11, 12, 22, 23, 27, 28
Best Days for Career: 4, 5, 14, 15, 18, 19, 25, 26

Venus, your family planet, remains 'out of bounds' this month (she has been 'out of bounds' since April 3). Family members and a parent or parent figure are outside their normal spheres. This is also true of friends. There are no solutions for them in the usual places and they must look elsewhere.

This month Mercury also goes 'out of bounds', from the 17th onwards, indicating that your intellectual tastes – the kinds of things you are reading, your taste in periodicals – are outside your norm. This is true in your spiritual life too. You are gravitating to systems and practices outside your norm. The New Moon of the 22nd is going to clarify your spiritual life over the next month (until the next New Moon).

Jupiter and Pluto are travelling together this month. This shows that children and children figures are prospering. They have many fine financial opportunities now. The transit favours speculations as well.

Your finances look good this month. Until the 29th your friends and social connections are playing an important role in your financial life. You have a good feeling for the world of technology and you seem more experimental than usual in finance. You are probably spending more on technology, but earning from it as well. A parent or parent figure is having a good financial month (though he or she is going outside their usual financial norms). On the 20th your financial planet moves into your spiritual 12th house, highlighting financial intuition. A flash of intuition is worth many years of hard labour, as our regular readers know. You will be more generous and charitable this period. You will experience more 'miracle money' rather than natural money. Be alert to your dreams and hunches over this period. There is good financial guidance there. Financial guidance will also come from astrologers, psychics, tarot readers, ministers and spiritual channels.

Retrograde activity increases this month, and by the end of the month 40 per cent of the planets will be moving backwards. Saturn's retrograde impacts on the love life. It slows things down. Venus's retrograde on the 13th (one of her rare retrogrades) also affects love, but more the family situation. Important family decisions shouldn't be made after the 13th. If you're buying high-tech equipment, try to do it before this date too.

June

Best Days Overall: 3, 4, 11, 12, 13, 21, 22, 28, 29
Most Stressful Days Overall: 1, 7, 8, 14, 15
Best Days for Love: 1, 2, 7, 8, 9, 10, 18, 19, 20
Best Days for Money: 1, 8, 9, 10, 18, 20, 21, 24, 27
Best Days for Career: 3, 4, 11, 12, 14, 15, 21, 22, 30

The Eastern half of your chart, the sector of self, is now the strongest it will ever be this year. It is not dominant – the Western, social sector is equally strong – but it is more pronounced than at any other time. Your 1st house is strong from the 21st onwards as well. So this is probably the best time to make the changes your need to make for your happiness. For the next few months you will be working to balance your own needs with the needs of others. You will be neither totally independent, nor totally dependent.

We have two eclipses this month. There is a lunar eclipse on the 5th and solar eclipse on the 21st. Both affect you strongly, so take it easy over those periods.

The lunar eclipse of the 5th occurs in your 6th house of health and work and announces job changes (this can be within your present company or with another one). There will be changes in your health regime too. This will go on for a few months. Sometimes there is a health scare, but your health looks good this month and this shouldn't amount to much. Children and children figures in your life are making important financial changes. Siblings and sibling figures are having dramas in the home. Since this eclipse impacts on Mars and Venus, it indicates dramas in the lives of parents or parent figures, career changes, and perhaps repairs in the home. Every lunar eclipse impacts you strongly because the Moon is the ruler of your Horoscope. It can bring a 'loss of honour' (temporary), slanders against you and sometimes a detox of the body. Once again, you are redefining yourself, your image and self-concept. Basically a healthy thing.

The solar eclipse of the 21st occurs in your own sign. All of you will feel this but those of you born early in the sign (June 21–22) will feel it most strongly. This eclipse brings dramatic financial changes. Your financial thinking and planning hasn't been realistic and thus they need some correction. The eclipse can also bring about a detox of the body and a redefinition of the self – the image and personality. You have to define yourself for yourself or others will do it for you and it won't be so pleasant. These internal changes you make will lead to wardrobe and image changes and changes in your outward presentation to others.

Planetary retrograde activity reaches the maximum for the year this month (although it will reach this point again in September). From the 23rd to the 25th 60 per cent of the planets are retrograde. After the 25th half will be in retrograde motion. This is a month for patience. Things are slowing down in the world.

July

Best Days Overall: 1, 9, 10, 19, 20, 27, 28
Most Stressful Days Overall: 4, 5, 11, 12, 25, 26, 31
Best Days for Love: 4, 5, 6, 7, 8, 15, 16, 17, 24, 25, 26, 31
Best Days for Money: 1, 4, 5, 9, 10, 14, 15, 20, 21, 22, 23, 24, 29, 31
Best Days for Career: 2, 3, 11, 12, 21, 22, 29, 30

Despite last month's solar eclipse, you are in a strong period of prosperity now. Your financial planet in your own sign is a wonderful financial signal. You receive windfalls. Money and opportunity seek you out. The money people in your life are very supportive. On the 22nd the Sun enters the money house – his own sign and house. This also shows increased earnings. The Sun is unusually powerful in his own sign and house, and you begin a yearly financial peak. But finance, though good, is not a smooth ride. You have to work harder for earnings, but if you put in the work you will prosper. Important financial changes are likely at the end of the month.

We have another eclipse this month – a third lunar eclipse on the 5th. This one occurs in your 7th house of love. A love relationship is getting tested. Usually repressed grievances – the dirty laundry – surface to be dealt with. Sometimes there are dramas in the life of the beloved that stress your relationship. A fundamentally sound relationship will survive, but flawed ones are in danger. This eclipse indirectly impacts on three other planets – Mercury, Jupiter and Mars. Thus there can be career changes, job changes, disruptions at the workplace or in the upper management of your company. The impact on Mercury affects cars and communication equipment. It will also affect the spiritual life, spiritual or charitable organizations that you're involved with and guru figures in your life. Like the eclipse of last month, there will be changes in your health regime. Reduce your schedule over this period.

Mars, your career planet, will have his solstice between the 7th and the 16th. He pauses in his latitudinal motion and then changes direction. So a pause in your career and change of direction is happening. This will be good.

Saturn moves back into Capricorn on the 1st. He is once again in stressful alignment with you. Health will need watching. You can enhance the health in the ways mentioned in the yearly report. The most important thing is to maintain high energy levels. Make sure you don't leave yourself vulnerable by being overtired.

Like last month, your challenge in July is to balance your own interests with the interests of others. Don't go too far in either direction.

August

Best Days Overall: 5, 6, 15, 16, 23, 24
Most Stressful Days Overall: 1, 2, 8, 9, 21, 22, 28, 29
Best Days for Love: 1, 2, 3, 4, 11, 15, 16, 20, 23, 24, 28, 29
Best Days for Money: 2, 8, 9, 11, 17, 18, 19, 20, 28, 29
Best Days for Career: 8, 9, 17, 18, 25, 26, 27

Venus moves into your sign on the 7th and stays there for the rest of the month. The personal appearance shines. Your sense of style and fashion is super, although perhaps you are more moody than usual. Family members, and especially a parent or parent figure, seem very devoted to you. Though your personal attractiveness is good, love is complicated. All the planets in your 7th house of love are retrograde this month. There is love in your life but it seems to lack direction.

You are still in the midst of a yearly financial peak until the 22nd. There is some financial upheaval from the 1st to the 3rd but it's a short-term problem. There could be some financial conflict between you and the beloved. The good news is that parents and parent figures in your life are supportive of your financial goals. Bosses too. Pay rises (official or unofficial) can happen. Speculations seem favourable.

On the 22nd your financial planet, the Sun, moves into your 3rd house. This aspect favours sales, marketing, PR, advertising, writing, blogging and retailing. Whatever you do, good use of the media, good marketing, becomes important. Until the 22nd you seem very keen on speculations. You're a free spender. Now you are more conservative. The financial judgement is better. The financial planet in Virgo favours the health field and favours earning money through work and service.

You are probably spending more on health, but you can also earn from this. People in the health field can be important financially. You are probably spending more on books, magazines and communication equipment too.

Four long-term planets are in stressful alignment with you, so your health needs keeping an eye on. As always, make sure you're getting enough rest. Keep your focus on the really important things in life and don't waste your energy on frivolities. You have the energy to do the important things. Enhance your health in the ways mentioned in the yearly report.

Retrograde activity increases again this month, with half the planets retrograde from the 15th onwards, close to the maximum for the year again. Things go slow in the world. The retrograde of Uranus impacts on the finances of the beloved. Finances are more uncertain and happen more slowly.

September

Best Days Overall: 1, 2, 3, 11, 12, 20, 21, 29, 30
Most Stressful Days Overall: 4, 5, 18, 19, 24, 25
Best Days for Love: 2, 3, 8, 13, 14, 17, 22, 23, 24, 25
Best Days for Money: 6, 7, 14, 15, 16, 17, 24, 25, 26
Best Days for Career: 4, 5, 14, 15, 22, 23

Health is the major concern this month. At least 60 per cent, sometimes 70 per cent of the planets will be in stressful alignment with you. This is no joke. With your 6th house empty you have a tendency to ignore your health, and this wouldn't be good. You'll have to force yourself to focus here. Enhance the health in the ways mentioned in the yearly report. Also, as we have mentioned many times, make sure you get enough rest and maintain high energy levels. High energy is the best defence against disease. If you can manage to spend more time in a health spa, or schedule more massages or reflexology treatments, that would be a big help. As was said last month, stay focused on your priorities and let lesser things go.

The good news is that your health planet Jupiter starts to move forward again on the 13th. So you will have more clarity here.

Retrograde activity will peak again for the year (matching the peak we had in June). Between the 9th and the 12th 60 per cent of the planets will be retrograde; and after the 12th it will be 50 per cent. With events in the world slowing down, this could be a good month to take a vacation or some time off.

Your career planet Mars goes retrograde on the 9th and will stay that way until November 14. Career issues are not clear now, and only time will resolve them, so you can take a breather from career and pay more attention to the home and family – especially from the 22nd onwards.

Though home and family haven't been as important this year as usual, this month, from the 22nd onwards, they do become important. This is Cancerian heaven. You're spending more on the home and the family but earning from there too. Family support will be good and family connections will be important financially. Your financial aspects seem easier before the 22nd than after. You'll just have to work harder after that date. There can be financial conflicts with children, children figures, and the spouse, partner or current love.

On the 6th Venus moves into the money house and stays there for the rest of the month. This too shows family support or family connections involved with finance. Friends also seem helpful.

October

Best Days Overall: 9, 10, 17, 18, 26, 27
Most Stressful Days Overall: 1, 2, 15, 16, 21, 22, 28, 29, 30
Best Days for Love: 3, 5, 14, 21, 22
Best Days for Money: 4, 5, 9, 10, 11, 12, 13, 14, 17, 18, 21, 23, 26, 31
Best Days for Career: 1, 2, 11, 12, 19, 20, 28, 29, 30

Health is still a major issue this month. Keep in mind our discussion of last month. The good news is that there is improvement after the 23rd. But even so, health still needs attention.

Your 4th house of home and family is one of the strongest in the Horoscope this month – although your 7th house of love is equally powerful. Mars, your career planet, is still retrograde all month, so it pays to focus more on the home and family – you probably won't be missing out on any career opportunities.

Personal independence has not been strong this year, and this month it gets even weaker as the planetary power shifts to the Western social sector. By the end of the month at least 70 per cent (sometimes 80 per cent) of the planets are in the West. Your focus is on others and their needs. Your good comes through the grace of others and not from your personal initiative. Likeability – social good will – is more important than personal skills.

Finances are good this month, but they will be better after the 23rd than before. Until then there can be financial disagreements with the spouse, partner or current love, and with children or children figures in your life. Perhaps there are extra expenses related to them. On the 23rd your financial planet enters Scorpio and earnings become easier. You should end the month in better financial shape than when you began.

With the Sun in Scorpio from the 23rd onwards, it is a good period to cut expenses and detox your financial life. Prune it. Declutter it. It is a good time for tax planning. If you are of the appropriate age it is good for estate planning too.

Pluto moves forward on the 4th after many months of retrograde motion. This, coupled with the Sun's move into Pluto's house on the 23rd, tends to mean that you are more speculative at this time – and your speculations tend to work out. You spend more on the children and children figures in your life, but can also earn from them. This is a period for happy money – money that is enjoyed, both in the making and in the spending.

The New Moon of the 16th is a 'Super New Moon'. It occurs with the Moon at her closest distance to earth so it is more powerful than usual. This will be a great financial day for you. The Full Moon of the 31st occurs right on Uranus, showing unexpected happenings. Best to take things easy that day.

November

Best Days Overall: 5, 6, 14, 15, 22, 23
Most Stressful Days Overall: 12, 18, 19, 25, 26
Best Days for Love: 2, 3, 11, 12, 18, 19, 21, 22
Best Days for Money: 5, 6, 2, 7, 8, 11, 14, 15, 19, 24, 25
Best Days for Career: 7, 8, 16, 25, 26

Last month on the 23rd you entered one of your yearly personal pleasure peaks. This continues until November 21. So have some fun and 'sit loose to life'. Joy itself is a great healer.

Health is much improved over last month but still needs watching. If you got through the past two months with health and sanity intact, you did very well. You can consider yourself successful. Continue to enhance your health in the ways mentioned in the yearly report. The good news is that health becomes more prominent in your Horoscope after the 21st as the Sun enters your health house. Focus is what is needed these days.

Retrograde activity is rapidly declining this month. After the 14th 80 per cent of the planets are moving forward, and after the 29th it is 90 per cent. Events in the world and in your life are moving forward. You have greater clarity on things. Hopefully you have used the intense retrograde activity to review your goals and formulate plans for the future – the whole purpose of these retrogrades. Now you should be in a good position to implement your plans and progress should be much faster.

The fourth and final lunar eclipse of the year occurs on the 30th. Every lunar eclipse affects you strongly, but this one less so than usual. It occurs in your 12th house of spirituality and impacts on your spiritual life – your teachings, practice and teachers. Usually spiritual changes come from 'revelation' – a new truth is seen, a new insight comes – and the old methodologies no longer apply. There are shake-ups in spiritual or charitable organizations that you're involved with and personal dramas in the lives of gurus or guru figures. Friends are forced to make dramatic financial changes. The beloved can experience job changes and changes in the health regime. And, as with every lunar eclipse, you are forced, once again, to redefine yourself – to upgrade your image and self-concept. This has been going on all year and the process continues until you get it right.

The New Moon of the 15th is a 'Super New Moon' that occurs with the Moon in perigee, at her closest to earth. It should be a super financial day. The spouse, partner or current love will have a super social day.

December

    Best Days Overall: 2, 3, 11, 12, 19, 20, 21, 29, 30, 31
    Most Stressful Days Overall: 9, 10, 15, 16, 22, 23
    Best Days for Love: 2, 3, 8, 9, 11, 12, 15, 16, 17, 22, 23, 27
    Best Days for Money: 5, 6, 8, 13, 14, 16, 24, 27
    Best Days for Career: 5, 6, 13, 14, 22, 23

This is a very eventful month with major changes going on. First of all, two long-term planets change signs this month. Saturn, your love planet, moves into Aquarius on the 18th (for the next two or so years) and Jupiter, your health planet, will also move into Aquarius two days later on the 20th. Jupiter will be here for almost all of 2021. Add to this a solar eclipse on the 14th and you have more change.

There is good news here too. Since two long-term planets are moving away from their stressful aspect to you, your health and energy will improve next year. You might have difficult months, caused by short-term planetary transits, but nothing like you have endured this year.

Saturn's move into Aquarius affects the love life. It becomes more erotic. Sexual magnetism seems the most important factor for singles. And even in the case of those who are married or already in a relationship, good sex will cover many sins. There will be greater experimentalism in love too.

Jupiter's move into your 8th house shows changes in your health regime and attitudes. You will become more experimental here as well. For the past year you've been pretty conservative in health matters; this will change. The ankles and calves will need more attention. The spine, knees and skeleton should be OK.

The solar eclipse of the 14th occurs in your 6th house of health and work and seems to announce the coming changes in the health regime.

There can be job changes – either within your present company or with another one. The conditions of work change. This eclipse brings needed financial corrections for both you and for children or children figures in your life. The money people in your life have personal dramas. Since this eclipse impacts on Neptune, the ruler of your 9th house, college-level students are affected. There can be changes of schools, courses or educational plans. Legal issues (if you are involved in them) will take a dramatic turn one way or another. They will move forward. Religious, theological and philosophical beliefs will get tested – some will be dropped, some will get revised.

Health needs some attention after the 21st, but the stress will be nowhere near as intense as in September and October. It is more of a short-term situation. Be sure to get more rest.

There can be job changes, but there is nothing to fear here. You will have ample job opportunities this month. Your 6th house is strong. You are in the mood for work.

Leo

Ω

THE LION

Birthdays from
21st July to
21st August

Personality Profile

LEO AT A GLANCE

Element – Fire

Ruling Planet – Sun
  Career Planet – Venus
  Love Planet – Uranus
  Money Planet – Mercury
  Planet of Health and Work – Saturn
  Planet of Home and Family Life – Pluto

Colours – gold, orange, red

Colours that promote love, romance and social harmony – black, indigo, ultramarine blue

Colours that promote earning power – yellow, yellow-orange

Gems – amber, chrysolite, yellow diamond

Metal – gold

Scents – bergamot, frankincense, musk, neroli

JASON 8/7/76

Quality – fixed (= stability)

Quality most needed for balance – humility

Strongest virtues – leadership ability, self-esteem and confidence, generosity, creativity, love of joy

Deepest needs – fun, elation, the need to shine

Characteristics to avoid – arrogance, vanity, bossiness

Signs of greatest overall compatibility – Aries, Sagittarius

Signs of greatest overall incompatibility – Taurus, Scorpio, Aquarius

Sign most helpful to career – Taurus

Sign most helpful for emotional support – Scorpio

Sign most helpful financially – Virgo

Sign best for marriage and/or partnerships – Aquarius

Sign most helpful for creative projects – Sagittarius

Best Sign to have fun with – Sagittarius

Signs most helpful in spiritual matters – Aries, Cancer

Best day of the week – Sunday

Understanding a Leo

When you think of Leo, think of royalty – then you'll get the idea of what the Leo character is all about and why Leos are the way they are. It is true that, for various reasons, some Leo-born do not always express this quality – but even if not they should like to do so.

A monarch rules not by example (as does Aries) nor by consensus (as do Capricorn and Aquarius) but by personal will. Will is law. Personal taste becomes the style that is imitated by all subjects. A monarch is somehow larger than life. This is how a Leo desires to be.

When you dispute the personal will of a Leo it is serious business. He or she takes it as a personal affront, an insult. Leos will let you know that their will carries authority and that to disobey is demeaning and disrespectful.

A Leo is king (or queen) of his or her personal domain. Subordinates, friends and family are the loyal and trusted subjects. Leos rule with benevolent grace and in the best interests of others. They have a powerful presence; indeed, they are powerful people. They seem to attract attention in any social gathering. They stand out because they are stars in their domain. Leos feel that, like the Sun, they are made to shine and rule. Leos feel that they were born to special privilege and royal prerogatives – and most of them attain this status, at least to some degree.

The Sun is the ruler of this sign, and when you think of sunshine it is very difficult to feel unhealthy or depressed. Somehow the light of the Sun is the very antithesis of illness and apathy. Leos love life. They also love to have fun; they love drama, music, the theatre and amusements of all sorts. These are the things that give joy to life. If – even in their best interests – you try to deprive Leos of their pleasures, good food, drink and entertainment, you run the serious risk of depriving them of the will to live. To them life without joy is no life at all.

Leos epitomize humanity's will to power. But power in and of itself – regardless of what some people say – is neither good nor evil. Only when power is abused does it become evil. Without power even good things cannot come to pass. Leos realize this and are uniquely qualified to wield power. Of all the signs, they do it most naturally. Capricorn,

the other power sign of the zodiac, is a better manager and administrator than Leo – much better. But Leo outshines Capricorn in personal
grace and presence. Leo loves power, whereas Capricorn assumes
power out of a sense of duty.

Finance

Leos are great leaders but not necessarily good managers. They are
better at handling the overall picture than the nitty-gritty details of
business. If they have good managers working for them they can
become exceptional executives. They have vision and a lot of
creativity.

Leos love wealth for the pleasures it can bring. They love an opulent
lifestyle, pomp and glamour. Even when they are not wealthy they live
as if they are. This is why many fall into debt, from which it is sometimes difficult to emerge.

Leos, like Pisceans, are generous to a fault. Very often they want to
acquire wealth solely so that they can help others economically. Wealth
to Leo buys services and managerial ability. It creates jobs for others
and improves the general well-being of those around them. Therefore
– to a Leo – wealth is good. Wealth is to be enjoyed to the fullest.
Money is not to be left to gather dust in a mouldy bank vault but to be
enjoyed, spread around, used. So Leos can be quite reckless in their
spending.

With the sign of Virgo on Leo's 2nd money house cusp, Leo needs
to develop some of Virgo's traits of analysis, discrimination and purity
when it comes to money matters. They must learn to be more careful
with the details of finance (or to hire people to do this for them). They
have to be more cost-conscious in their spending habits. Generally,
they need to manage their money better. Leos tend to chafe under
financial constraints, yet these constraints can help Leos to reach their
highest financial potential.

Leos like it when their friends and family know that they can depend
on them for financial support. They do not mind – and even enjoy –
lending money, but they are careful that they are not taken advantage
of. From their 'regal throne' Leos like to bestow gifts upon their family
and friends and then enjoy the good feelings these gifts bring to every-

body. Leos love financial speculations and – when the celestial influences are right – are often lucky.

Career and Public Image

Leos like to be perceived as wealthy, for in today's world wealth often equals power. When they attain wealth they love having a large house with lots of land and animals.

At their jobs Leos excel in positions of authority and power. They are good at making decisions – on a grand level – but they prefer to leave the details to others. Leos are well respected by their colleagues and subordinates, mainly because they have a knack for understanding and relating to those around them. Leos usually strive for the top positions even if they have to start at the bottom and work hard to get there. As might be expected of such a charismatic sign, Leos are always trying to improve their work situation. They do so in order to have a better chance of advancing to the top.

On the other hand, Leos do not like to be bossed around or told what to do. Perhaps this is why they aspire so for the top – where they can be the decision-makers and need not take orders from others.

Leos never doubt their success and focus all their attention and efforts on achieving it. Another great Leo characteristic is that – just like good monarchs – they do not attempt to abuse the power or success they achieve. If they do so this is not wilful or intentional. Usually they like to share their wealth and try to make everyone around them join in their success.

Leos are – and like to be perceived as – hard-working, well-established individuals. It is definitely true that they are capable of hard work and often manage great things. But do not forget that, deep down inside, Leos really are fun-lovers.

Love and Relationships

Generally, Leos are not the marrying kind. To them relationships are good while they are pleasurable. When the relationship ceases to be pleasurable a true Leo will want out. They always want to have the freedom to leave. That is why Leos excel at love affairs rather than commitment. Once married, however, Leo is faithful – even if some Leos have a tendency to marry more than once in their lifetime. If you are in love with a Leo, just show him or her a good time – travel, go to casinos and clubs, the theatre and discos. Wine and dine your Leo love – it is expensive but worth it and you will have fun.

Leos generally have an active love life and are demonstrative in their affections. They love to be with other optimistic and fun-loving types like themselves, but wind up settling with someone more serious, intellectual and unconventional. The partner of a Leo tends to be more political and socially conscious than he or she is, and more libertarian. When you marry a Leo, mastering the freedom-loving tendencies of your partner will definitely become a life-long challenge – and be careful that Leo does not master you.

Aquarius sits on Leo's 7th house of love cusp. Thus if Leos want to realize their highest love and social potential they need to develop a more egalitarian, Aquarian perspective on others. This is not easy for Leo, for 'the king' finds his equals only among other 'kings'. But perhaps this is the solution to Leo's social challenge – to be 'a king among kings'. It is all right to be regal, but recognize the nobility in others.

Home and Domestic Life

Although Leos are great entertainers and love having people over, sometimes this is all show. Only very few close friends will get to see the real side of a Leo's day-to-day life. To a Leo the home is a place of comfort, recreation and transformation; a secret, private retreat – a castle. Leos like to spend money, show off a bit, entertain and have fun. They enjoy the latest furnishings, clothes and gadgets – all things fit for kings.

Leos are fiercely loyal to their family and, of course, expect the same from them. They love their children almost to a fault; they have to be careful not to spoil them too much. They also must try to avoid attempting to make individual family members over in their own image. Leos should keep in mind that others also have the need to be their own people. That is why Leos have to be extra careful about being over-bossy or over-domineering in the home.

Horoscope for 2020

Major Trends

Health, work and career are the major headlines this year, Leo. If some of you are unemployed there are many job opportunities awaiting you. It is a work-oriented year ahead. More on this later.

Though your health is good you seem very involved in health matters this year. Probably you're involved in preventive measures and making sure you have a healthy lifestyle. In many cases you will be involved in the health of others. More details later.

The career is perhaps the most exciting area this year. This began last year and will go on for many more years. Excitement implies change and drama. If things are going steadily there is no drama, no excitement. Even the good can get a little boring. Not so this year. You are learning to cope with career instability. More on this later.

Uranus's move into your 10th career house in March last year also affects the love life. Your attitudes change. You are mixing with important people and furthering your career by social means. It is a positive signal for love, but it will get tested. There's more on this later.

Neptune, the most spiritual of all the planets, has been in your 8th house of regeneration for many years now and he will be there for many more; a long-term trend and we have discussed this in previous reports. The sex life and sexual practices are becoming spiritualized and more refined. Little by little the sex life is becoming more an act of worship than mere animal lust.

Mars will spend more than six months in your 9th house this year. This is good for college students as it shows focus on their studies, which indicates success. There could also be legal issues that take a lot of your time.

Though your 12th house of spirituality is not strong this year, we will have four lunar eclipses – twice as many as usual. With the Moon as your spiritual planet, there is much spiritual change happening for you, many course corrections. (Two eclipses, one solar and one lunar, will actually occur in your 12th house, reinforcing what is being said.)

Your major areas of interest this year are health and work; love, romance and social activities; sex, personal transformation and occult studies; religion, philosophy, higher education and foreign travel (from June 28 onwards); and career.

Your paths of greatest fulfilment in the year ahead will be spirituality (until May 6); the body and image (from May 6 onwards); health and work (until December 20); and love, romance and social activities (after December 20).

Health

(Please note that this is an astrological perspective on health and not a medical one. In days of yore there was no difference, both these perspectives were identical. But now there could be quite a difference. For a medical perspective, please consult your doctor or health practitioner.)

Health is basically good this year. For most of the year there will be only one long-term planet – Uranus – in stressful alignment with you. Saturn will make a brief foray into stressful alignment from March 23 to July 1, but for not long enough to cause serious

Important foot reflexology points for the year ahead
Try to massage all of the foot on a regular basis – the top of the foot as well as the bottom – but pay extra attention to the points highlighted on the chart. When you massage, be aware of 'sore spots' as these need special attention. It's also a good idea to massage the ankles and below them.

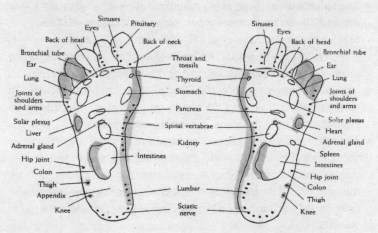

problems. However, from December 18 onwards Saturn and Jupiter both move into stressful alignment, and that will be a time to rest and relax more and pace yourself better. For most of the year you're fine and dandy.

Your 6th house of health is easily the strongest in your Horoscope. In one sense this is good, as preventive measures you take now will stand you in good stead for later on (and next year). In another sense this focus is not so good. It can give a tendency to magnify little things into big things and to create problems where none really exists. You have be careful of this. The South Node of the Moon, an abstract point which denotes a feeling of deficiency, will be in your 6th house until May 6. This could also contribute to the focus on health. Perhaps you feel deficient here.

This focus on health could also show, as was mentioned, that you are involved in other people's health – the health of family members and children, or people who are like family to you.

Good though your health is you can make it even better. Give more attention to the following – the vulnerable areas of your Horoscope (the reflex points are shown in the chart above):

- The heart is always important for Leo and, as always, good heart health means avoiding worry and anxiety. These are the root causes of heart problems.
- The spine, knees, teeth, skin and overall skeletal alignment. These are also always important for Leo. Good back care is vital and regular back massage, regular visits to the chiropractor or osteopath would be good. The knees should also be massaged and given more support when exercising. Maintain good dental hygiene. Therapies such as the Alexander Technique (which works on posture), Rolfing and Feldenkrais are good. Yoga and Pilates are good exercises for the spine and overall alignment.
- The colon, bladder and sexual organs have become important areas since 2008, when Pluto entered your 6th house, and they will remain so for years to come. Safe sex and sexual moderation are important. A herbal colon cleanse every now and then would also be beneficial, especially if you feel under the weather.

- The liver and thighs will be important until December 20. Regular thigh massage will not only strengthen the liver and thighs, but the lower back as well – very important for you.
- The ankles and calves. These gain in importance after December 18 and will remain so for the next few years as Saturn, your health planet, moves into Aquarius. So regular ankle and calf massage will be beneficial. Calf massage will not only strengthen that area, but also the reproductive system – so important these days.

Pluto is the ruler of your 4th house of home, family and emotional life. His position in the 6th house shows that for you good health means a healthy family and domestic life. Problems here could impact on the actual physical health. So if, God forbid, problems arise, restore the harmony here as quickly as possible. Moods need to be kept positive and constructive. Meditation will be a big help.

Jupiter in your house of health shows that relations with the children and children figures in your life are important. Problems here could impact on your actual physical health. So do your best to keep the harmony here. This transit would also indicate the therapeutic value of a creative hobby. There is a need to express the creative urges this year.

Home and Family

Though your 4th house is basically empty this year (only short-term planets move through there), Pluto, your family planet, receives much stimulation. The empty 4th house would tend to the status quo, but the impact on Pluto signals much change.

Pluto is receiving contradictory influences this year which really complicates the family situation. Both Saturn and Jupiter (opposites really) are impacting on Pluto. Saturn is restrictive and controlling. Jupiter is expansive and freedom-loving. There are various ways to read this and all of them would be true.

Family members could exhibit extreme ambivalence this year. They can alternate from conservatism and coldness (the Saturn influence) to warmth and generosity (the Jupiter influence). Saturn would tend to frugality. Jupiter would tend to generosity. So family members and parent figures are like that. A parent figure can be over-controlling one moment and warm and generous the next. Most likely he or she feels that the controlling part – the sternness – is a form of benevolence. He or she would feel like a benevolent dictator. The other parent figure is just the opposite. He or she seems rebellious, wants personal freedom, wants to be free of all responsibility. If they are still together, they seem to get along, but between March 23 and July 1, and from December 18 onwards, they clash. Their marriage gets tested.

A part of you would like to move (the Jupiter influence) while another part fears it and wants to stay put (the Saturn influence). So moves could happen but with glitches and delays involved. The question is will the Jupiter force be stronger than the Saturn force? Or vice versa? I would say that the Saturn force – the urge to stay put – would be stronger. Saturn in Capricorn is dignified and powerful. He is in his own sign and house. Jupiter, by contrast, is in his 'fall' – his weakest possible position. So though a move could happen it is more likely that you will stay put and make better use of the space that you have.

For many years now – and we have discussed this in previous years' reports – you have been working to make the home 'healthier'. Probably you have spent money on getting rid of environmental or other toxins from the home and grounds. You have installed health equipment – exercise equipment or other kinds of health gadgets. You're making the home as much a spa as a home. This year the tendency for this is even stronger.

You've also been making the home a workplace, installing home offices and office equipment. Many of you are working from home or in a home-based business. This trend is also stronger this year.

However this year, in addition, you are also making the home a place of entertainment. You don't need to go out to have fun. It's right there at home.

Finance and Career

Your money house hasn't been strong for a number of years, and this is still the case in 2020. Only short-term planets will move through the money house. On the positive side this shows a contentment with things as they are. There is no special need to make dramatic changes and no special need to overly focus here. On the negative side, you may be ignoring an important area of life. If financial problems arise this could be the root cause. You will need to start focusing more.

In spite of this I see prosperity this year. Your 6th house of health and work is the strongest in the Horoscope; I doubt whether there will be any unemployed Leos this year. There are many job opportunities and offers - and good ones. Even those who are already employed will have offers for second jobs or overtime (and you'll probably take them). Your work ethic is unusually strong these days. This is noticed by superiors and helps the career.

Your financial planet Mercury is a fast-moving and often erratic kind of planet. And this is reflected in your financial life. Sometimes earnings come quickly, sometimes slowly, sometimes they stand still and sometimes they seem to go backwards. They tend to mirror Mercury's movements in the heavens. Because Mercury moves so quickly there will be many short-term financial trends that depend on where Mercury is at any given time and the kinds of aspects he receives. These are best dealt with in the monthly reports.

Career is more of a headline than finances these days, Leo. Uranus entered your 10th house of career in March 2019 and will stay for many years. There are many, many messages here. First of all, as was mentioned earlier, it shows instability in the career - constant change. Because of this, it favours a freelance career over a steady job working for others. You need more freedom in the career. If a steady position allows for this freedom it could work for you.

Instability is another name for excitement and change. Anything can happen at any time. No matter how bleak things may appear, the situation can change in an instant. Career opportunities happen out of the blue. Uranus in your 10th house would favour the world of technology - computers, programming, online activities and the like. If they are involved in entertainment and the arts, even better. Whatever you're doing your technological expertise is an important factor.

Uranus is also your love planet. This too gives many messages. A lot of your socializing is career- or business-related. Who you know - your social contacts - can be more important than your actual skills. In general your social grace - your likeability - plays a huge role in career success, and thus it is good to cultivate the social graces this year. (The Western social sector of your chart is the dominant sector, reinforcing what we are saying here.) You further your career by social means, by attending or hosting the right kind of parties and gatherings. You have a special ability to meet, on a social level, exactly the right people who can help you.

There is another way to read this too – and just as accurate. The love planet near the Mid-heaven – its most elevated position – often shows that your mission this year (and for many more to come) is to be there for the beloved and your friends. You might be involved in worldly affairs, but your real mission is your friends and partner.

Your career planet, Venus, is a fast-moving planet. Usually she moves through your whole chart in a given year, although this year (because of her retrograde) she will only move through 11 houses instead of 12. Still, this is a lot of movement. Thus there are many short-term career trends that depend on where Venus is and the aspects she receives. We will cover this in the monthly reports.

Love and Social Life

The love and social life is very important this year. First of all, your 7th house will become powerful from March 23 to July 1, and then again from December 18 onwards. But even more important than that is your love planet Uranus's position on the Mid-heaven of your chart. The Mid-heaven – the top of the chart – is the most powerful place for a planet to be. Just as the Sun is most powerful at noon (its Mid-heaven point) so too are the other planets most powerful here. Add to this the dominance of the Western, social sector and we see a year where the social grace and gifts are very much accentuated. It is a year for focusing on others. There will be times, as the year progresses, where the Eastern sector of self gets stronger, but it will never dominate.

The love planet on the Mid-heaven shows that power and prestige are important allurements in love – perhaps more so than the usual ones. You gravitate to powerful people, to people above you in status, to those who can help you get to where you want to go. You are meeting these kinds of people too.

Often this indicates romantic opportunities with bosses and superiors. It favours the office romance. (Your work planet, Saturn, moves into your 7th house of love between March 23 and July 1, and again from December 18 onwards, and this too favours the office romance.) Many companies have rules about this, and there are other scenarios indicated too. Bosses, superiors or co-workers can play Cupid in your love life, make proper introductions, etc. They seem very involved in romance one way or another.

Your love planet is in conservative Taurus all year. Saturn is also a conservative planet. Thus you seem more cautious in love these days (very different from the way you were from 2012 to 2019). This I read as a good thing. In the past you were too quick here. A sense of caution is a good thing.

Jupiter's move into your 7th house at the end of the year is often a signal for a marriage or serious relationship (a relationship that is like marriage). This would be more likely next year than in 2020. But even so, it is not wise to rush into anything. Saturn will also be in your 7th house and he tends to delay things.

On an overall level your best love and social periods will be from January 1 to January 20; April 20 to May 20; August 23 to September 22; and December 22 to the end of the year.

For those working on their second marriage there is romance after June 28, but it seems very challenging. Things will get easier from December 18 onwards. Those working on their third marriage have a quiet, stable kind of year.

Self-improvement

Pluto, the generic ruler of sex, has been in your 6th house of health for many years. Thus safe sex and sexual moderation have been important, healthwise, for a long time. Neptune, the most spiritual of all the planets, has been occupying your 8th house of sex and regeneration for many years too. So we have a strong message from the Horoscope. There is a need to elevate the sexual act, to make it an act of worship rather than an act of lust. This elevation is the 'real' safe sex. So, these days, you are a candidate for some of the spiritual teachings and practices of sex. It would be good to study Tantra or Kundalini yoga if you are of the Eastern bent. Westerners can study Karezza or Hermetic science which also deal with these things.

As we mentioned earlier, the four lunar eclipses this year impact very directly on the spiritual life. There will be two eclipses that actually occur in the 12th house – a lunar eclipse on January 10 and a solar eclipse on June 21. So there is much change and turmoil happening here. The events of life are going to test your spiritual attitudes, practices, teachings and teachers. If you belong to a spiritual organization there is much upheaval and disruption happening. This is also the case in charitable organizations that you're involved with. These things need not be bad. Often spiritual changes – changes in direction and practice – happen because of inner revelation. This is a good thing. A practice that might have been good for a while is no longer necessary and you progress to other disciplines. Those of you not yet on a spiritual path are likely to get on one this year.

Jupiter and Pluto in your 6th house of health show a need for good emotional health, as we have said, and for a healthy creative life. It's very important to avoid depression these days. The good news is that Leos are generally optimistic people and not prone to depression. But you need to feel that you're enjoying your life, that life is fun and happy. Joy itself is a powerful healing force and this year more so than usual. Therapies such as laughter yoga would be very powerful for you. Meditation will be a great help here too, and for maintaining emotional stability.*

Month-by-month Forecasts

January

Best Days Overall: 2, 3, 12, 20, 21, 29, 30, 31
Most Stressful Days Overall: 5, 6, 18, 19, 24, 25, 26
Best Days for Love: 4, 5, 13, 14, 18, 19, 22, 24, 25, 26, 27, 28
Best Days for Money: 5, 6, 14, 15, 22, 23, 25, 26
Best Days for Career: 5, 6, 13, 14, 18, 19, 27, 28

---

* Those of you who want to go deeper into these things can visit my blog, where we discuss these issues in greater detail: www.spiritual-stories.com.

The planetary momentum is overwhelmingly forward this month. On the 11th, as Uranus moves forward, *all* the planets will be in forward motion. Events, both personally and on a world level, move forward swiftly. The pace of life is fast, just as you like it.

Health is good and you seem focused here. Your 6th house of health and work is easily the strongest in your Horoscope this month and it is doubtful that there are any unemployed Leos these days. In fact the opposite is more likely – many of you are working multiple jobs.

Health will need more attention after the 20th, although there's nothing serious afoot. It is just not one of your best health periods. It's a short-term issue. Enhance the health in the ways mentioned in the yearly report.

The Western, social sector of your Horoscope is overwhelmingly dominant this month – in fact, this will be the tendency for the entire year ahead. You are in a strong social cycle. The needs of others come before your own. Your social grace determines what happens in your life. This is especially so from the 20th onwards as the Sun enters your 7th house of love and you begin a yearly love and social peak. Uranus's forward motion also helps the love life. Social popularity is a wonderful thing, but sometimes it can complicate an existing relationship. The spouse, partner or current love doesn't take kindly to it. Be more patient with the beloved from the 21st to the 23rd.

A lunar eclipse on the 10th occurs in your 12th house. Its effects are basically benign for you but it won't hurt to reduce your schedule. This eclipse shows spiritual changes – changes in teachers, teachings and practices. Spiritual attitudes change. (Keep in mind that the Moon is your spiritual planet and this eclipse is like a double hit on this area.) It brings upheavals in spiritual or charitable organizations you belong to and dramas in the lives of gurus and guru figures. The beloved can experience job changes and changes in the health regime.

Mercury, your financial planet, will be 'out of bounds' from the 1st to the 12th. Thus in financial matters you are outside your normal sphere. On the 16th Mercury moves into your 7th house, indicating that the favour of others will be important financially. You are putting the financial interest of others ahead of your own and it seems to work for you. Mercury in Aquarius is his most powerful position. It should be a good financial month.

February

Best Days Overall: 8, 9, 16, 17, 26, 27
Most Stressful Days Overall: 1, 2, 14, 15, 21, 22, 28, 29
Best Days for Love: 1, 7, 8, 9, 10, 16, 17, 18, 21, 22, 26, 27, 28
Best Days for Money: 1, 2, 6, 7, 10, 11, 14, 15, 19, 20, 23, 24, 25, 28, 29
Best Days for Career: 1, 2, 7, 8, 16, 17, 26, 27, 28, 29

You are still in a yearly love and social peak, until the 19th, and relations with the beloved are much improved. Love seems happy and you are popular.

Last month, the upper half of your Horoscope became stronger than the lower half. Dawn is breaking in your year. It is time to be up and about and focused on your outer affairs. Home, family and emotional issues can be put on the back burner now.

Finances are good this month, but become more complicated as your financial planet starts to retrograde on the 17th. So make important purchases, investments or financial decisions before then. After the 17th take a 'wait and see' attitude. Gather more facts. See where financial improvements can be made and hold off important financial moves.

From the 3rd, Mercury will be in your 8th house. Thus there is still a need this month to focus on the financial interests of others ahead of your own. This must be uppermost in your mind. To the degree that you can enrich others, to that degree will your personal prosperity happen. This transit is also good for a financial detox – getting rid of redundant accounts or expenses. Good to declutter both the financial life and your personal possessions. (Whatever things you don't use should be sold or given to charity.) It is a good month (especially until the 17th) for tax planning or insurance purchases (money can come from these sources too). If you are of the appropriate age it is good for estate planning too.

Mercury in the sign of Pisces enhances the financial intuition. After the 17th, however, your intuition should be verified. It could be correct, but your interpretation could be amiss.

Venus, your career planet, has her solstice from the 8th to the 10th. She pauses in the heavens and then changes direction (in latitude). So a pause in career matters is happening and then a change of direction. Venus will be in your 9th house from the 7th onwards. This often indicates career-related travel, and educational opportunities related to the career. These are helpful to you.

Mars enters your 6th house on the 16th, so exercise and good muscle tone become important for your health.

Your 8th house is very powerful this month, especially from the 19th onwards. Thus the month ahead favours projects involving personal transformation – giving birth to your ideal self, the person that you want to be. It favours detox regimes on all levels, physical, emotional and mental.

March

Best Days Overall: 6, 7, 14, 15, 24, 25
Most Stressful Days Overall: 1, 12, 13, 19, 20, 27, 28
Best Days for Love: 1, 8, 16, 17, 18, 19, 20, 26, 27, 28
Best Days for Money: 1, 8, 9, 10, 11, 17, 18, 22, 23, 27, 28
Best Days for Career: 1, 8, 17, 18, 27, 28

Saturn's move into your 7th house on the 23rd is not a full-blown transit but only a flirtation, a harbinger of things to come. Love is getting tested. Singles are probably dating less. There is a need to focus on quality rather than quantity. You find health professionals or people involved in your health alluring. Mars moving into your 7th house on the 31st will also test love. Good relationships will survive these testings.

More importantly, your health planet's move shows a need to focus more on health. Your health and energy are not up to their usual standards. This is especially so next month. Enhance the health in the ways discussed in the yearly report. From the 23rd onwards good health means a healthy love life. So, strive to maintain harmony here. Problems in love and with friends can be a root cause of physical problems.

Mercury moves erratically this month. He starts out in your 8th house, retrogrades back into your 7th house on the 4th and then returns to your 8th house on the 16th. We get the impression that some unfinished business has to be taken care of before you move forward again – something neglected. The good news is that, with Mercury's forward motion on the 10th, the financial faculties are back to normal – in fact from the 10th to the 16th they are supernormal. And financial intuition is back on target from the 16th.

The Sun travelling with spiritual Neptune on the 8th and 9th signals various things. It brings spiritual breakthroughs, enhanced ESP, prophetic dreams and perhaps an erotic encounter. (These erotic encounters often happen in dreams.) The Full Moon of the 9th is not technically a 'Super Full Moon' – but it is close. It occurs with the Moon very near perigee – her closest distance to earth. This too will bring an active dream life, enhanced ESP, supernatural-type experiences and perhaps a spiritual breakthrough.

On the 20th the Sun moves into your 9th house – a beautiful transit for you. Leo always tends to shine, but now the light is much brighter. The Sun is in his most exalted position in the sign of Aries. So you are super-creative, super-fun-loving these days. One needs sun glasses to look at you. This is a wonderful transit for college-level students; they should do well in their studies. Foreign travel is likely to be on the agenda too – opportunities will be there.

A happy career meeting – it seems like a social meeting – happens between the 6th and the 9th.

April

Best Days Overall: 3, 4, 11, 12, 20, 21, 22
Most Stressful Days Overall: 9, 10, 15, 16, 23, 24
Best Days for Love: 5, 7, 8, 13, 15, 16, 17, 23, 25, 26
Best Days for Money: 1, 2, 5, 6, 10, 11, 14, 20, 21, 24, 30
Best Days for Career: 7, 8, 15, 16, 17, 23, 24, 25, 26

Jupiter and Pluto are travelling together all month. A move or the fortunate sale or purchase of a home could happen. A parent or parent figure prospers. The family as a whole prospers.

Mars and Saturn travel together on the 1st and 2nd. Health can be enhanced through exercise and by scalp and face massage. Your job could take you to foreign countries. Perhaps there is a job opening in a foreign land.

The main issue this month is health, especially from the 19th onwards. Five, sometimes six planets will be in stressful alignment with you. This is serious. Yes, you're busy. The career is successful and demanding, but without good health what good is it? There are other issues too. Things that you did easily just a few months ago are now becoming difficult. Maybe you climbed that ladder to fix the roof a few months ago and it was a breeze. Maybe you were able to cycle 20 miles no sweat. Now, you probably can't. If you push things, problems can happen. So, succeed in your career – you are in a yearly career peak from the 19th onwards. The focus here is fully justified. But don't allow yourself to get overtired. Concentrate on the essential things in your life – you have the energy for those things – but let the trivialities go. Enhance the health in the ways mentioned in the yearly report. If possible, spend some time in a health spa or schedule in extra massages or reflexology treatments.

Love is still being tested this month, but there is a happy romantic meeting between the 24th and 26th. This could involve the career. It can be with someone involved in your career as well.

Mercury, your financial planet, has his solstice from the 14th to the 16th. He pauses in the heavens and then reverses direction (in latitude). So a pause in finances is likely. It is a good pause, natural and cosmic, and nothing to be alarmed about. When it is over you will have a change of financial direction. Finances look good this month. First off, Mercury is moving speedily. Progress is quick, confidence is good. Money and financial opportunity can happen in many ways and through various people. Until the 11th financial detoxing is still in order. It is a good time either to pay off debts or to take on a loan, depending on your need. You have good access to capital. If you have good ideas it is good for attracting outside investors to your projects. From the 11th to the 27th Mercury is in Aries, your beneficent 9th house: a very positive indicator for finance. Earnings are increased. Financial decisions are made quickly. But be careful of excessive risk-taking. You are generally a speculative kind of person, but this period even more so. From the 27th Mercury will be in your 10th house of career. Here he becomes more conservative. Pay rises (official or unofficial) can happen.

May

Best Days Overall: 1, 8, 9, 18, 19, 27, 28
Most Stressful Days Overall: 6, 7, 13, 14, 20, 21
Best Days for Love: 2, 4, 5, 10, 13, 14, 20, 23, 24
Best Days for Money: 2, 3, 12, 13, 22, 23, 24, 29, 30
Best Days for Career: 4, 5, 13, 14, 20, 21, 23, 24

Venus, your career planet, went 'out of bounds' on April 3, and will be 'out of bounds' for the entire month ahead. This is highly unusual for any planet. Thus your career is taking you way outside your normal sphere. Perhaps career responsibilities are pulling you – stretching you – outside your normal limits.

We see a similar situation in finance: Mercury is 'out of bounds' from May 17 onwards. So there are probably no financial solutions to be found in the normal places and you must go outside them. The money people in your life also seem outside their normal borders.

Health still needs attention this month, especially until the 20th. Still, it is improving day by day. The situation is nowhere near as serious as last month. Mercury moves away from his stressful aspect on the 12th. Mars stops stressing you on the 13th. And on the 20th the Sun begins making harmonious aspects. Until the 19th enhance the health in the ways mentioned in the yearly report. Most importantly, rest when tired.

Career is going well and you are successful – at the top of your game. People look up to you and you have status and appreciation. Financially things also look good. Until the 12th money comes from your good career reputation, or from the career itself. Pay rises (official or unofficial) can happen. Bosses, elders, parents or parent figures are supporting your financial goals. Mercury in your career house indicates financial focus – it is high on your list of priorities. Mercury, like any other planet, is always stronger at the top of your chart. But Mercury is strong after the 12th too, when he moves into his own sign and house where he is most comfortable. This is good for earnings. It signals the financial favour of friends and a good feeling for technology, computers and the online world. On the 29th your financial planet enters your 12th house. You become more generous (even more so than usual) and charitable. You have an instinct for the spiritual perspective on wealth. Financial guidance comes in dreams, through hunches and astrologers, psychics, tarot readers and spiritual channels. Sometimes something in a newspaper or flyer will jump out at you and give you a financial message. The invisible world is supporting your financial goals.

Love is tricky this month, but friendships are good. Some months (and some years) are like that.

June

Best Days Overall: 5, 6, 14, 15, 24, 30
Most Stressful Days Overall: 3, 4, 9, 10, 16, 17, 18, 28, 29
Best Days for Love: 1, 7, 8, 9, 10, 16, 17, 19, 20, 26, 27
Best Days for Money: 3, 4, 8, 11, 12, 18, 21, 22, 26, 27
Best Days for Career: 1, 9, 10, 16, 17, 18, 19, 20

Career is slowing down a bit now. Your career planet, Venus, went retrograde on May 13 and will be this way until the 25th, so career issues are not clear and only time will bring clarity here. But the slow down is not only in the career. This month, retrograde activity hits its maximum level for the year. Between the 23rd and 25th 60 per cent of the planets will be retrograde, and after the 25th it will still be 50 per cent. (Retrograde activity will hit another maximum in September.) The pace of life is slower now, and so this is a good month for spiritual practice. The worldly doors might be closed, but the spiritual doors are always open.

We have two eclipses this month. On the 5th there is a lunar eclipse that occurs in your 5th house, and on the 21st a solar eclipse occurs in your 12th house. Both eclipses affect your spiritual life, spiritual or charitable organizations you're involved with, and the guru figures in your life.

The lunar eclipse of the 5th impacts on the children and children figures in your life. They should take things easy and be kept out of harm's way. Let them spend more quiet time at home. Perhaps they have encounters with death. Generally these are psychological encounters such as close calls, surgery (recommended or actual), or dreams or thoughts of death. The eclipse affects the income of a parent or parent figure – he or she is forced to make some dramatic changes over the next few months. Students at college are affected, and they have to deal with changes in educational plans or disruptions at school. Foreign travel is not recommend over this period. Your personal philosophy and theology gets tested and there will be changes here over the next few months.

The solar eclipse of the 21st in your 12th house impacts you and your spiritual life, as was mentioned earlier. Every solar eclipse affects you because the Sun, the eclipsed planet, is the ruler of your Horoscope. There is a need to redefine yourself for yourself. Your image and presentation to the world – in terms of 'look' and 'appearance' – will reflect these inner changes. You want others to look at you in a completely different way. Good to reduce your schedule during this period.

Mercury goes retrograde on the 18th, so try to wrap up important purchases or investments before then. Your financial intuition is good until the 18th, but after then it needs more verification.

July

Best Days Overall: 2, 3, 11, 12, 21, 22, 29, 30
Most Stressful Days Overall: 1, 6, 7, 8, 14, 15, 27, 28
Best Days for Love: 4, 6, 7, 8, 14, 16, 17, 24, 25, 26
Best Days for Money: 1, 4, 5, 9, 10, 14, 15, 19, 20, 23, 24, 27, 28, 31
Best Days for Career: 6, 7, 8, 14, 15, 16, 17, 25, 26

Health is dramatically improved this month: Saturn moves away from his stressful aspect on the 1st. The short-term planets are in harmonious alignment or leaving you alone, and your ruler the Sun moves into your own sign on the 22nd. Your energy is back. And though you are focused on health, there is nothing really wrong. Even pre-existing conditions are more or less in abeyance.

The Western, social sector of your chart is still the strongest sector this month. Yet, you are in a period of maximum independence for the year. (You have been more independent in other years and will be so in future years as well – but this year, this is the max.) Next month, too, will be a period of maximum independence, with the short-term planets in their most Eastern positions. The needs of others still come first, but you can give some time to your personal desires too. If you need to make changes in your life this is the time to do it.

We have the third lunar eclipse of the year this month, on the 5th. This eclipse occurs in your 6th house. Thus there are job changes afoot. These can be actual job changes, either within your present company or with another one, or changes in the conditions of work. Perhaps the rules of the workplace change. Job changes shouldn't alarm you. You have many employment opportunities and seem a hot item in the job market now. Those of you who employ others can experience employee turnover (often it is because of dramas in their lives, and not because of you). There will be changes in the health regime too. Often there are changes of doctors or therapists, changes in diet or medications. Often the changes are deeper ones – philosophical changes, changes in your approach to health. Children and children figures in your life are making important financial changes. Parents and parent figures have issues with their siblings or sibling figures. And, as has been the case almost all year, there are spiritual changes. You need course corrections in your spiritual life, in your practice and attitudes. There are dramas and upheavals in spiritual and charitable organizations that you are involved with. Gurus and guru figures have personal dramas – their marriages or partnerships are getting tested.

This eclipse impacts, although not directly, three other planets: Mercury, Jupiter and Mars. So there are minor financial changes – minor course corrections. Computers, software and high-tech gadgetry can be more temperamental. There are dramas in the lives of children and children figures and, for college students, changes in educational plans. There can be dramas in the lives of the worship leaders in your place of worship as well. But these don't seem too serious. Bumps on the road.

August

Best Days Overall: 8, 9, 17, 18, 25, 26, 27
Most Stressful Days Overall: 3, 4, 10, 11, 23, 24, 30, 31
Best Days for Love: 1, 2, 3, 4, 10, 11, 15, 16, 19, 20, 23, 24, 28, 29, 30, 31
Best Days for Money: 2, 8, 11, 17, 18, 19, 20, 28, 29
Best Days for Career: 3, 4, 10, 11, 15, 16, 23, 24

Health is wonderful this month, as there is only one long-term planet in stressful alignment with you. The short-term planets are moving in your favour too. (Sometimes the Moon will exert some stress, but this passes quickly.) With increased energy all kinds of doors open up for you. Things that seemed impossible when your energy was low are now entirely possible.

You look good. The Sun in your sign until the 22nd brings good self-esteem and self-confidence. You are more your natural Leo self. You are comfortable in your own skin. You have charisma and star quality. Mercury moves into your sign on the 5th signalling financial windfalls and financial opportunities that seek you out. You dress expensively and spend on yourself. You project the appearance of a prosperous person. Money is earned easily and spent freely; you seem 'happy go lucky' with money. This changes as the month progresses, however. On the 20th your financial planet moves into your money house, followed by the Sun on the 22nd. You begin a yearly financial peak. The month ahead is prosperous.

But the prosperity is even stronger than we say. Your financial planet is part of a Grand Trine in the Earth signs – a very fortunate aspect. Money is earned easily. Your financial judgement is sound. You're not likely to overspend and will get value for your cash. You handle all the little details of finance very well. You have the Midas touch this period. In addition, the Sun in the money house shows a personal focus on finance. This, in my opinion, is even more important than the fortunate aspects. By the spiritual law, we get what we focus on – good, bad or indifferent.

Love is rocky as the month begins. The 1st and 2nd seem stressful. You and the beloved seem in conflict. But this passes as the month

progresses, and the love life shines from the 22nd. Those in relationships have harmony with the beloved. Those not yet in a relationship
– or in between relationships – have romantic meetings. The only
complication in love is Uranus's retrograde, which begins on the 15th.
This won't stop romance, however. Singles will still date and go out.
But it slows things down and introduces glitches and delays. Love
takes longer to develop. The person you court is not sure of his or her
feelings.

September

Best Days Overall: 4, 5, 14, 15, 22, 23
Most Stressful Days Overall: 6, 7, 8, 20, 21, 26, 27
Best Days for Love: 2, 3, 6, 7, 13, 14, 16, 17, 22, 23, 24, 25, 26,
    27
Best Days for Money: 6, 7, 9, 16, 17, 18, 19, 24, 25, 26, 27
Best Days for Career: 2, 3, 6, 7, 8, 13, 14, 22, 23

Retrograde activity surges to a yearly maximum again this month. Half
the planets are retrograde all month, and between the 9th and 12th 60
per cent of them will be retrograde. (This equals the rate we saw in
June.) So the pace of life slows down once more. You can reduce (but
probably not eliminate) delays by being perfect in all that you do. Spend
time getting the details of things right. Avoid short cuts (which are
often not short cuts at all) and make progress slowly and methodically.
There are some good points about retrogrades, though they are not
usually comfortable. We learn patience – something fiery Leo needs to
learn. But they also provide a space for review and reflection. A good
time to review your goals and formulate plans for the future. Thus,
when the planets start moving forward again (and they will) you will be
in a good position to move forward as well.

Health is good this month, but all the planets involved with health
are moving backwards. So there's no need to make major dietary or
health changes just yet. Study things more. If you read about some
miracle supplement, cure or diet, take it with a pinch of salt. Chances
are it is not what you think it is. The same holds true for job opportunities. They are out there for you, no question, but may not be quite

what they're advertised. Do more research. If you're hiring others, the same holds true.

Though the pace of life is slower, financially things are moving briskly. Mercury is in his speedy mode this month. Until the 5th he is in your money house and part of a fortunate (and rare) Grand Trine in Earth. So there is prosperity. You're still in the midst of a yearly financial peak until the 22nd. Mercury's move into Libra on the 5th shows the need for social grace in your financial dealings. From the 5th onwards you'll be working harder for earnings but they will come. Mercury in your 3rd house until the 27th indicates the importance (more than usual) of good sales, marketing, advertising and PR in whatever you are doing. People have to know about your product or service. You spend more on books, lectures, seminars and magazines – on educational items. Financial opportunities occur in your neighbourhood and perhaps with neighbours. Siblings and sibling figures seem involved in your finances. On the 27th, Mercury enters Scorpio, your 4th house. There can be some financial shakeups this period. Perhaps a need to make sudden changes. Perhaps a sudden, unexpected, expense. There is some financial disagreement with the beloved too. In spite of all this you prosper this month.

With the Sun in your 3rd house this is a good month for students below college level. They should do well in their studies. It is a good month to pursue your education – regardless of your age. The mind is sharper and learns better.

October

Best Days Overall: 1, 2, 11, 12, 19, 20, 28, 29, 30
Most Stressful Days Overall: 4, 5, 17, 18, 23, 24, 25, 31
Best Days for Love: 3, 4, 5, 13, 21, 22, 23, 24, 25, 31
Best Days for Money: 4, 5, 9, 10, 13, 14, 17, 18, 21, 23, 26, 31
Best Days for Career: 3, 4, 5, 21, 22, 31

The Eastern sector of your chart, the sector of the self, hasn't been strong all year, but this month it becomes even weaker. Personal independence, such as it was, is not an issue now. The month ahead – and future months – is all about catering to others and their interests. This is hard for you Leo, but it is a good spiritual lesson. It is good now and then to take a vacation from oneself. Many psychological problems have their origin in excessive self-centredness, so there is a therapeutic dimension to this. What you have been learning all year is that as you take care of others, your own needs get met as well, with little effort or attention.

Venus, your career planet, moves into your money house on the 2nd. This is a good financial signal as it shows that you have the financial favour of bosses, parents, parent figures and the authority figures in your life. This can bring pay rises (official or unofficial) and would also show focus. Right now, you measure career success in hard cash – in monetary terms – not in terms of prestige or status.

Career, however, is not a big issue this month. The lower, night side of your Horoscope is the dominant side now. So this is a period of preparation, a period for doing all the 'behind the scenes work' that makes career success possible. It is about getting into emotional harmony and making sure the home and family situation is solid. Those of you involved in psychological therapies should make good progress from the 23rd onwards, as the Sun enters your 4th family house. Even those of you not in any 'official' therapy will make progress. The 4th house is Nature's therapeutic system, where the past is close and memories are unsealed. The hidden traumas and experiences that hold you back are easily seen, perhaps in dreams or through the events of life. Thus they get re-interpreted in a better way – based on your present understanding of things.

Your career planet Venus will have her solstice from October 29 to November 2. This shows a pause in your career and then a change of direction – a change of attitude.

Finances get more complicated after the 14th as Mercury starts to retrograde. So, as always, try to make important purchases, investments or financial decisions before that date. Afterwards, shop for necessities of course, but better to take a 'wait and see' attitude on financial affairs.

Mercury will be in your 4th house until the 24th. This shows various things. You spend more on the home and family and are perhaps earning from them as well. There is good family support that goes both ways.

November

Best Days Overall: 7, 8, 16, 25, 26
Most Stressful Days Overall: 1, 14, 15, 20, 21, 27, 28
Best Days for Love: 1, 2, 3, 9, 10, 12, 17, 18, 20, 21, 22, 27
Best Days for Money: 2, 3, 4, 10, 11, 13, 14, 19, 22, 23
Best Days for Career: 1, 2, 3, 12, 21, 22, 27, 28

Retrograde activity reached its crescendo in September and has been diminishing ever since; by the end of this month 90 per cent of the planets will be moving forward. Life moves forward. The pace of events quickens. Hopefully you have used the retrograde period properly and prepared yourself to leap forward with great confidence.

Health needs watching this month, especially until the 21st. The good news is that your 6th house of health is very strong and you are on top of things. You're paying attention. Good emotional health will lead to good physical health, and this is a good month for getting into good emotional health. Your 4th house of home and family is even stronger than last month. A move could happen this month – either a literal move or a renovation of the home, something that makes the home 'like' a new one. The family circle seems to expand. Usually this is through a birth or marriage, but sometimes it's through meeting people who are 'like' family to you. Children and children figures in your life are having a spiritual period. Parents or parent figures are prospering. Family members of childbearing age are more fertile.

Mars has been retrograde since September 9 and remains so until the 14th. The past few months haven't been the best for foreign travel – though many of you have done it. College-level students are uncertain about their studies. Legal issues have been delayed. But on the 14th things start moving forward again.

Like last month, this is a home and family kind of month. Career is on the back burner for a while. Indeed, on the 21st your career planet, Venus, moves into your 4th house. This can be read in a few ways. In one, home and family *is* the career, *is* the mission this period. Sometimes it shows that you are pursuing the career from home. Family and family connections are playing a big role in the career. Most importantly this shows that getting the emotional life right – the family situation right – will lead, eventually, to career success. Stay in emotional harmony and the career will fall into place.

The final lunar eclipse of the year occurs on the 30th. It happens in your 11th house and thus affects friends and professional or trade organizations you're involved with. There are shakeups in the lives of friends and in these organizations. Computers, software and high-tech equipment can be temperamental over this period and sometimes repairs or upgrades are needed. And, as always with every lunar eclipse, the spiritual life changes. There are more shakeups in spiritual and charitable organizations that you're involved with. Parents or parent figures are making important financial changes.

December

Best Days Overall: 5, 6, 13, 14, 22, 23
Most Stressful Days Overall: 11, 12, 17, 18, 24, 25, 26
Best Days for Love: 2, 3, 7, 11, 12, 15, 17, 18, 22, 23, 24, 25
Best Days for Money: 5, 6, 7, 8, 13, 14, 16, 24, 27
Best Days for Career: 2, 3, 11, 12, 22, 23, 24, 25, 26

The final eclipse of the year, a solar eclipse, occurs on the 14th in your 5th house. You, children and children figures in your life are affected. Keep them out of harm's way over this period. Things that have to be done should be done, but anything non-essential – especially if it is stressful – is better off being rescheduled. You and the children or children figures in your life are going into another period of redefinition of the self – the self-concept, the image, the personality. The self will get upgraded in the coming months and this will be reflected in the way you dress and your accessories. This eclipse impacts strongly on Neptune, the ruler of your 8th house. Thus important financial changes are happening with the spouse, partner or current love. Bankers or investors you're involved with have personal dramas. The money people in your life are having their marriages tested. There can be confrontations with death (usually on the psychological level). Sometimes there are near-death experiences or close calls. Sometimes surgery is recommended. Sometimes there are dreams of death. The purpose is to remind you to focus on the reason you were born, to focus on your mission in life. 'Life is short and can end at any time,' says the Dark Angel. 'Get down to the reason for your incarnation.'

Though the eclipse shakes things up, the month ahead is happy. You're in the midst of one of your yearly personal pleasure peaks. Even an eclipse is not going to dim your joy – not for too long anyway.

Saturn moves out of Capricorn and into Aquarius on the 18th and Jupiter follows suit on the 20th. This will impact on the health. You will feel it more next year rather than now, but health will need more attention.

Saturn's move into your 7th house is going to test your current relationship, and this will be a long-term thing. Since only the best will do for you, relationships get subjected to stress tests to see how well they hold up. A relationship that can withstand the next two years can pretty much withstand anything.

While Saturn is testing love, Jupiter will be expanding it. Jupiter's presence in your 7th house will bring romantic opportunities for singles. Usually this kind of transit would suggest marriage or a relationship that is 'like' marriage. But Saturn in the 7th house suggests more caution.

Virgo

♍

THE VIRGIN

Birthdays from
22nd August to
22nd September

Personality Profile

VIRGO AT A GLANCE

Element – Earth

Ruling Planet – Mercury
  Career Planet – Mercury
  Love Planet – Neptune
  Money Planet – Venus
  Planet of Home and Family Life – Jupiter
  Planet of Health and Work – Uranus
  Planet of Pleasure – Saturn
  Planet of Sexuality – Mars

Colours – earth tones, ochre, orange, yellow

Colour that promotes love, romance and social harmony – aqua blue

Colour that promotes earning power – jade green

Gems – agate, hyacinth

Metal – quicksilver

Scents – lavender, lilac, lily of the valley, storax

ZAC 9/10/98

Quality – mutable (= flexibility)

Quality most needed for balance – a broader perspective

Strongest virtues – mental agility, analytical skills, ability to pay attention to detail, healing powers

Deepest needs – to be useful and productive

Characteristic to avoid – destructive criticism

Signs of greatest overall compatibility – Taurus, Capricorn

Signs of greatest overall incompatibility – Gemini, Sagittarius, Pisces

Sign most helpful to career – Gemini

Sign most helpful for emotional support – Sagittarius

Sign most helpful financially – Libra

Sign best for marriage and/or partnerships – Pisces

Sign most helpful for creative projects – Capricorn

Best Sign to have fun with – Capricorn

Signs most helpful in spiritual matters – Taurus, Leo

Best day of the week – Wednesday

Understanding a Virgo

The virgin is a particularly fitting symbol for those born under the sign of Virgo. If you meditate on the image of the virgin you will get a good understanding of the essence of the Virgo type. The virgin is, of course, a symbol of purity and innocence – not naïve, but pure. A virginal object has not been touched. A virgin field is land that is true to itself, the way it has always been. The same is true of virgin forest: it is pristine, unaltered.

Apply the idea of purity to the thought processes, emotional life, physical body and activities and projects of the everyday world, and you can see how Virgos approach life. Virgos desire the pure expression of the ideal in their mind, body and affairs. If they find impurities they will attempt to clear them away.

Impurities are the beginning of disorder, unhappiness and uneasiness. The job of the Virgo is to eject all impurities and keep only that which the body and mind can use and assimilate.

The secrets of good health are here revealed: 90 per cent of the art of staying well is maintaining a pure mind, a pure body and pure emotions. When you introduce more impurities than your mind and body can deal with, you will have what is known as 'dis-ease'. It is no wonder that Virgos make great doctors, nurses, healers and dieticians. They have an innate understanding of good health and they realize that good health is more than just physical. In all aspects of life, if you want a project to be successful it must be kept as pure as possible. It must be protected against the adverse elements that will try to undermine it. This is the secret behind Virgo's awesome technical proficiency.

One could talk about Virgo's analytical powers – which are formidable. One could talk about their perfectionism and their almost superhuman attention to detail. But this would be to miss the point. All of these virtues are manifestations of a Virgo's desire for purity and perfection – a world without Virgos would have ruined itself long ago.

A vice is nothing more than a virtue turned inside out, misapplied or used in the wrong context. Virgos' apparent vices come from their inherent virtue. Their analytical powers, which should be used for healing, helping or perfecting a project in the world, sometimes get misapplied and turned against people. Their critical faculties, which should be used constructively to perfect a strategy or proposal, can sometimes be used destructively to harm or wound. Their urge to perfection can turn into worry and lack of confidence; their natural humility can become self-denial and self-abasement. When Virgos turn negative they are apt to turn their devastating criticism on themselves, sowing the seeds of self-destruction.

Finance

Virgos have all the attitudes that create wealth. They are hard-working, industrious, efficient, organized, thrifty, productive and eager to serve. A developed Virgo is every employer's dream. But until Virgos master some of the social graces of Libra they will not even come close to fulfilling their financial potential. Purity and perfectionism, if not handled correctly or gracefully, can be very trying to others. Friction in human relationships can be devastating not only to your pet projects but – indirectly – to your wallet as well.

Virgos are quite interested in their financial security. Being hard-working, they know the true value of money. They do not like to take risks with their money, preferring to save for their retirement or for a rainy day. Virgos usually make prudent, calculated investments that involve a minimum of risk. These investments and savings usually work out well, helping Virgos to achieve the financial security they seek. The rich or even not-so-rich Virgo also likes to help his or her friends in need.

Career and Public Image

Virgos reach their full potential when they can communicate their knowledge in such a way that others can understand it. In order to get their ideas across better, Virgos need to develop greater verbal skills and fewer judgemental ways of expressing themselves. Virgos look up to teachers and communicators; they like their bosses to be good communicators. Virgos will probably not respect a superior who is not their intellectual equal – no matter how much money or power that superior has. Virgos themselves like to be perceived by others as being educated and intellectual.

The natural humility of Virgos often inhibits them from fulfilling their great ambitions, from acquiring name and fame. Virgos should indulge in a little more self-promotion if they are going to reach their career goals. They need to push themselves with the same ardour that they would use to foster others.

At work Virgos like to stay active. They are willing to learn any type of job as long as it serves their ultimate goal of financial security. Virgos may change occupations several times during their professional lives, until they find the one they really enjoy. Virgos work well with other people, are not afraid to work hard and always fulfil their responsibilities.

Love and Relationships

If you are an analyst or a critic you must, out of necessity, narrow your scope. You have to focus on a part and not the whole; this can create a temporary narrow-mindedness. Virgos do not like this kind of person. They like their partners to be broad-minded, with depth and vision. Virgos seek to get this broad-minded quality from their partners, since they sometimes lack it themselves.

Virgos are perfectionists in love just as they are in other areas of life. They need partners who are tolerant, open-minded and easy-going. If you are in love with a Virgo do not waste time on impractical romantic gestures. Do practical and useful things for him or her – this is what will be appreciated and what will be done for you.

Virgos express their love through pragmatic and useful gestures, so do not be put off because your Virgo partner does not say 'I love you' day-in and day-out. Virgos are not that type. If they love you, they will demonstrate it in practical ways. They will always be there for you; they will show an interest in your health and finances; they will fix your sink or repair your video recorder. Virgos deem these actions to be superior to sending flowers, chocolates or Valentine cards.

In love affairs Virgos are not particularly passionate or spontaneous. If you are in love with a Virgo, do not take this personally. It does not mean that you are not alluring enough or that your Virgo partner does not love or like you. It is just the way Virgos are. What they lack in passion they make up for in dedication and loyalty.

Home and Domestic Life

It goes without saying that the home of a Virgo will be spotless, sanitized and orderly. Everything will be in its proper place – and don't you dare move anything about! For Virgos to find domestic bliss they need to ease up a bit in the home, to allow their partner and children more freedom and to be more generous and open-minded. Family members are not to be analysed under a microscope, they are individuals with their own virtues to express.

With these small difficulties resolved, Virgos like to stay in and entertain at home. They make good hosts and they like to keep their friends and families happy and entertained at family and social gatherings. Virgos love children, but they are strict with them – at times – since they want to make sure their children are brought up with the correct sense of family and values.

Horoscope for 2020

Major Trends

Looks like a healthy and happy year ahead, Virgo. Enjoy! Your 5th house of fun, creativity and children is easily the most powerful in your chart, so this is your year for fun, for enjoying the rapture aspect of life. Being a Virgo, even fun involves discipline and work – but that's just your nature. Work is fun.

Real Virgo heaven will happen from March 23 and July 1, and from December 18 onwards, as your 6th house of work becomes very strong. You will be enjoying your work – your job – even more than usual.

The health looks good this year. There is only one long-term planet in stressful alignment with you. All the others are either in harmonious aspect or leaving you alone. More on this later.

Uranus has been in your 9th house since March of last year, and he will be there for the next seven or so years. This shows that your religious and philosophical beliefs – your personal religion – is getting tested, probably by scientific findings. By the time Uranus is finished with you, you will have a new personal religion and new perspective on life. This transit also affects college-level students and brings much instability here. There will probably be serial changes of schools and subjects. There is also much instability in your place of worship.

Four lunar eclipses this year – twice the usual number – show that there are major dramas in the lives of friends. This could test friendships. It would also show the testing of your high-tech equipment and gadgets multiple times.

Neptune has been in your 7th house of love for many years and we've discussed this in previous years' reports. The love life is becoming more idealistic, more spiritual and refined. You are attracting spiritual and artistic friends and love interests. More on this later.

Venus will spend an unusually long time (over four months) in your 10th house of career. This is a good career signal and indicates pay rises (official or unofficial) this year. More details later.

Though your 12th house of spirituality is empty this year, with only short-term planets moving through there, spirituality seems fulfilling and successful in 2020. The abstract North Node of the Moon will be moving into the 12th house on May 6.

Mars will spend more than six months (an unusually long time) in your 8th house of transformation this year; he will be there from June 28 to the end of the year. This would show a more sexually active kind of period and a focus on personal transformation. There could be psychological encounters with death as well. Perhaps surgery is recommended to you or to people close to you.

Your major areas of interest this year are children, fun and creativity; health and work (from March 23 to July 1 and from December 18 onwards); sex, personal transformation and occult studies (from June 28); and religion, philosophy, higher education and foreign travel.

Your paths of greatest fulfilment will be children, fun and creativity (until December 20); health and work (from December 20 onwards); friends, groups and group activities (until May 6); and spirituality (after May 6).

Health

(Please note that this is an astrological perspective on health and not a medical one. In days of yore there was no difference, both these perspectives were identical. But now there could be quite a difference. For a medical perspective, please consult your doctor or health practitioner.)

Health, as we have said, is good this year. If forced to make a judgement I'd say that the early part of the year is better than later on, but the whole year will be good. With energy levels high pre-existing conditions seem in abeyance. With high energy, things that were once considered impossible become eminently doable.

Health is always important for Virgo, for this is what Virgo is all about. But early in the year, until March 23, it will be less important than usual. The focus increases from March 23 to July 1 and from December 18 onwards, when your 6th house becomes powerful.

Good though your health is you can make it even better. Give more attention to the following – the vulnerable areas of your horoscope this year (the reflex points are shown in the chart opposite):

- The small intestine – always important for Virgo.
- The ankles and calves. These too are always important for Virgo, as Uranus, the ruler of these areas, is your health planet. Regular ankle and calf massage should be part of your normal health regime, and be sure to give the ankles good support when exercising.
- The neck and throat. These became important for you last year (and will remain so for years to come). Regular neck massage will be very beneficial; tension tends to collect there and needs to be released. Craniaosacral therapy is also excellent for the neck.
- The spine, knees, teeth, skin and overall skeletal alignment become important from March 23 to July 1 and from December 18 onwards. Good spinal and skeletal health is vital, and regular back and knee massage will be good – as will regular visits to the chiropractor or osteopath. The vertebrae need to be kept in alignment through good posture. Therapies such as the Alexander Technique, Feldenkrais or Rolfing and exercises such as Yoga and Pilates are all good for the spine and skeletal

Important foot reflexology points for the year ahead

Try to massage all of the foot on a regular basis – the top of the foot as well as the bottom – but pay extra attention to the points highlighted on the chart. When you massage, be aware of 'sore spots' as these need special attention. It's also a good idea to massage the ankles and below them.

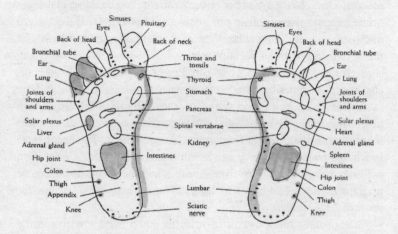

alignment. Give the knees support when exercising. Don't neglect dental hygiene (Virgo is not likely to do this, but a reminder is always useful).

- The liver and thighs become important from December 20, when Jupiter, the ruler of these areas, enters your 6th house. (They will be important for most of 2021 as well.) Thighs should be massaged. This will not only strengthen the thighs but the liver and the lower back as well. Diet will also become more important, as well as the need for good emotional health.

Home and Family

Your 4th house of home and family is not strong this year. Instead it is practically empty, and only short-term planets will move through there. It was much stronger last year, when many of you moved or renovated the home. This year you seem more or less content with things as they are and have little need to make dramatic changes.

Jupiter, your family planet, spends most of the year in your 5th house and this gives various messages. You're enjoying the family more. You are more focused on children or children figures in your life. Women of childbearing age seem more fertile than usual, but a pregnancy seems complicated. It is likely that you are making the home more of a fun place – a place of entertainment. You could be installing home cinema systems, buying more toys (for both adults and children) and perhaps installing sports/gym equipment. No need to leave the home to have fun and entertainment.

Jupiter will move into your 6th house of health and work on December 20, signalling that you will strive to make the home and the family healthier. You could spend on removing harmful substances from the building or the grounds. You could be buying health equipment for the home and perhaps exercise equipment. The home is as much like a doctor's surgery as a home. This is natural for a Virgo. You will also be working more from home – setting up home offices or perhaps even a home-based business. These trends will continue for most of 2021 as well.

Siblings and sibling figures in your life could move later on in the year, but it's not a smooth endeavour. There are many delays involved. Their marriages or current relationships are being tested these days; this began in 2019 and will continue for many more years. They are experiencing much social instability.

A parent or parent figure is working very hard but will have a good financial year. A move is not likely, though there is nothing against it. The other parent or parent figure is making major financial changes this year, but the home life seems stable.

Children or children figures in your life are taking on more responsibility these days and they will prosper next year. They seem to binge and then diet. They alternate between the two. They could renovate the home this year, but a move is not likely.

Grandchildren (if you have them), or those who play that role in your life, seem very unsettled. They have a need for personal freedom these days. They are travelling a lot, perhaps living in different places for extended periods, but a formal move is not likely.

If you're planning major renovations to the home, January 3 to February 16 would be a good period for this. If you're planning to beautify the home, to redecorate or to buy art objects for the home, November 21 to the end of the year would be a good time.

Finance and Career

The financial area hasn't been a point of focus (a house of power) for many years now. This has both good and bad points. On the good side, it shows contentment – satisfaction – with things as they are and there's no need to give finances special attention. Things sort of happen on their own in their pre-ordained way. It tends to the status quo. The negative side of this could be a lack of attention to a vital area of life. If financial problems arise this is the probable root cause.

Still, I expect the year ahead to be prosperous. First of all, you will have happy job opportunities this year – at least two. (And next year the job prospects look even better.) Secondly, your financial planet, Venus, will spend an unusual amount of time (four times longer than normal) in your 10th house of career. This is a prominent position, the top of your Horoscope, and tends to be more powerful than other areas. Venus will be there from April 3 to August 7 and her presence indicates a focus on finance, which is 90 per cent of the battle. It shows that it is high on your agenda. It shows increased earning power. Pay rises (official or unofficial) are likely. Your good professional reputation brings extra earnings to you. The authority figures in your life – parents, parent figures, bosses and elders – are supportive of your financial goals.

Because your financial planet is so fast moving – Venus will move through 11 of your 12 houses this year – money or financial opportunity can come to you in various ways and through various people. This is just your nature. These short-term trends are best discussed in the monthly reports.

Venus as your financial planet signals the importance of social contacts and good social skills in the financial life. These are perhaps just as important as your professional skills. This year the social skills – your ability to gain cooperation from others – are even more important as the Western, social sector of your chart is overwhelmingly dominant. Keep the focus on others and your own good will come to you naturally and with little effort.

Career, too, is not that big an issue this year. Some years are like that. The cosmos aims at a rounded development and different years will emphasize different activities. Your 10th house for the most part will be empty, with only short-term planets moving through there. However, as we mentioned, Venus will spend four months in your career house between April and August. Aside from the financial benefits outlined above, it shows career-related travel – foreign travel. It indicates educational opportunities that relate to the career, which you should take. It shows success for college students and for those applying to college. Legal issues go back and forth but seem ultimately successful.

There is a lunar eclipse on November 30 that occurs in your 10th house. This will bring changes and course corrections in the career. There can be shifts in the management of your company or industry. Perhaps the government enacts changes to the rules and regulations that affect your industry. The rules of the game will change.

Your career planet Mercury is, next to the Moon, the fastest of all the planets. During the course of a year he will move through your entire chart. Thus career opportunities can come in a variety of ways and through a variety of people. This is just the way things work for you. You have great flexibility in career matters. These short-term trends are best dealt with in the monthly reports.

Love and Social Life

Love has been important for many years now, Virgo. Your 7th house has been strong and will remain so for many more years. This year the love and social life seem even stronger than they have been. The Western, social sector of your chart – the sector that focuses on other people – is overwhelmingly dominant this year. So you are more focused on others. Your social grace is stronger than usual. You are probably more popular than usual too.

Aside from this, the love trends are pretty much as they have been for many years and we have written about them before. Not trying to be repetitive here, we're just describing what is.

You are always idealistic in love, always searching for the perfect love. You like perfection in everything but especially in love. And these days even more so. Your standards for love are very high. And, in many cases, no mere mortal could ever live up to them. This produces a subtle sense of disappointment or disillusionment even in the best of relationships. They can be good, but not of the ultimate standard.

For a Virgo it is always helpful to understand that perfection is a process. It is rarely handed to us on a silver platter. Perfection is something we create – or allow to manifest. So, as long as we are constantly improving – as long as the relationship is better today than last week or last month – we are on the road to perfection, though not yet there.

Neptune, as our regular readers know, is the most spiritual of planets, and he is the ruler of your 7th house. A very powerful position. The spiritual force is very strong these days, especially in love and the social life. Thus, if you are looking for love in nightclubs and bars you're probably wasting your time. You might find sex there, but not love. For love you should attend spiritual or charitable-type gatherings: meditation seminars or lectures, prayer meetings, the yoga studio, charity events or events sponsored by or involving altruistic kinds of causes.

In love you need a spiritual-type person – ministers, mystics, spiritual channels, psychics and the like. But you would also be attracted to artistic types – poets, musicians, dancers, film-makers or people involved in the film industry.

Perhaps the main danger in love – and this too has been the case for many years – is the tendency to over-idealize your partner. You tend to put him or her on such a pedestal that no human can occupy. And when your partner proves to be human there is disappointment.

The love life will sparkle from February 3 to March 3 (though there will be twists and turns as your ruler Mercury will go retrograde during this period); March 16 to April 11; May 29 to August 4 (there will be twists and turns this period too, with another Mercury retrograde); September 27 to October 28 (again Mercury's retrograde complicates things); and November 11 to December 1.

With your 5th house very strong all year there will be plenty of opportunities for love affairs – fun, unserious kinds of relationships. These are not likely to lead to marriage.

There is much turmoil in your friendships this year. Four lunar eclipses affect this area and two eclipses occur in your 11th house of friends. So friendships are getting tested. Friends are having many dramas this year.

Self-improvement

Virgos are not known for their spirituality. We think of them as intellectuals, doctors, healers, programmers, engineers and productive types of people. Yet, there is deep spirituality here and all these other attributes stem from this spirituality. Keep in mind that the ruler of the 12th house, the Sun, is in Virgo. They just express this spirituality in the form of service to others and through health. One of the hidden talents of Virgo, rarely mentioned in astrology texts, is their power over the body. They have an innate capacity to mould and shape their bodies by spiritual means. The knowledge is innate. But it tends to manifest over time.

With the Sun as their spiritual planet, Virgo is comfortable with the solar-oriented religions – Christianity, Judaism and Krishna Yoga.

For many years now spirituality is manifesting in the love and social life. The love life is becoming ever-more refined and spiritual. The sensuous, common forms of romance are losing their lustre. Virgo wants something more. These days Virgo wants a relationship that produces spiritual growth – that furthers their spiritual path. Where once you might have looked at the physical appearance, the sexual magnetism or the financial worthiness of the partner, now you are looking at their spiritual development. Here is the allurement.

There is something even deeper going on, which we have also written about in past years' reports. You are being led, step by step, to spiritual love. Many people confuse this with romantic love – the love of a specific person or object. But spiritual love is much wider than that. The ancients called it *agape* – unconditional love, with or without an object. The cosmic force of love flowing through the body, mind and emotions. With spiritual love the person doesn't seek love from outside. The person is merely a channel for the love force to flow through. The person channels love into the world, rather than taking it from the world. Not everyone will return it, but you can be sure that love will come back to you. Whether you are in a relationship or not, it's basically the same. You always feel loved. In a relationship there

are certain pleasures and out of a relationship there are other pleasures. Either way you feel loved. You are happy with either situation.
This is the real Ideal Love that you seek. Humans can only love with
limitations; the Divine will love without limitations.

Month-by-month Forecasts

January

Best Days Overall: 5, 6, 14, 22, 23
Most Stressful Days Overall: 1, 7, 8, 20, 21, 27, 28
Best Days for Love: 1, 9, 10, 13, 14, 18, 19, 27, 28
Best Days for Money: 5, 6, 13, 14, 16, 18, 19, 22, 23, 27, 28
Best Days for Career: 5, 6, 7, 8, 14, 15, 25, 26

A down-to-earth kind of month for a down-to-earth kind of person.
Very comfortable for you. Progress happens swiftly this month as, after
the 11th, *all* the planets are moving forward. Health and energy are
super and life is beautiful.

Even a Lunar Eclipse on the 10th will not dim the goodness of the
month. It just adds a little spice and excitement to life. Too much ease
can be boring. In fact, you might find that the disruptions and changes
that the eclipse brings are actually good. They clear barriers and open
doors.

The eclipse of the 10th occurs in your 11th house of friends. It also
impacts on the ruler of your 11th house – the Moon. So this is the
message of the eclipse. Friendships will get tested. Those that are
flawed might go by the wayside, but good ones will remain. There are
likely to be dramatic events in their lives (and this will be the case for
the entire year ahead). A parent or parent figure will need to make
financial course corrections. The events of the eclipse will show that
his or her financial thinking has been amiss. Children and children
figures will have their marriages and relationships (if they are of appropriate age) tested. Computer and high-tech equipment is likely to be
erratic during this period, and sometimes repairs or replacements are
necessary. It would be good to back up important files regularly and to
maintain up-to-date anti-virus, anti-hacking software.

Finance is good this month. Until the 13th money comes to you the old-fashioned way, through work and productive service. After the 13th earnings will be much stronger. Venus, your financial planet, enters Pisces, her most exalted and powerful position. This signals increased earning power. It shows good financial intuition and a spiritual approach to wealth. You are more generous in your charitable giving this period. Social connections are always important financially, but even more so after the 13th. Take note of your dreams on the 26th and 27th as they have financial import.

February

Best Days Overall: 1, 2, 10, 11, 18, 19, 20, 28, 29
Most Stressful Days Overall: 3, 4, 5, 16, 17, 23, 24, 25
Best Days for Love: 6, 7, 8, 14, 15, 16, 17, 23, 24, 25, 26, 27
Best Days for Money: 1, 2, 7, 8, 10, 11, 12, 13, 16, 17, 19, 20, 26, 27, 28, 29
Best Days for Career: 3, 4, 5, 6, 7, 14, 15, 23, 24, 25

The Western social sector of your chart contains all the planets this month (with the exception of the Moon between the 3rd and the 15th), which is highly unusual. Even the ruler of your Horoscope, Mercury, spends all month in the West, and most of the month in your 7th house of love. Your 7th house will be unusually strong, while your 1st house will be empty (only the Moon passes through there on the 10th and 11th). So we have a clear message. This is a social month. It's all about others and not about yourself. Your good comes through the good grace of others and not because of your self-assertion or initiative. Indeed you seem comfortable with this. You are personally very popular. Even Mercury's retrograde on the 17th plays well into this. It might weaken self-confidence and self-esteem, but you don't need too much of that this month. Let others have their way (and you seem to be doing that), so long as their way isn't destructive.

There are two powerful houses in your chart this month – both of equal power – your 5th house of fun, creativity and children and your 7th house of love. So the month ahead is about fun and love. (Indeed, the power in your 6th house of work until the 19th could just add to this – Virgo loves work, finds fulfilment in work.) Thus you're having fun this month. Singles have many romantic opportunities; the problem (especially after the 17th and Mercury's retrograde) is in 'who to choose' – you don't seem sure.

Health is less easy than usual after the 19th. On an overall level, health is excellent. This is merely a short-term blip and nothing to worry about. Still, it is a good idea to get more rest. Enhance the health in the ways mentioned in the yearly report.

Finances look good. They come more easily until the 7th. Earnings will happen afterwards too but will take more work. Until the 7th trust your financial intuition. After the 7th more direct action is necessary. Venus, your financial planet, will be in your 8th house after that date, signalling that this is a good period for a financial detox. You prosper by 'cutting back' – by reducing waste and needless expenses. (You never cut essentials – just the inessential.) It's good to get rid of possessions that you don't need or use. They just take up space and clog the arteries of supply. Even in finance, others come first. You don't ignore your personal financial interest, but you keep the financial interest of others at the forefront. It is a good period for paying down or taking on debt – depending on your need. If you have good business ideas this is a good time to attract outside investors for your projects.

March

Best Days Overall: 1, 8, 9, 17, 18, 27, 28
Most Stressful Days Overall: 2, 3, 14, 15, 22, 23, 29, 30
Best Days for Love: 4, 5, 8, 12, 13, 17, 18, 22, 23, 27, 28
Best Days for Money: 1, 8, 9, 10, 11, 17, 18, 27, 28
Best Days for Career: 2, 3, 10, 11, 22, 23, 29, 30

The planetary momentum is overwhelmingly forward this month. Mercury is the only planet in retrograde motion – and this will end on the 10th. So the world moves ahead speedily. Personally, there is speedy progress to your goals.

You are still in a yearly love and social peak until the 20th and personal popularity is still very strong. The problem in love is mostly you. You're not sure. You lack direction. You back away from love. This will change after the 10th as social confidence and thinking are clarified.

On the 7th and 8th, as the Sun and Neptune travel together, there is a romantic opportunity with someone spiritual. He or she could be some sort of guru figure. Perhaps he or she is counselling you about love. In general it is a very spiritual time. Pay attention to your dream life. Your personal ESP abilities will be much stronger than usual.

Two powerful planets enter your 6th house this month – Saturn on the 23rd and Mars on the 31st, bringing changes in health. The spine, knees, teeth and good skeletal alignment become more important, and exercise and scalp massage will be beneficial after the 31st. Though the health needs change, health is much improved from the 20th onwards. The entry of these planets into your 6th house also signals new job opportunities or offers.

Your financial planet Venus has been in Aries since early February. Thus you have been more speculative and risk-taking in your finances. Perhaps even overly impulsive in your spending. But this month, on the 5th, Venus enters conservative Taurus and the financial judgement improves. Venus travels with Uranus from the 6th to the 9th, which gives several messages. Sudden, unexpected money can come. Sometimes this transit shows an unexpected expense too – but the money for it will also occur. A job opportunity is likely. From the 9th onwards there is prosperity – and it happens rather easily. Venus will spend the rest of the month in your beneficent 9th house.

Mercury, the ruler of your Horoscope, moves back into your 7th house of love on the 16th, indicating personal popularity. You are totally focused on others. You go out of your way for your friends or current love. People feel this.

Your family planet Jupiter travels with Pluto all month, signalling that siblings or sibling figures in your life are prospering. This is an excellent financial month for them. It is also good for students below college level – they seem successful in their studies.

April

Best Days Overall: 5, 6, 13, 14, 23, 24
Most Stressful Days Overall: 11, 12, 18, 19, 25, 26
Best Days for Love: 1, 2, 7, 8, 9, 10, 15, 16, 17, 18, 19, 25, 26, 28, 29
Best Days for Money: 6, 7, 8, 14, 15, 16, 17, 24, 25, 26
Best Days for Career: 1, 2, 10, 11, 20, 21, 25, 26, 30

The planetary momentum is still forward, but towards the end of the month – on the 25th – Pluto will start to move backwards. Since Pluto rules your 3rd house of communication you will need to be more careful in this area, and will need to be so for many months. Take the time to make sure that others have received your message the way you intended, and that you have got their message. A little care in the beginning can save much heartache later on.

Jupiter and Pluto are still travelling together this month, so this can show a new car or new communication equipment (try to make any purchase before the 25th). It is still very good for students below college level, as was mentioned last month, and it is a good transit for teachers, writers, marketers and PR people. Buying and selling – trading – also seems profitable.

There are interesting things happening in your financial life this month. On the 3rd Venus, your financial planet, enters Gemini, your 10th career house. This is also a good transit for teachers, writers, marketers, PR people and traders. But it shows other things too. Venus will be at the top of your chart, and she is powerful there. This can bring pay rises (official or unofficial) and the financial favour of bosses, elders, parents or parent figures. Even the government seems kindly disposed to your finances. Earnings can come from your good career reputation. Venus will go 'out of bounds' from the 3rd onwards. Thus in financial matters there are no answers to be found within your normal circles and you need to look further afield. The money people in your life are also going outside their usual environments.

Mercury travels with Neptune, your love planet, on the 3rd and 4th. For singles this brings a romantic meeting, probably with a spiritual-type person in a spiritual-type setting. For those already in a relationship, this shows a particular closeness with the beloved. A highly romantic period.

Mercury, the ruler of your Horoscope, has a solstice, from the 14th to the 16th. He will pause in the heavens and then change direction (in latitude). So a pause in your affairs is likely and then a change of direction. This is a good pause; a pause that refreshes. It is as if Mercury is taking a nice deep breath before he moves again.

The Sun travelling with Uranus, your health planet, from the 24th to the 27th shows that you will benefit from some spiritual healing. Health is good, but some new insight comes to you.

May

Best Days Overall: 2, 3, 10, 11, 20, 21, 29, 30
Most Stressful Days Overall: 8, 9, 15, 16, 23, 24
Best Days for Love: 4, 5, 6, 7, 13, 14, 15, 16, 23, 24, 25, 26
Best Days for Money: 3, 4, 5, 12, 13, 14, 22, 23, 24
Best Days for Career: 2, 3, 12, 13, 23, 24

The upper, day side of your Horoscope has been getting stronger and stronger since February. This month, especially after the 13th when Mars crosses from the lower half to the upper half of your chart, it dominates. So, outer affairs are where the focus should be now. In addition, keep in mind that your career house will become very strong from the 20th onwards – another signal to focus on the career and let family matters slide for a while. (The timing here is very interesting. Your family planet, Jupiter, will start to retrograde on the 14th, just before your 10th house becomes powerful.) The month ahead is going to be very successful.

The only complication this month is the increase in planetary retrograde activity. Though we are still far from the maximum amount for the year, 40 per cent of the planets will be retrograde after the 14th – a high percentage. The pace of life is beginning to slow down. There are more glitches and delays to deal with.

Finances also become more complicated this month. Venus remains 'out of bounds' all month, and on the 13th she starts to move backwards in a rare, once every two years, retrograde. So try to wrap up important purchases or investments before the 13th. After that take a 'wait and see' attitude to finance. You're in a period for gaining more clarity in finance. The financial picture is not the way you've imagined it.

Venus 'out of bounds' shows that you are still in 'unknown' financial territory, and her retrograde shows the need for more facts and clarity. The unknown always suggests a need for caution.

Things are slowing down in the world, but you seem to be moving quickly. Mercury moves rapidly this month. Until the 12th he is in your 9th house, which suggests foreign travel, and from the 12th to the 29th he is in your 10th house of career, showing personal success and elevation. You are at the top of your world, the top of your chart. People look up to you. You are appreciated both for your professional skills and for who you are. On the 20th, as the Sun enters your career house, you further the career through pro bono and charitable activities. You can be recognized as much for your spiritual attainments as for your professional and personal ones.

Mercury will also be 'out of bounds' from the 17th onwards. So you are not only outside your normal sphere financially, but personally as well. Perhaps career responsibilities are sending you to unknown places.

June

Best Days Overall: 7, 8, 16, 17, 18, 26, 27
Most Stressful Days Overall: 5, 6, 11, 12, 13, 19, 20, 30
Best Days for Love: 1, 3, 4, 9, 10, 11, 12, 13, 19, 20, 21, 22, 28, 29
Best Days for Money: 1, 8, 9, 10, 18, 19, 20, 27
Best Days for Career: 3, 4, 11, 12, 19, 20, 21, 22

Health has needed more attention since May 20, and this remains the case until the 21st. A lunar eclipse on the 5th is also stressful on health, so make sure to get enough rest. This is the most important thing. Reduce your schedule until the 22nd and especially around the eclipse period. Health will start to improve after the 22nd and particularly after the 28th. Enhance the health in the ways mentioned in the yearly report.

The lunar eclipse this month occurs in your 4th house, bringing dramas in the lives of family members, and especially with a parent or parent figure. Repairs might be needed in the home. Passions can run high at home too, so be more patient with the family. Once again friendships, computers and high-tech equipment get tested. High-tech gadgets in the home seem particularly vulnerable. There are shakeups in professional and trade organizations you're involved with. Bosses, parents or parent figures have to make important financial changes. You too (and the spouse, partner or current love) will be making important financial changes. Foreign travel is not a good idea during this period, but if you must travel, try to schedule it around the eclipse. College-level students experience shakeups in their school and in their educational plans.

There is a second eclipse this month; a solar eclipse on the 21st is more benign to you but it won't hurt to take a more relaxed schedule. This eclipse occurs in your 11th house of friends, bringing yet more testing of friendships and more drama in their personal lives. Once again there are shakeups in professional and trade organizations – and spiritual or charitable organizations – you're involved with. There are spiritual changes, changes in practice, teachings, teachers and attitudes, and there are personal dramas in the lives of guru figures.

You're still in a yearly career peak this month, until the 21st. So in spite of the eclipses there is still success.

Your financial planet Venus is impacted by the lunar eclipse of the 5th and so changes are happening in finance. However, you might want to study and research these changes more until after the 25th when Venus will start moving forward again. After the 25th financial confidence and clarity return. In addition, Venus moves back 'in bounds' from the 2nd onwards, so financially you're in more secure (and known) territory.

Retrograde activity will hit its maximum level for the year this month. Between the 23rd and the 25th 60 per cent of the planets will be retrograde. After the 25th 50 per cent of the planets will be moving backwards. So be patient. Life slows down.

July

Best Days Overall: 4, 5, 14, 15, 23, 24, 31
Most Stressful Days Overall: 2, 3, 9, 10, 16, 17, 29, 30
Best Days for Love: 1, 6, 7, 8, 9, 10, 16, 17, 19, 20, 25, 26, 27, 28
Best Days for Money: 4, 5, 6, 7, 8, 14, 15, 16, 17, 23, 24, 25, 26, 31
Best Days for Career: 1, 9, 10, 16, 17, 19, 20, 27, 28

Another lunar eclipse on the 5th – the third this year – yet again shakes up professional organizations, friendships and your high-tech equipment (which is behaving erratically). This eclipse occurs in your 5th house of children, fun and creativity. So children and children figures in your life are affected here. They should take it easy during this time. If they are involved in a romantic relationship it is getting tested now. If they are too young for that, there is social instability. Once again we see a need for parents and parent figures (perhaps bosses as well) to make important financial changes. Their financial thinking hasn't been realistic and corrections are in order.

This eclipse affects three other planets – Mercury, Jupiter and Mars. Thus there can be some dramas in your career and personal life – you need to adjust your image and personal appearance. The spouse, partner or current love is making some financial changes. There can be dramas at home and with the family (but these don't look too serious). Since Mars is also affected (slightly), there can be dreams of death or encounters with death – generally on the psychological level. It would be good to avoid stressful activities during this eclipse period.

Personal finance looks very strong now. Venus is still at the top of your chart. She is moving forward. She is strong on your behalf. It should be a prosperous month. The financial planet in Gemini still favours teachers, writers, lecturers, marketers, PR people and traders. The authority figures in your life are kindly disposed to your financial goals. Your good career reputation brings extra earnings. Perhaps more important than all of the above is your strong financial focus. Finance is your priority these days, and by the spiritual law we get what we focus on.

Retrograde activity decreases slightly this month. Until the 12th half the planets are in retrograde motion; after the 12th the figure is 40 per cent. So though it is a bit easier than last month, these are still high numbers. With nothing much happening in the world you can focus more on your spiritual practice. This becomes important from the 22nd onwards. The world might seem in gridlock, but spirit never is.

This is a good month for love. Neptune, your love planet, receives very nice aspects. Only he is retrograde. So, you have opportunities, but go slow.

August

Best Days Overall: 1, 2, 10, 11, 19, 20, 28, 29
Most Stressful Days Overall: 5, 6, 13, 14, 25, 26, 27
Best Days for Love: 3, 4, 5, 6, 15, 16, 23, 24
Best Days for Money: 2, 8, 11, 17, 18, 20, 21, 22, 28, 29
Best Days for Career: 8, 13, 14, 17, 18, 28, 29

Retrograde activity increases again this month, and from the 15th onwards 50 per cent of the planets are moving backwards. Continue to focus on your spiritual life until the 22nd and then on your body and image after that date. You might as well. There's nothing much going on in the world.

This year hasn't been an especially strong year for personal independence. The Eastern sector of self has never been stronger than the Western, social sector. This has been a year for focusing on others and their needs and you have needed the grace of others to get anything done. But now, the short-term planets are moving to their maximum Eastern position. This is the strongest the East will be this year. And although the social sector is still much stronger, you have a wee bit more independence these days.

The month ahead looks happy. Saturn moved back into your 5th house on July 2 and this house of fun, creativity and children is the strongest in your Horoscope. Add to this the Sun's move into your own sign on the 22nd (and Mercury moves in on the 20th) and you have a recipe for a fun kind of month. (With all the retrograde motion going on you might as well have some fun.)

Health is super this month. There is only one long-term planet – Neptune – in stressful alignment with you. (The Moon will make occasional stressful aspects, of short duration.) Also, from the 20th onwards, we will have a Grand Trine in the Earth signs – your native element. You are very comfortable with this. Personal creativity is super and you have a 'happy go lucky' approach to life. The Sun in your sign makes the personal appearance shine. You have an other-worldly glamour. You have the ability to mould and shape the body by spiritual means. Mercury in your sign also improves the appearance. It gives you the aura, the image, of success. People see you this way.

Venus has spent more than four months in your 10th house of career, but on the 7th she finally moves on into your 11th house. Though your financial intuition remains good and you have the financial cooperation of the beloved, there are more challenges involved in finances this month. You need to work harder than usual for earnings. And, finance doesn't seem the major focus that it was in previous months. If you put in the extra work you will prosper. The question is, do you have the interest?

September

Best Days Overall: 6, 7, 8, 16, 17, 24, 25
Most Stressful Days Overall: 1, 2, 3, 9, 10, 22, 23, 29, 30
Best Days for Love: 1, 2, 3, 11, 12, 13, 14, 20, 21, 22, 23, 29, 30
Best Days for Money: 2, 3, 6, 7, 13, 14, 16, 17, 18, 19, 22, 23, 24, 25
Best Days for Career: 9, 10, 18, 19, 26, 27

Retrograde activity once again reaches a crescendo for the year. Between the 9th and the 12th 60 per cent of the planets are retrograde – equalling the highpoint of June. Before and after this period, half the planets are retrograde. So, the pace of life slows down again. Yet, for you, the important things are going forward. Mercury is moving speedily this month, showing that you are moving speedily and covering much ground. You have confidence and the career is moving forward. Your financial planet Venus is also moving forward, so earnings don't seem affected by the retrogrades.

You remain in one of your yearly personal pleasure peaks until the 22nd. Personal appearance shines. You still have the ability to shape and mould the body by spiritual means – more than usual.

Last month, the planetary power shifted from the upper, day side of your chart to the lower, night side. It is time to focus more on the home, family and emotional wellness. It is time to build the psychological infrastructure upon which future career success will be built. The timing here is very good. Your family planet, Jupiter, will start moving forward on the 13th. There is clarity in the home and family and your actions will be sound.

We still have a Grand Trine in the Earth signs until the 22nd. Being an Earth sign you are very comfortable with this, and it is excellent for health. Your management decisions and organizational abilities – always strong – will be even stronger. Your spiritual life also shines and your ESP and intuition are working well.

On the 22nd the Sun enters your money house and you begin a yearly financial peak. The focus is on finance. Your financial planet moves into your spiritual 12th house on the 6th, which also increases earnings. Venus moves away from her stressful aspect with three long-term planets and starts to receive more positive aspects. This month you will learn that spirit wants you to prosper and is vitally concerned about this issue. Your spiritual planet, the Sun, and your financial planet are guests in each other's houses. This is called 'mutual reception' and shows great cooperation between finance and spirituality. Usually the focus on material things is a distraction to the spiritual practice. But not this period. They both work together. You will find it easy to apply the spiritual laws of affluence. You will, no doubt, experience 'miracle money' this period too. (Natural money will also come, but the miracle money is the most fun.)

Love will improve after the 5th, and improves even further after the 22nd.

October

Best Days Overall: 4, 5, 13, 14, 21, 23, 31
Most Stressful Days Overall: 6, 7, 19, 20, 26, 27
Best Days for Love: 3, 9, 10, 17, 18, 21, 22, 26, 27
Best Days for Money: 3, 4, 5, 13, 14, 15, 16, 21, 22, 23, 31
Best Days for Career: 6, 7, 9, 10, 17, 18, 26

The month ahead is very prosperous. You're still in the midst of a yearly financial peak until the 23rd. More importantly Venus, your financial planet, moves into your own sign on the 2nd and stays there until the 28th. This kind of transit brings prosperity in its own right. But this time Venus's largesse is stronger than usual. She is part of a Grand Trine in Earth – a very fortunate configuration. Financial windfalls will come to you – larger than usual. Clothing and personal accessories will also come. (This is a good period to buy these kinds of things – especially before the 14th.) Financial opportunities will come to you with little effort on your part and there will be opportunities for foreign travel. You will dress expensively and stylishly. There will be a tendency to show off your wealth. People see you as a money person. On the 28th Venus moves into your money house where she is also very strong: she will be in her own sign and house and thus more powerful on your behalf. The New Moon of the 16th will occur in the money house as well. This is not only a powerful financial day, but its effects will go on until the next New Moon and will clarify financial issues. Everything you need to know in order to make a good decision will come to you – very naturally.

Health is good this month. There is only one long term planet in stressful alignment with you (although the Moon will sometimes make brief discordant aspects). This is not enough to cause problems. Most of the planets are either supporting you or leaving you alone. The personal appearance is good too – better than usual. Venus in your sign not only brings money but a sense of style and beauty.

Love is improved over last month, but your love planet Neptune is still retrograde. So let things develop at their own pace. Neptune's retrograde doesn't stop love from happening, but it does introduce delays, glitches and indecision.

Mercury, the ruler of your Horoscope, will go retrograde on the 14th. So self-confidence and self-esteem will not be quite what they should be. It will also slow down the career – which should be slowed down anyway! The power is in the bottom, night side of your chart now.

Retrograde activity is still high, but less than last month. It is gradually diminishing month by month.

November

Best Days Overall: 1, 10, 18, 19, 27, 28
Most Stressful Days Overall: 2, 3, 4, 16, 22, 23, 30
Best Days for Love: 2, 3, 5, 6, 12, 14, 15, 21, 22, 23
Best Days for Money: 2, 3, 11, 12, 19, 21, 22
Best Days for Career: 2, 3, 4, 13, 14, 22, 23, 30

Jupiter and Pluto are once again travelling together. This brings prosperity to the family as a whole and especially to a parent or parent figure. A move or renovation could happen as well (though it seems complicated). The family circle expands.

Venus, your financial planet, will be in your 2nd money house until the 21st – a powerful position. Earnings are high but you will have to work harder for them. There are more obstacles to deal with.

Retrograde activity will practically disappear this month. After the 14th 80 per cent of the planets will be moving forward; 90 per cent after the 29th. The pace of life quickens. You make faster progress to your goals.

Mercury will move forward on the 3rd restoring your sense of direction and self-confidence. Career issues also become clearer. On the 16th and 17th Mercury opposes Uranus. This can bring some disturbance at work. There can be dramas with parents, parent figures or bosses. It wouldn't hurt for all of you (yourself included) to take it easy over these days.

We have our fourth and final lunar eclipse of the year on the 30th. This one affects you strongly, so you should take it easy that period. It occurs in your 10th house and shows career changes. These can manifest as shakeups in the management of your company or industry, and more dramas in the lives of bosses, parents, parent figures or elders –

the authority figures in your life. Often the government changes the regulations for your industry, and so the rules of the game change. Once again (it has been relentless this year) there are dramas in the lives of friends and the testing of friendships. There are shakeups in trade and professional organizations that you belong to. Computers and technological equipment will get tested. Make sure important files are backed up and that your anti-virus, anti-hacking software is up to date.

Health needs some attention after 21st, and especially around the eclipse period. There is nothing serious afoot, as your long-term health is good. It is just a temporary blip in your energy levels. Enhance the health in the ways mentioned in the yearly report. And, as always, make sure you get enough rest.

December

    Best Days Overall: 7, 8, 15, 16, 24, 25, 26
    Most Stressful Days Overall: 1, 13, 14, 19, 20, 21, 27, 28
    Best Days for Love: 2, 3, 11, 12, 19, 20, 21, 22, 23, 29, 30
    Best Days for Money: 2, 3, 8, 9, 10, 11, 12, 16, 22, 23, 27
    Best Days for Career: 1, 5, 6, 13, 14, 24, 27, 28

This is a very eventful month for you, Virgo. The chess pieces are being re-arranged on the cosmic chessboard. Two long-term planets will change signs this month – always a headline. Add to that a solar eclipse on the 14th and you have a classic recipe for change.

This is a home and family kind of month. Your 4th house is very strong. Even your career planet, Mercury, will be in your 4th house until the 21st. It is a very clear message. Your mission, your career, is the home and family – to be there for them. This often indicates someone who is pursuing their career from home – working from home, etc. The solar eclipse of the 14th occurs in the 4th house as well. So, though family issues are going rather well, there are some shakeups and changes. Often hidden flaws are found in the home and need repair. You might never have known they existed if not for the eclipse. Passions run high in the family. Family members are more temperamental than usual. There can be personal dramas in the lives of family members and of a parent or parent figure. Siblings and sibling figures are making important financial changes. Children and children figures in your life are making important spiritual changes – and this is so for you as well. Spiritual changes often happen due to a new revelation, always good. It leads to changes in the practice, teachings and teachers. Spiritual or charitable organizations you are involved with are in some disarray. Guru figures have personal dramas. The dream life at this time shouldn't be given too much weight. Much of it at the moment is the result of disturbances in the 'dream world' – the astral plane – caused by the eclipse.

Saturn moves out of your 5th house into your 6th on the 18th. Many of you will find jobs that are more enjoyable in the coming year. Children and children figures are more focused on finance.

Jupiter will leave your 5th house on the 20th and he too will enter your 6th house. This also shows very happy job opportunities coming to you in 2021. (It can even happen at the end of the month.)

Mercury is 'out of bounds' from the 13th onwards. Thus you and perhaps parents or parent figures are moving outside your normal sphere. It could be that career demands are the cause. There are no answers for you in the usual places and you must seek outside them.

Libra

☖

THE SCALES

Birthdays from
23rd September to
22nd October

Personality Profile

LIBRA AT A GLANCE

Element – Air

Ruling Planet – Venus
   Career Planet – Moon
   Love Planet – Mars
   Money Planet – Pluto
   Planet of Communications – Jupiter
   Planet of Health and Work – Neptune
   Planet of Home and Family Life – Saturn
   Planet of Spirituality and Good Fortune – Mercury

Colours – blue, jade green

Colours that promote love, romance and social harmony – carmine, red, scarlet

Colours that promote earning power – burgundy, red-violet, violet

Gems – carnelian, chrysolite, coral, emerald, jade, opal, quartz, white marble

Chuck 9/25/47

Metal – copper

Scents – almond, rose, vanilla, violet

Quality – cardinal (= activity)

Qualities most needed for balance – a sense of self, self-reliance, independence

Strongest virtues – social grace, charm, tact, diplomacy

Deepest needs – love, romance, social harmony

Characteristic to avoid – violating what is right in order to be socially accepted

Signs of greatest overall compatibility – Gemini, Aquarius

Signs of greatest overall incompatibility – Aries, Cancer, Capricorn

Sign most helpful to career – Cancer

Sign most helpful for emotional support – Capricorn

Sign most helpful financially – Scorpio

Sign best for marriage and/or partnerships – Aries

Sign most helpful for creative projects – Aquarius

Best Sign to have fun with – Aquarius

Signs most helpful in spiritual matters – Gemini, Virgo

Best day of the week – Friday

Understanding a Libra

In the sign of Libra the universal mind – the soul – expresses its genius for relationships, that is, its power to harmonize diverse elements in a unified, organic way. Libra is the soul's power to express beauty in all of its forms. And where is beauty if not within relationships? Beauty does not exist in isolation. Beauty arises out of comparison – out of the just relationship between different parts. Without a fair and harmonious relationship there is no beauty, whether it in art, manners, ideas or the social or political forum.

There are two faculties humans have that exalt them above the animal kingdom: their rational faculty (expressed in the signs of Gemini and Aquarius) and their aesthetic faculty, exemplified by Libra. Without an aesthetic sense we would be little more than intelligent barbarians. Libra is the civilizing instinct or urge of the soul.

Beauty is the essence of what Librans are all about. They are here to beautify the world. One could discuss Librans' social grace, their sense of balance and fair play, their ability to see and love another person's point of view – but this would be to miss their central asset: their desire for beauty.

No one – no matter how alone he or she seems to be – exists in isolation. The universe is one vast collaboration of beings. Librans, more than most, understand this and understand the spiritual laws that make relationships bearable and enjoyable.

A Libra is always the unconscious (and in some cases conscious) civilizer, harmonizer and artist. This is a Libra's deepest urge and greatest genius. Librans love instinctively to bring people together, and they are uniquely qualified to do so. They have a knack for seeing what unites people – the things that attract and bind rather than separate individuals.

Finance

In financial matters Librans can seem frivolous and illogical to others. This is because Librans appear to be more concerned with earning money for others than for themselves. But there is a logic to this financial attitude. Librans know that everything and everyone is connected and that it is impossible to help another to prosper without also prospering yourself. Since enhancing their partner's income and position tends to strengthen their relationship, Librans choose to do so. What could be more fun than building a relationship? You will rarely find a Libra enriching him- or herself at someone else's expense.

Scorpio is the ruler of Libra's solar 2nd house of money, giving Libra unusual insight into financial matters – and the power to focus on these matters in a way that disguises a seeming indifference. In fact, many other signs come to Librans for financial advice and guidance.

Given their social grace, Librans often spend great sums of money on entertaining and organizing social events. They also like to help others when they are in need. Librans would go out of their way to help a friend in dire straits, even if they have to borrow from others to do so. However, Librans are also very careful to pay back any debts they owe, and like to make sure they never have to be reminded to do so.

Career and Public Image

Publicly, Librans like to appear as nurturers. Their friends and acquaintances are their family and they wield political power in parental ways. They also like bosses who are paternal or maternal.

The sign of Cancer is on Libra's 10th career house cusp; the Moon is Libra's career planet. The Moon is by far the speediest, most changeable planet in the horoscope. It alone among all the planets travels through the entire zodiac – all twelve signs and houses – every month. This is an important key to the way in which Librans approach their careers, and also to what they need to do to maximize their career potential. The Moon is the planet of moods and feelings – Librans need a career in which their emotions can have free expression. This is why so many Librans are involved in the creative arts. Libra's ambitions wax and wane with the Moon. They tend to wield power according to their mood.

The Moon 'rules' the masses – and that is why Libra's highest goal is to achieve a mass kind of acclaim and popularity. Librans who achieve fame cultivate the public as other people cultivate a lover or friend. Librans can be very flexible – and often fickle – in their career and ambitions. On the other hand, they can achieve their ends in a great variety of ways. They are not stuck in one attitude or with one way of doing things.

Love and Relationships

Librans express their true genius in love. In love you could not find a partner more romantic, more seductive or more fair. If there is one thing that is sure to destroy a relationship – sure to block your love from flowing – it is injustice or imbalance between lover and beloved. If one party is giving too much or taking too much, resentment is sure to surface at some time or other. Librans are careful about this. If anything, Librans might err on the side of giving more, but never giving less.

If you are in love with a Libra, make sure you keep the aura of romance alive. Do all the little things – candle-lit dinners, travel to exotic locales, flowers and small gifts. Give things that are beautiful, not necessarily expensive. Send cards. Ring regularly even if you have nothing in particular to say. The niceties are very important to a Libra. Your relationship is a work of art: make it beautiful and your Libran lover will appreciate it. If you are creative about it, he or she will appreciate it even more; for this is how your Libra will behave towards you.

Librans like their partners to be aggressive and even a bit self-willed. They know that these are qualities they sometimes lack and so they like their partners to have them. In relationships, however, Librans can be very aggressive – but always in a subtle and charming way! Librans are determined in their efforts to charm the object of their desire – and this determination can be very pleasant if you are on the receiving end.

Home and Domestic Life

Since Librans are such social creatures, they do not particularly like mundane domestic duties. They like a well-organized home – clean and neat with everything needful present – but housework is a chore and a burden, one of the unpleasant tasks in life that must be done, the quicker the better. If a Libra has enough money – and sometimes even if not – he or she will prefer to pay someone else to take care of the daily household chores. However, Librans like gardening; they love to have flowers and plants in the home.

A Libra's home is modern, and furnished in excellent taste. You will find many paintings and sculptures there. Since Librans like to be with friends and family, they enjoy entertaining at home and they make great hosts.

Capricorn is on the cusp of Libra's 4th solar house of home and family. Saturn, the planet of law, order, limits and discipline, rules Libra's domestic affairs. If Librans want their home life to be support-ive and happy they need to develop some of the virtues of Saturn – order, organization and discipline. Librans, being so creative and so intensely in need of harmony, can tend to be too lax in the home and too permissive with their children. Too much of this is not always good; children need freedom but they also need limits.

Horoscope for 2020

Major Trends

Although the year ahead is not an especially strong career year – your 10th house is basically empty, almost all of the long-term planets are on the night side of your chart, and your 4th house of home and family is much, much stronger than your career house – we do see many career changes happening this year. There will be four lunar eclipses this year, twice as many as usual. And, since the Moon is your career planet, there is much change, turmoil and disruption going on. More on this later.

Your 4th house of home and family is easily the strongest house in your Horoscope this year – at least up until December 18. This is where the action will be. It is a year for 'behind the scenes' activity – preparation – setting the stage for future career progress. More details later.

Since his move in March 2019, Uranus is now in your 8th house of transformation for the long haul – for approximately the next seven years. This shows a tendency to sexual experimentation. The old rule books get thrown out and you learn what works best for you. So long as this experimentation is not destructive, it is probably a good thing.

This is how we learn. Personal transformation is not an exact science. You are very involved with these kinds of projects and you will be experimental here too.

Health is an issue for you this year, Libra. There are many long-term planets in stressful alignment with you. The good news is that you are on the case: your 6th house of health is strong. More on this later.

The love and social life are active this year. *All* the long-term planets are in the Western, social sector of your chart. In a sense this is Libra heaven. The year ahead is all about other people and getting on with them. Romantic opportunities for singles are developing from June 28 onwards, as Mars makes an extremely long transit through your 7th house of love. Details below.

Venus, the ruler of your Horoscope, will spend a long time (four times her usual length of stay in a sign) in your 9th house, from April 3 to August 7. This shows foreign travel and happy educational opportunities.

Your areas of greatest interest and focus this year will be home and family; children, fun and creativity (from March 23 to July 1 and from December 18 onwards); sex, personal transformation and occult studies; health; love, romance and social activities (from June 28 onwards); and religion, philosophy, higher education and foreign travel (from April 3 to August 7).

Your paths of greatest fulfilment this year are the career (until May 6); friends groups and group activities (after May 6); home and family (until December 20); and children, fun and creativity (from December 20 onwards).

Health

(Please note that this is an astrological perspective on health and not a medical one. In days of yore there was no difference, both these perspectives were identical. But now there could be quite a difference. For a medical perspective, please consult your doctor or health practitioner.)

Health, as we mentioned, is delicate this year. For much of the year three, and sometimes four, long-term planets are in stressful alignment with you. But things really become dicey when the short-term planets also move into stressful alignment; these periods will be from

January 1 to January 20, March 20 to April 19 and June 21 to July 22. These are periods to rest and relax more and to book more massages or other preventive treatments. The important thing will be to maintain high energy levels. High energy is the best preventive against disease.

The good news is that your 6th house of health is strong this year and so you will be paying attention. It would be much more dangerous if you were just ignoring things. After December 18, you should see a big improvement in your health and energy; 2021 will be much better healthwise than 2020.

More good news. There is much you can do to enhance the health and prevent problems from developing. And even when you can't totally prevent the problem (due to strong karmic momentum) you can soften it to a great extent. It need not be devastating. Give more attention to the following – the vulnerable areas of your Horoscope (the reflex points are shown in the chart below):

Important foot reflexology points for the year ahead

Try to massage the whole of the foot on a regular basis – the top of the foot as well as the bottom – but pay extra attention to the points highlighted on the chart. When you massage, be aware of 'sore spots' as these need special attention. It's also a good idea to massage the ankles and below them.

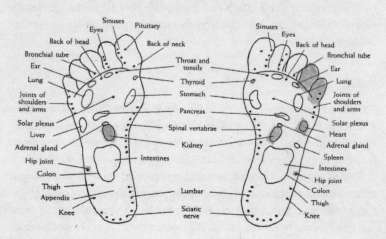

- The kidneys and hips, which are always important for Libra. Regular hip massage should be part of your normal health regime. A herbal kidney cleanse every now and then would be a good idea too, especially if you feel under the weather.
- The feet. These are also always important for you, as Neptune, the planet that rules the feet, is your health planet. Of late, with Neptune in your 6th house, the feet have become even more important (and this will be a trend for many years to come). So regular foot massage is vital. This will not only strengthen the feet but the whole body as well. There are inexpensive gadgets that will massage the feet automatically, while you're watching TV or sitting at the computer, and this would be a good investment this year. As would gadgets that give foot whirlpool treatments
- The heart has become important over the past two years as Saturn has started to travel with Pluto in Capricorn. And when Jupiter moved into Capricorn late last year it became even more important. The important thing with the heart is to develop more faith – reduce worry and anxiety, the two emotions that stress it out. The good news is that by the end of the year, from December 18 onwards, the heart will be less vulnerable. Next year it won't be an issue.

With Neptune as your health planet you always respond well to spiritual-type therapies; now, with Neptune strongly positioned and in his own sign and house, you respond to these even better. If you feel under the weather, see a spiritual healer.

You have a good connection to the healing power of the Water element these days too. You will benefit being near water – oceans, rivers, lakes and springs. Natural bodies of water are always best. Good to soak in these waters. Swimming, boating and water sports are good exercises. So are yoga and tai chi. Spiritual-type exercises will be beneficial. When you are in the shower, imagine that the water is washing you inside as well as outside. The healing powers of water are considerable. For those of you interested in learning more there is much information in my blog – www.spiritual-stories.com.

Home and Family

Home and family has been important for many years, since 2008 in fact, when Pluto moved into your 4th house. In the past two years it has become even more important as Saturn moved in. This year it is easily the most important area of your chart as Jupiter will spend almost all year here too.

This area of life looks bittersweet, although it seems better – happier – than last year. Jupiter is bringing more happiness and prosperity to the family.

Saturn in your 4th house signals that family life is a bit of a burden. A discipline. You sort of grit your teeth and handle things. Expressing your true feelings has been difficult for the past two years and probably you bottled them up. This year it is a bit easier to express your feelings. Writing them out seems like a good way.

Women of childbearing age are more fertile than usual this year. But the pregnancy seems complicated. Not a smooth ride. Fertility will be very strong after December 20 and for almost all of next year.

You seem in two minds about moving. Part of you would like to move, while another part, the more conservative side of you, wants to stay put and make better use of the existing space. You've felt cramped in the home for some years now. Which side of you will win? This seems a free will decision this year, but if you do decide to move it will be complicated.

You've had a tendency to earn money from the home for many years, and the trend is even stronger in the year ahead. You're spending more on the home and family but can earn from them as well. Family support looks strong.

A parent or parent figure in your life seems pessimistic and over-controlling, but he or she is prospering these days. He or she seems very involved in your finances. This parent figure might be doing renovations in the home (or perhaps even building a home) but an actual move is not likely. The other parent or parent figure has many personal crises this year. He or she will be redefining the personality, the self-concept and the image that he or she projects to the world. But that parent figure is not likely to move.

Siblings and sibling figures seem closer to the family this year – especially to one of the parents. They are prospering, but a move is not likely. There is nothing against it, but there is nothing especially supporting it either.

Children and children figures in your life will be taking on more responsibility from March 23 to July 1, and after December 18. They have to get more serious about life. They also seem more fertile than usual (if they are of childbearing age). They can have multiple moves and/or renovations of the home this year and in the coming years. Their domestic situation seems unstable. Grandchildren (if you have them) or those who play that role in your life are having a quiet kind of family year.

If you're planning renovations or major repairs to the home, almost all year would be good for this, but February 16 to March 13 seems the best period. If you're doing some cosmetic redecoration in the home or buying art objects for it, March 5 to March 23, April 3 to July 1 and October 2 to October 28 seem good times.

Finance and Career

Though your money house is empty this year – only short-term planets will move through there – the year ahead looks prosperous. You don't have the chart of a lottery winner; you will have to earn your prosperity, but it will happen. Your financial planet Pluto is receiving strong stimulation.

Pluto is a very slow-moving planet. He stays in a sign for anything between fifteen and thirty years, so many of the trends we have written about in previous years are still very much in effect – perhaps even stronger.

Pluto has been in your 4th house for since 2008, signalling good family support for finances. You can earn through your own family business or through a business that is 'run like a family'. You are attracted to these kinds of businesses these days. You have a good feeling for residential real estate, the food business, restaurants and hotels. Also for companies that cater to homeowners – landscapers, furniture companies, interior designers and the like.

Generically Pluto rules inheritance, taxes and debt. This gives various messages. Good tax planning, tax efficiency, is important in earnings and probably many financial decisions are influenced by this. Many of you have received inheritances in past years and this can also happen in the year ahead. You could be named in someone's will or be appointed to some administrative position in an estate. We often see this aspect in people who deal with estates – antique dealers and auction houses. This is a good year to either pay off debts or to borrow – it depends on your need. You can earn through the creative use of debt. If you have good business ideas, the year ahead is excellent (better than last year) for attracting outside investors to your projects. You have good access to outside money this year.

Those of you of the appropriate age are doing estate planning this year, and probably making changes here.

Your financial planet travels with both Saturn and Jupiter – two opposite kinds of planets. Saturn is ultra-conservative and risk averse (and especially so these past two years). Jupiter, on the other hand, is more optimistic, more willing to speculate, more risk-taking. Jupiter can be over-confident. Saturn tends to be pessimistic. These two forces conflict in your mind. One urges caution and care and the other says 'things will work out, let's take a chance'. Satisfying both these urges is a challenge, but your best investments will be those that satisfy both your pessimistic and optimistic sides.

The family as a whole gets richer this year.

Jupiter rules your 3rd house of communication and intellectual interests. His position near your financial planet shows that earnings can come through siblings or sibling figures, through neighbours, through writing, sales, marketing, advertising, PR and trading – buying and selling. Teachers and writers should have an especially good financial year.

As we mentioned earlier, your 10th house of career is not prominent this year. The focus is mostly on the home and family. And even your success in earning is probably motivated by family concerns rather than a need for prestige or status. The night side of your chart – and especially the 4th house – can be compared to the 'behind the scenes' activity in a film or theatrical production, while the 10th house equates to the final product – the actual film or play. Without the behind-the-scenes activity, activity that the audience never sees, the finished product would never see the light of day. So don't discount the importance of this year. The stage is being set for future success.

Love and Social Life

As we said before, the year ahead will be very social. The Western, social sector of the Horoscope is totally dominant. Sure, the Eastern sector will strengthen a bit as the year progresses, but it will never overpower the West. So though there will be periods of relative independence, the year ahead is about exercising your social genius (which is considerable).

More importantly Mars, your love planet, will spend over six months in your 7th house of love, from June 28 onwards. He is very powerful here in his own sign and house, and this increases your social magnetism even further. It shows that there is a relationship happening. For singles it shows romance. But it doesn't seem a smooth ride, however; family obligations and duties interfere. Perhaps the family or a parent figure is obstructive. But Libra knows how to handle challenging relationships.

With Mars in your 7th house you tend to fall in love quickly. You tend to jump into relationships quickly too. You would also attract similar people – impulsiveness is the main problem this year. A little caution, a little more 'stepping back' might be a good idea.

You could be attracted to athletic types of people. People in the military or police would also be alluring. You like independent, bold people. The sexual magnetism would be the prime attraction.

Romantic opportunities happen in the usual places this year – at parties, weddings and social gatherings. They can happen at the gym or sports field too. These would be interesting places to go on dates as well.

Those in or working on their second or third marriages (and many of you are) will socialize more, but love tends towards the status quo.

Mars is not a very fast-moving planet, but neither is he very slow. This year he will move through six signs and houses of your chart so there are short-term trends in love that are best dealt with in the monthly reports.

While Mars is in your 7th house he will make one of his rare retrogrades – from September 9 to November 14. This will add complication to the relationship. Important decisions about love shouldn't be made during that retrograde period.

Jupiter's move into your 5th house of fun and creativity at the end of the year indicates a possible love affair. There will be plenty of opportunities for love affairs in 2021 as well.

Self-improvement

The 4th house has deeper meanings than just home and family. It is really about your moods and general emotional life. This, psychologically speaking, is where you live. The denizens of your emotional home are your emotional family. So, the power in the 4th house is showing that this is a year for psychological progress. For emotional healing. Those of you involved in psychological therapies will make much progress. The desire to heal is 90 per cent of the battle.

Pluto, in your 4th house for so many years, as well as being your financial planet, generically is the ruler of deep psychology. This transit signals that you are going very deep into the psyche and are cutting away the negativity – the old patterns and the traumas of the past – that block you going forward. Often this manifests as a death in the family or a near-death experience for a family member. These kinds of experiences have certainly happened over the years. Sometimes it shows the 'death' or 'near death' of the family itself. And then, the resurrection on a better level.

Saturn, your family planet, has been in your 4th house for the past two years and spends most of the coming year there as well. This has a few interpretations. On one level it shows (and we have written about this in past years) a tendency to repress your true feelings. Usually people don't feel safe expressing them and they hold them back. But this can't go on for too long. Eventually these things will surface and usually in an unbalanced and destructive kind of way. On a deeper level, Saturn moving through your 4th house shows a need to manage the emotions, to take charge of them and to direct them according to your will. We were not created to be victims of our emotions (especially negative ones) but masters of them. Spiritually speaking this has been your task for the past two years. Management and control doesn't mean repression. Repression is not healthy. Management means being able to express destructive feelings (and the thoughts behind them) in a safe, non-destructive way. There are various methods for doing this. You can write out your bad feelings on a piece of paper (a method I like this year) and then throw the paper away. Don't reread it. Another method is 'touch and let go'. Take a piece of paper, write down five things that bother you, then touch the paper and let it go. Repeat this for 15 minutes or so.*

After you've done these exercises you'll find that you have more emotional control. Those of you who meditate will find that your meditation goes better too.

Month-by-month Forecasts

January

Best Days Overall: 7, 8, 16, 24, 25, 26
Most Stressful Days Overall: 2, 3, 9, 10, 22, 23, 29, 30, 31
Best Days for Love: 1, 2, 3, 12, 13, 14, 18, 19, 20, 21, 27, 28, 29, 30, 31
Best Days for Money: 5, 6, 14, 15, 18, 19, 22, 23
Best Days for Career: 5, 6, 9, 10, 14, 15, 24, 25

An emotionally and physically stressful kind of month. Keep in mind that the universe never gives more than can be handled. If it is given, by definition, you can handle it.

Health is the major concern this month. At least half, and sometimes it's 60 per cent, of the planets are in stressful alignment with you – including two heavy hitters, Saturn and Pluto. So it is very important to maintain high energy levels. Be sure to rest when tired. Keep your focus on the essential things in life and drop the trivialities and distractions. You have the energy for the important things, but not for frivolities. Enhance the health in the ways mentioned in the yearly report. If

---

* There is more information on these subjects in my blog – www.spiritual-stories. com – and in my book *A Technique for Meditation*.

it is possible, schedule more massages or other health treatments this month. You should see improvement in your energy from the 20th onwards. But health still needs watching.

A lunar eclipse on the 10th also affects you strongly so try to take it easy that period. The things that you must do should be done, but non-essentials are better off rescheduled. This eclipse occurs in your 10th house of career and impacts on your career planet, the Moon, so it has a double effect here. There can be career changes and upheavals. There can be shakeups in the management of your company or industry. The government can change the rules regarding your industry. Bosses, parents, parent figures – people in authority over you – are having personal dramas. This eclipse has an impact on three other planets – Saturn, Pluto and Mercury – making it even stronger than we have said. Its impact on Saturn signals dramas at home and with the family. Repairs might be needed in the home. The impact on Pluto shows a need for financial change. The events of the eclipse will show where your financial thinking hasn't been realistic. There are dramas in the lives of the money people in your life. The impact on Mercury indicates that students are affected. They can change schools or educational plans. Cars and communication equipment will be tested.

Though the eclipse affects the career, this is not the main focus this month. Home and family is. Emotions can run high in the family this month so be more patient with them. It is a good month to get the emotional life in order, and for psychological kinds of therapies. Also good for building the psychological infrastructure for future career success.

February

Best Days Overall: 3, 4, 5, 12, 13, 21, 22
Most Stressful Days Overall: 6, 7, 18, 19, 20, 26, 27
Best Days for Love: 7, 8, 9, 16, 17, 18, 26, 27, 28, 29
Best Days for Money: 1, 2, 10, 11, 14, 15, 19, 20, 28, 29
Best Days for Career: 3, 4, 6, 7, 12, 13, 23, 24

Health is still a concern this month, especially after the 16th when Mars joins the gang of planets in discordant alignment with you. The good news is that your 6th house of health becomes very powerful after the 19th, which at least means that you are on the case, focused on health. Enhance the health in the ways mentioned in the yearly report, and if you feel under the weather see a spiritual-type healer.

Last month, on the 20th, you entered a yearly personal pleasure peak and this continues until the 19th. Having fun, relaxing and indulging in things that bring you joy will certainly improve your mood and your health. Children and children figures in your life are having a good social period now. Social and romantic opportunities pursue them rather than the other way around.

The power in your 6th house is excellent for job seekers; there are many opportunities coming. Even those who are already employed will have opportunities for overtime or second jobs. Those who employ others also have an abundance of applicants.

The bottom half – the night side – of your Horoscope is the dominant one this year. So the focus needs to be on the home, family and your emotional wellness. When you find your point of emotional harmony, you can easily succeed in your outer career from that point. But first comes emotional harmony. Career comes later.

Venus, the ruler of your Horoscope, has her solstice from the 8th to the 10th. She pauses in the heavens and then reverses direction (in her latitudinal motion). So a pause in your life and then a reversal of direction is happening. A good thing. A natural thing. Nothing to be concerned about.

From the 16th onwards your favourite sector – the Western, social sector – contains *all* the planets. You are in Libra heaven. The focus is on others and their needs. This is when you get to exercise your social genius to the full. Libra always tends to be popular, but especially so now. Venus enters your 7th house on the 7th and stays there for the rest of the month. You are socially proactive. Perhaps your self-confidence is not what it should be, but it doesn't need to be. You go out of your way for your friends. They feel this and respond to it.

March

Best Days Overall: 2, 3, 10, 11, 19, 20, 29, 30
Most Stressful Days Overall: 4, 5, 17, 18, 24, 25
Best Days for Love: 1, 8, 9, 17, 18, 24, 25, 27, 28
Best Days for Money: 1, 8, 9, 12, 13, 17, 18, 27, 28
Best Days for Career: 4, 5, 12, 13, 24, 25

Health is still a major concern this month, so keep in mind our previous discussions of this. Focus on health until the 20th and it will stand you in good stead for afterwards.

In spite of your lowered energy levels, many nice things are happening. Jupiter travels with Pluto, your financial planet, all month so the weeks ahead are prosperous. Very prosperous. Money can come from family support or family connections. Your intellectual property can be marketable. There is good fortune in trading – buying and selling. Job opportunities are still plentiful.

Like last month, all the planets (with the exception of the Moon between the 4th and 15th) are in the Western social sector. On the 20th the Sun enters your 7th house of love and you begin a yearly love and social peak. So, like last month – but even more so – the month ahead is social. Your love planet Mars will spend almost all month (until the 31st) in your 4th house. This gives many messages. A lot of your socializing will be at home, with the family or family connections. You like people with whom you can bond emotionally – people you can share feelings with. Emotional intimacy is just as important as the physical side of a relationship. Romantic opportunities are close to home this month. From the 15th to the 21st your love planet travels with Jupiter. This brings romantic opportunities in your neighbourhood and perhaps with neighbours. Educational and school functions can also be a venue for romance. For singles we see two relationships this month.

The Sun in your 7th house shows that being involved with groups and group activities can lead to romance too. From the 6th to the 9th your ruling planet Venus travels with Uranus. This can bring an opportunity for a love affair, but this doesn't seem serious. Just fun and games.

Saturn will move out of your 4th house on the 23rd – but this is only a temporary move for a few months, a signal of things to come next year. A parent or parent figure is more focused on finance. Perhaps he or she tries to inhibit your fun or creativity. The transit can signal pregnancy for women of childbearing age, but it's not a smooth ride.

Venus will be in your 8th house from the 5th onward. This is excellent for weight loss or detox regimes. It would tend to be a more sexually active kind of period too. (Regardless of your age and stage of life the libido will be stronger than usual.)

April

Best Days Overall: 7, 8, 15, 16, 17, 25, 26
Most Stressful Days Overall: 1, 2, 13, 14, 20, 21, 22, 28, 29
Best Days for Love: 7, 8, 15, 16, 17, 20, 21, 22, 25, 26
Best Days for Money: 6, 8, 10, 14, 24
Best Days for Career: 1, 2, 3, 4, 12, 23, 28, 29

Health is still a major concern until the 19th. However, there is good news here too. After that date you should see dramatic improvement. In the meantime, as always, make sure to get enough rest and try to schedule more health treatments – massage, reflexology, shiatsu, acupuncture and the like. You want therapies that boost your energy. A visit to a spiritual healer might be a good idea.

You're still in the midst of a yearly love and social peak until the 19th. All the planets are still in the social Western half of your chart (only the Moon will visit the East, from the 1st to the 12th and from the 28th to the 30th) so you are in a social month of a very social year. Love seems happy this month. You seem in harmony with the current love. Singles will find harmonious romantic partners. But none of this seems too serious. Just amusement (and nothing wrong with that). Your love planet Mars spends the month in your 5th house of fun and you find romantic opportunities in the usual places – at parties, resorts, places of entertainment, sporting events.

Venus, the ruler of your Horoscope and a most important planet in your chart, enters your 9th house on the 3rd, where she'll spend the next four months. This gives many messages. It is a wonderful transit for college-level students as it signals focus and interest. This spells success. Foreign lands will call to you and there will be opportunities for foreign travel. You have a strong personal interest in religion, philosophy and theology and philosophical breakthroughs are likely over this period. The 9th house is also very 'upbeat' – optimistic. So there is personal happiness and optimism about life.

Venus goes 'out of bounds' after the 13th: she moves outside her usual boundaries in the heavens. So, you are doing this too. You are outside your usual sphere. Your normal environment isn't interesting and so you go outside it. Travelling to exotic places would fit the symbolism here, but it would also apply to your philosophical and theological studies – they are outside your normal sphere.

Your 8th house becomes powerful after the 19th. This favours detox and weight-loss regimes. It favours projects involving personal transformation – becoming the person that you want to be.

Finances look super. Jupiter is still travelling with your financial planet all this month, continuing a trend that we saw last month. The only complication is Pluto's retrograde on the 25th. This might slow things down but earnings will still come.

May

Best Days Overall: 4, 5, 13, 14, 23, 24
Most Stressful Days Overall: 10, 11, 18, 19, 25, 26
Best Days for Love: 4, 5, 13, 14, 15, 18, 19, 23, 24, 25, 26
Best Days for Money: 3, 6, 7, 11, 12, 21, 22
Best Days for Career: 2, 3, 11, 23, 25, 26

In spite of Pluto's retrograde, prosperity is still happening. Perhaps it is not as much as it could be or slows down somewhat, but it is still happening. Your financial planet will be retrograde for many more months; you can't stop your life because of this, but you can take a more cautious approach to finance. More research and due diligence will be needed over the next few months – especially if you're considering large expenditures or investments.

You've had excellent financial judgement for many years. You've been conservative and by now you've probably built up savings and investments. But now it's time to be even more conservative. Resolve all doubts before making major purchases.

Health is not perfect, but it's good. Most of the planets are either in harmonious aspect or leaving you alone. Good health is another form of wealth – though we often take it for granted. Mars will move into your 6th house of health on the 13th, indicating that you benefit from face and scalp massage and physical exercise (as well as the things mentioned in the yearly report).

Mars is your love planet. So good health for you also means good social health – a healthy love life, marital harmony. Problems here could impact on your physical health. So if health problems arise (God forbid) restore harmony here as quickly as you can.

Love is complicated this month. You will have to work harder to achieve your social goals. Mars in your 6th house shows an attraction to health professionals and to people involved in your health. It often shows an office romance – a romance with a co-worker. But it is complicated. You would also be attracted to someone more spiritual, artistic and creative. Good spiritual compatibility would be important. Venus's rare (once in two years) retrograde also complicates love. You're not sure what you want. You have doubts.

Your 9th house is easily the most powerful in your Horoscope this month – especially from the 20th onwards. So, like last month, there is a focus on religion, philosophy and theology. Some thinkers have said that 'man is a theological animal'. This is certainly true of you these days. It is your theology – conscious or unconscious – that determines how you will live your life.

June

Best Days Overall: 1, 9, 10, 19, 20
Most Stressful Days Overall: 7, 8, 14, 15, 21, 22
Best Days for Love: 1, 3, 4, 9, 10, 11, 12, 14, 15, 19, 20, 21, 22, 30
Best Days for Money: 3, 4, 8, 18, 27, 28, 29
Best Days for Career: 1, 9, 10, 20, 21, 22

Health is once again an issue this month. Not only are there many planets in discordant alignment with you, but we have two eclipses as well – both of which affect you strongly. You will feel the stress more after the 21st, but health should be heeded even before. Review our discussion of health in the yearly report. In addition, face and scalp massage and physical exercise will be beneficial until the 28th. As always, do your best to get enough rest. Keep your focus on the real priorities of your life and let lesser things go. Don't waste your energy on non-essentials.

The lunar eclipse of the 5th occurs in your 3rd house and affects students below college level (although college-level students can also be slightly affected). There are changes in educational plans and perhaps changes of school. There can be disturbances at school and disturbances in the neighbourhood. Siblings and sibling figures are forced to redefine themselves – their image and self-concept. This will manifest as changes in their wardrobe and overall 'look' and presentation and will go on for a few months. Cars and communication equipment will get tested, and will often need repair or replacement. There can be problems with the mail as well.

Since the Moon is your career planet, her eclipse signals career changes (this is going on all year). The career is in a state of flux. There can be management changes in your company or industry, and regulations concerning your industry can also change. There are personal dramas in the lives of bosses, parents, parent figures and authority figures in your life. Since this eclipse impacts, pretty directly, on both Venus and Mars – two important planets in your Horoscope – you and the beloved have a need to redefine yourselves. This eclipse can test your relationship. Often such an eclipse brings a detox of the body. It will be a good idea to drive more carefully over this period.

The solar eclipse of the 21st also has a strong impact on you (though those born early in Libra – from September 22 to 24 – will feel it most strongly). This eclipse occurs in your 10th house and once again shakes up the career in the ways mentioned previously. Again there are personal dramas in the lives of bosses, parents, and other authority figures in your life. Friendships get tested. Often this is not because of the friendship per se but because of crises happening in your friends' lives. Computers and high-tech gadgetry get tested again, and can act erratically.

Because this eclipse occurs on one of the Cardinal points (0 degrees in Aries, Cancer, Libra and Capricorn) it has a worldwide effect, not just a personal one.

July

Best Days Overall: 6, 7, 8, 16, 17, 25, 26
Most Stressful Days Overall: 4, 5, 11, 12, 19, 20, 31
Best Days for Love: 2, 3, 6, 7, 8, 11, 12, 16, 17, 21, 22, 25, 26, 29, 30
Best Days for Money: 1, 4, 5, 14, 15, 23, 24, 27, 28, 31
Best Days for Career: 1, 9, 10, 19, 20, 21, 22, 29

We have another lunar eclipse this month that almost replicates the previous one of last month. This too occurs on the 5th and affects you strongly, so reduce your schedule during that period. (You should be taking things more easily anyway, but especially that period.)

This third lunar eclipse of the year occurs in your 4th house of home and family. So both sets of parents or parent figures are affected. They can have personal dramas or crises. They have a need to redefine themselves – their images and personalities. There can be body detoxes too. This eclipse brings upheavals and changes in both the home and the career. Passions in the family run high and family members are more temperamental and on edge. Your dream life will probably be more active too, but don't give your dreams too much weight; the dream world (the astral plane) is stirred up and so weird dreams can happen. Siblings and sibling figures in your life are forced to make financial changes. Repairs could be needed in the home. Course corrections in the career are necessary.

This eclipse sideswipes three other planets – Mercury, Jupiter and Mars. Happily the effect on these areas will be mild. The impact on Mars indicates a testing of a current love relationship and perhaps some drama in the life of the beloved. The impact on Mercury and Jupiter suggests a need to avoid needless travel during this period. (Essential travel is another story: only you can decide which is which.) Again, it will be a good idea to drive more carefully. Cars and communication equipment get tested again. Students at all levels have dramas in school and changes in their educational plans.

Health needs attention all month, but especially until the 22nd. Enhance the health by maintaining high energy levels, resting when tired and scheduling more massages or foot reflexology treatments.

Mars entered your 7th house on June 28 and will be there for the rest of the year. So love is happening, but it is not a smooth road right now. Your love planet has his solstice from the 7th to the 16th. He stays in the same degree of latitude that period and then changes direction. He is pausing in the heavens. So a pause in your love and social life is happening and then a change of direction. This is nothing to fear. It is as natural as the sunrise and is essentially good.

Career is important this month, but so is the home and family. Your challenge is to balance both. Many have this challenge, but for you it is very dramatic this month.

August

Best Days Overall: 3, 4, 13, 14, 21, 22, 30, 31
Most Stressful Days Overall: 1, 2, 8, 9, 15, 16, 28, 29
Best Days for Love: 3, 4, 8, 9, 15, 16, 17, 18, 23, 24, 25, 26, 27
Best Days for Money: 2, 11, 20, 23, 24, 29
Best Days for Career: 8, 9, 15, 16, 18, 19, 28

Health is slightly improved compared with last month, but still needs attention. Four long-term planets are in stressful alignment with you so, as always, watch your energy and make health a priority. Review our health discussion in the yearly report.

In spite of lower energy levels, you seem successful these days. Last month you were in a yearly career peak. This month, on the 7th, your ruling planet Venus enters your 10th house. So, you are on top of your world. You are appreciated and honoured as much for who you are as for your professional achievements. Others aspire to be like you.

Finances have been good this year and they are OK in the month ahead. Just slower than usual. Your financial planet Pluto is still retrograde. It is still good to take a 'wait and see' attitude to important purchases or investments. Finances will improve after the 22nd, but earnings can happen with a delayed reaction.

Love is important this month and active, but very complicated. There are many challenges involved. But Libra more than any other sign knows how to handle social challenges.

The Eastern sector of your chart – the sector of the self – is about as strong as it will ever be this year, although the Western social side is still more dominant. The month ahead is still about others and their needs, but there is a wee bit more personal independence than usual. The planetary power will be at its maximum Eastern point for the next two months, so it might be easier to start making some of the changes you need to make. But others still come first.

Retrograde activity peaked in June but is still strong in the month ahead. Half of the planets are moving backwards after the 15th. The pace of life is slow and there's not much happening in the world. You might as well focus on your spiritual practice, especially from the 22nd onwards. In the outer world doors might be closed, but the spiritual doors are always open.

Children or children figures in your life have a love crisis on the 1st and 2nd. Happily their love life improves dramatically after the 22nd.

Your 11th house of friends is strong until the 22nd. Thus it is a social kind of month – both romantically and in terms of friendships. The 11th house is a beneficent house, so there is more optimism around, and the attainment of fondest hopes and wishes.

September

Best Days Overall: 9, 10, 18, 19, 26, 27
Most Stressful Days Overall: 4, 5, 11, 12, 24, 25
Best Days for Love: 2, 3, 4, 5, 13, 14, 15, 22, 23
Best Days for Money: 6, 7, 16, 17, 20, 21, 24, 25
Best Days for Career: 6, 7, 11, 12, 17, 26

Retrograde activity this month equals the maximum level reached in June. Between the 9th and the 12th 60 per cent of the planets are in retrograde motion, and for the rest of the month it is 50 per cent. These are very high numbers. (Children born under these aspects will be late bloomers in life.) With the pace of life so slow, you might as well focus on your spiritual life – especially until the 22nd. When everything seems in gridlock, Spirit is unaffected. Its doors are always open. Also, spiritual work helps to keep a person positive.

Your love planet Mars starts to retrograde on the 9th. This is a rarity as he only goes into retrograde motion once every two years. Singles will still date and the social life won't stop completely, but things slow down. A current relationship could seem to go backwards instead of forward. It won't be wise to make important love decisions after the 9th. Let things develop as they will.

Health still needs watching but you will see improvement from the 22nd onwards. The Sun's move into your own sign tends to boost the energy levels.

Romance might be slowing down, but not friendships. Friends and opportunities for group activities will come to you from the 22nd onwards. Friends seem very devoted to you as well. Astrology becomes more interesting during this period. Many people have their Horoscopes done under these kinds of aspects. High-tech equipment or gadgetry will come your way. Venus, the ruler of your Horoscope, moves into your 11th house of friends on the 6th and this reinforces the above.

Mercury in your sign from the 5th to the 27th brings opportunities for foreign travel. He also brings a sense of optimism to life. Educational opportunities will seek you out.

On the 22nd the planetary power begins to shift from the upper, day side of your chart to the lower, night side. It is as if it is sunset in your year. It is time to let go of the activities of day (the outer affairs of life, the career) and focus more on the activities of night – the emotional life, home and family. It is time to prepare inwardly for your next career push, which will happen next year.

Jupiter starts to move forward on the 13th, which is good news for students. They seem to have more direction in their studies now and more confidence in their intellectual faculties. Jupiter has been in Capricorn all year. Thus the urge is to learn more slowly but to delve deeper into the subject. Depth is more important than just superficial knowledge.

October

Best Days Overall: 6, 7, 15, 16, 23, 24, 25
Most Stressful Days Overall: 1, 2, 9, 10, 21, 22, 28, 29, 30
Best Days for Love: 1, 2, 3, 11, 12, 19, 20, 21, 22, 28, 29, 30
Best Days for Money: 4, 5, 13, 14, 17, 18, 21, 22, 23, 31
Best Days for Career: 6, 7, 9, 10, 15, 16, 25

Finances have been good all year but they get even better in the month ahead. On the 4th your financial planet, Pluto, starts moving forward after many months of retrograde motion. And though he is not exactly conjunct to Jupiter, he is within range. This tends to expand earnings. You have more financial clarity, more of a sense of direction. On the 23rd the Sun enters your money house and you begin a yearly financial peak. So, the month ahead becomes steadily more prosperous. The 21st to the 23rd seems a particularly strong financial period.

Retrograde activity is less than last month, and it will steadily weaken over the coming months. Little by little, though not just yet, the pace of life quickens.

You entered one of your yearly personal pleasure peaks on September 22 and this continues until the 23rd. This is a good period both to pamper the body and get it into the shape that you want it to be. Like last month, you are at the peak of personal independence at the moment. (Keep in mind that this is relative. Other people and their needs still take precedence.)

The romantic life is still complicated. Your love planet Mars is retrograde all month and is receiving stressful aspects. This can show personal challenges in the life of the beloved and it could be this that's causing the complication. But you and the beloved seem more distant (especially after the 28th). You're far apart. This is not always physical distance, but psychological distance. The challenge will be to bridge your differences. Not so easy to do, but Libra, more than most, can do it.

Friends and the opportunity for friendship are still very much flagged in the Horoscope. They seek you out. They seem supportive and devoted. It seems a happy area of life.

Venus will be in your 12th house of spirituality for most of the month, from the 2nd to the 28th. So the month ahead is spiritual too. Your focus here will improve your personal appearance – it will be better than hosts of lotions and potions.

Venus will have her solstice from October 29 to November 2. She pauses in the heavens – occupies the same degree of latitude – during that period and then changes direction. So a pause in your affairs is called for. It will be natural and good. A breather. Then comes a change of direction.

November

Best Days Overall: 2, 3, 4, 12, 20, 21, 30
Most Stressful Days Overall: 5, 6, 18, 19, 25, 26
Best Days for Love: 2, 3, 7, 8, 12, 16, 21, 22, 25, 26
Best Days for Money: 2, 11, 14, 15, 19
Best Days for Career: 5, 6, 14, 15, 24, 25

Venus is in your sign until the 21st and is powerful here, in her own sign and house. She is strong both celestially and terrestrially. Love is challenging, but it's not because of your personal appearance – which shines now. You were born with strong social gifts and a double measure of grace, but now they are even stronger. This is a good month to buy clothing or accessories – things that enhance the image – as your sense of style is very strong.

Love will improve as the month unfolds. On the 14th Mars starts to move forward again, bringing more clarity in love. Things start to move forward. On the 21st, as Venus moves away from her stressful aspect to your love planet, conflict and differences between you and the beloved weaken as well.

Retrograde activity is declining rapidly now. After the 14th 80 per cent of the planets are moving forward, and after the 29th the figure is 90 per cent. The pace of life quickens and you experience more rapid progress towards your goals.

We have our final lunar eclipse of the year on the 30th, and this one has only a mild effect on you personally. It occurs in your 9th house and affects college-level students. They are changing educational plans and are forced to make important financial changes. Your religious, philosophical and theological beliefs get tested and challenged, and this will go on for another few months. This is a good thing, though not always pleasant. Some of these beliefs need to be modified or dropped completely. This is important as they shape how you live your life. The spouse, partner or current love can have challenges with siblings, sibling figures, cars and communication equipment. Your siblings or sibling figures will have their relationships tested. Once again there are career changes and dramas in the lives of bosses, parents, parent figures and authority figures in your life.

The month ahead is prosperous – in fact it is a banner financial month. You're in the midst of a yearly financial peak until the 21st and it might even continue after that date. Your financial planet Pluto is moving forward and in a pretty exact conjunction with Jupiter, the planet of abundance. A move could happen. The family circle is likely to expand. You have good aspects for buying or selling a home. Family support is great.

Health is not as stressed as it was in January or June and July, but it still needs watching. Keep in mind our previous discussions of this. Review the health section of the yearly report.

December

Best Days Overall: 1, 9, 10, 17, 18, 27, 28
Most Stressful Days Overall: 2, 3, 15, 16, 22, 23, 29, 30, 31
Best Days for Love: 2, 3, 5, 6, 11, 12, 13, 14, 22, 23
Best Days for Money: 8, 11, 12, 16, 25, 26, 27
Best Days for Career: 2, 3, 5, 6, 13, 14, 24, 29, 30, 31

Health is an issue this month, especially after the 21st. The good news is that it is nowhere near as stressful as earlier in the year. And, since two major planets are changing signs and moving away from their stressful aspects with you, health is going to be a lot better in 2021 than in 2020. So, review our discussion of this area in the yearly report. Do your best to maximize your energy levels. Rest when tired, and keep your focus on the really important things in your life and let lesser things go. Try to schedule in more massages, foot reflexology treatments or other health treatments over this period.

We have another eclipse this month – the sixth and final one of the year. It is a solar eclipse on the 14th that occurs in your 3rd house, affecting cars, phones, computers and other technological gadgetry. They can behave erratically and sometimes will require repairs or replacement. Perhaps upgrades are needed – this is the positive side of it. The money people in your life are making important financial changes. Siblings and sibling figures need to redefine themselves: their images, appearances and self-concepts. In the coming months this will manifest as wardrobe changes, changes of hair style and a new public image. Students below college level make changes in educational plans and perhaps change schools. There are disruptions in their schools. Parents or parent figures have spiritual changes. Friendships get tested and there are probably dramas in the lives of friends and shakeups in trade or professional organizations that you're involved with. This eclipse is relatively benign for you, but it won't hurt to take it easy this period anyway.

Love is happy until the 21st; after then there are more challenges. Two long-term planets in the 5th house from the 20th onwards – Jupiter and Saturn – signal a couple of love affairs, but these are more entertainment than love.

Finance should be good this month. Your financial planet is moving forward and receiving decent aspects. More importantly, Venus will be in your money house until the 15th. This shows focus and personal involvement. You spend on yourself and project an image of wealth to others. You are seen as a money person. Personal appearance and overall demeanour seem important in earnings.

Until the 21st there is a great focus on intellectual interests. The mind is sharper and learns better. You communicate well. It is a good period for students, teachers, writers, marketers and traders. After the 21st the focus is on home and family. Things seem a lot quieter and better here than they have been all year.

Scorpio

♏

THE SCORPION

Birthdays from
23rd October to
22nd November

Personality Profile

SCORPIO AT A GLANCE

Element – Water

Ruling Planet – Pluto
   Co-ruling Planet – Mars
   Career Planet – Sun
   Love Planet – Venus
   Money Planet – Jupiter
   Planet of Health and Work – Mars
   Planet of Home and Family Life – Uranus

Colour – red-violet

Colour that promotes love, romance and social harmony – green

Colour that promotes earning power – blue

Gems – bloodstone, malachite, topaz

Metals – iron, radium, steel

Scents – cherry blossom, coconut, sandalwood, watermelon

Quality – fixed (= stability)

Quality most needed for balance – a wider view of things

Strongest virtues – loyalty, concentration, determination, courage, depth

Deepest needs – to penetrate and transform

Characteristics to avoid – jealousy, vindictiveness, fanaticism

Signs of greatest overall compatibility – Cancer, Pisces

Signs of greatest overall incompatibility – Taurus, Leo, Aquarius

Sign most helpful to career – Leo

Sign most helpful for emotional support – Aquarius

Sign most helpful financially – Sagittarius

Sign best for marriage and/or partnerships – Taurus

Sign most helpful for creative projects – Pisces

Best Sign to have fun with – Pisces

Signs most helpful in spiritual matters – Cancer, Libra

Best day of the week – Tuesday

Understanding a Scorpio

One symbol of the sign of Scorpio is the phoenix. If you meditate upon the legend of the phoenix you will begin to understand the Scorpio character – his or her powers and abilities, interests and deepest urges.

The phoenix of mythology was a bird that could recreate and reproduce itself. It did so in a most intriguing way: it would seek a fire – usually in a religious temple – fly into it, consume itself in the flames and then emerge a new bird. If this is not the ultimate, most profound transformation, then what is?

Transformation is what Scorpios are all about – in their minds, bodies, affairs and relationships (Scorpios are also society's transformers). To change something in a natural, not an artificial way, involves a transformation from within. This type of change is radical change as opposed to a mere cosmetic make-over. Some people think that change means altering just their appearance, but this is not the kind of thing that interests a Scorpio. Scorpios seek deep, fundamental change. Since real change always proceeds from within, a Scorpio is very interested in – and usually accustomed to – the inner, intimate and philosophical side of life.

Scorpios are people of depth and intellect. If you want to interest them you must present them with more than just a superficial image. You and your interests, projects or business deals must have real substance to them in order to stimulate a Scorpio. If they haven't, he or she will find you out – and that will be the end of the story.

If we observe life – the processes of growth and decay – we see the transformational powers of Scorpio at work all the time. The caterpillar changes itself into a butterfly; the infant grows into a child and then an adult. To Scorpios this definite and perpetual transformation is not something to be feared. They see it as a normal part of life. This acceptance of transformation gives Scorpios the key to understanding the true meaning of life.

Scorpios' understanding of life (including life's weaknesses) makes them powerful warriors – in all senses of the word. Add to this their depth, patience and endurance and you have a powerful personality. Scorpios have good, long memories and can at times be quite vindictive – they can wait years to get their revenge. As a friend, though, there is no one more loyal and true than a Scorpio. Few are willing to make the sacrifices that a Scorpio will make for a true friend.

The results of a transformation are quite obvious, although the process of transformation is invisible and secret. This is why Scorpios are considered secretive in nature. A seed will not grow properly if you keep digging it up and exposing it to the light of day. It must stay buried – invisible – until it starts to grow. In the same manner, Scorpios fear revealing too much about themselves or their hopes to other people. However, they will be more than happy to let you see the finished product – but only when it is completely unwrapped. On the other hand, Scorpios like knowing everyone else's secrets as much as they dislike anyone knowing theirs.

Finance

Love, birth, life as well as death are Nature's most potent transformations; Scorpios are interested in all of these. In our society, money is a transforming power, too, and a Scorpio is interested in money for that reason. To a Scorpio money is power, money causes change, money controls. It is the power of money that fascinates them. But Scorpios can be too materialistic if they are not careful. They can be overly awed by the power of money, to a point where they think that money rules the world.

Even the term 'plutocrat' comes from Pluto, the ruler of the sign of Scorpio. Scorpios will – in one way or another – achieve the financial status they strive for. When they do so they are careful in the way they handle their wealth. Part of this financial carefulness is really a kind of honesty, for Scorpios are usually involved with other people's money – as accountants, lawyers, stockbrokers or corporate managers – and when you handle other people's money you have to be more cautious than when you handle your own.

In order to fulfil their financial goals, Scorpios have important lessons to learn. They need to develop qualities that do not come naturally to them, such as breadth of vision, optimism, faith, trust and, above all, generosity. They need to see the wealth in Nature and in life, as well as in its more obvious forms of money and power. When they develop generosity their financial potential reaches great heights, for Jupiter, the Lord of Opulence and Good Fortune, is Scorpio's money planet.

Career and Public Image

Scorpio's greatest aspiration in life is to be considered by society as a source of light and life. They want to be leaders, to be stars. But they follow a very different road than do Leos, the other stars of the zodiac. A Scorpio arrives at the goal secretly, without ostentation; a Leo pursues it openly. Scorpios seek the glamour and fun of the rich and famous in a restrained, discreet way.

Scorpios are by nature introverted and tend to avoid the limelight. But if they want to attain their highest career goals they need to open up a bit and to express themselves more. They need to stop hiding their light under a bushel and let it shine. Above all, they need to let go of any vindictiveness and small-mindedness. All their gifts and insights were given to them for one important reason – to serve life and to increase the joy of living for others.

Love and Relationships

Scorpio is another zodiac sign that likes committed, clearly defined, structured relationships. They are cautious about marriage, but when they do commit to a relationship they tend to be faithful – and heaven help the mate caught or even suspected of infidelity! The jealousy of the Scorpio is legendary. They can be so intense in their jealousy that even the thought or intention of infidelity will be detected and is likely to cause as much of a storm as if the deed had actually been done.

Scorpios tend to settle down with those who are wealthier than they are. They usually have enough intensity for two, so in their partners they seek someone pleasant, hard-working, amiable, stable and easy-going. They want someone they can lean on, someone loyal behind them as they fight the battles of life. To a Scorpio a partner, be it a lover or a friend, is a real partner – not an adversary. Most of all a Scorpio is looking for an ally, not a competitor.

If you are in love with a Scorpio you will need a lot of patience. It takes a long time to get to know Scorpios, because they do not reveal themselves readily. But if you persist and your motives are honourable, you will gradually be allowed into a Scorpio's inner chambers of the mind and heart.

Home and Domestic Life

Uranus is ruler of Scorpio's 4th solar house of home and family. Uranus is the planet of science, technology, changes and democracy. This tells us a lot about a Scorpio's conduct in the home and what he or she needs in order to have a happy, harmonious home life.

Scorpios can sometimes bring their passion, intensity and wilfulness into the home and family, which is not always the place for these qualities. These traits are good for the warrior and the transformer, but not so good for the nurturer and family member. Because of this (and also because of their need for change and transformation) the Scorpio may be prone to sudden changes of residence. If not carefully constrained, the sometimes inflexible Scorpio can produce turmoil and sudden upheavals within the family.

Scorpios need to develop some of the virtues of Aquarius in order to cope better with domestic matters. There is a need to build a team spirit at home, to treat family activities as truly group activities – family members should all have a say in what does and does not get done. For at times a Scorpio can be most dictatorial. When a Scorpio gets dictatorial it is much worse than if a Leo or Capricorn (the two other power signs in the zodiac) does. For the dictatorship of a Scorpio is applied with more zeal, passion, intensity and concentration than is true of either a Leo or Capricorn. Obviously this can be unbearable to family members – especially if they are sensitive types.

In order for a Scorpio to get the full benefit of the emotional support that a family can give, he or she needs to let go of conservatism and be a bit more experimental, to explore new techniques in childrearing, be more democratic with family members and to try to manage things by consensus rather than by autocratic edict.

Horoscope for 2020

Major Trends

The bottom half – the night side – of your Horoscope is dominant this year. There is only one long-term planet above the horizon. And while the day side will get stronger as the year progresses, it will never outweigh the night side. So the year ahead is more about home, family and emotional issues – psychological issues – rather than outer activities. More on this later.

Health looks good most of the year. (Next year will be a different story, however; you'll have to work harder on health.) This year there is only one (sometimes two) long-term planets in stressful alignment. More later.

Your 3rd house of communication and intellectual interests is easily the strongest in your Horoscope this year, which is good for students. It shows a focus on their studies. They are working hard and this spells success. It is also a good aspect for teachers, writers, marketing and PR people. They work hard but there is success.

Four lunar eclipses this year (twice as many as usual) impact on college-level students, signalling much change and disruption. They can change schools, change courses, change their educational plans. These eclipses will also test your personal religion and philosophy. Your beliefs get tested multiple times. Some will have to be revised, some will be discarded. It will not be wise to travel during these eclipse periods. (We will discuss them more fully in the monthly reports.)

Finances look excellent this year, Scorpio. Your financial planet, Jupiter, travels with Pluto and Saturn on and off during the year. This shows that you earn your money in enjoyable ways and there is luck in speculations. More on this later.

Spiritual Neptune has been in your 5th house for many years now and will be there for many more to come. So your tastes in entertainment are being refined and spiritualized. There is a greater affinity for the fine arts. Children and children figures in your life seem more spiritual as well.

Love is perhaps the most challenging area this year (and for years to come). Love is exciting, but unstable. Existing relationships are being severely tested. More on this later.

Your most important areas of interest this year are communication and intellectual pursuits; home and family (from March 23 to July 1 and from December 18 onwards); children, fun and creativity; health and work (from June 28 onwards); and love, romance and social activities.

Your paths of greatest fulfilment this year will be communication and intellectual interests (until December 20); home and family (after December 20); religion, philosophy, higher learning and foreign travel (until May 6); and career (from May 6 onwards).

Health

(Please note that this is an astrological perspective on health and not a medical one. In days of yore there was no difference, both these perspectives were identical. But now there could be quite a difference. For a medical perspective, please consult your doctor or health practitioner.)

Health, as we mentioned above, looks good this year – especially early in the year. From March 23 to July 1, Saturn will join Uranus in stressful alignment with you, but this is generally not enough to cause serious problems. Your 6th house becomes strong after the end of June, showing more focus on health which is exactly what is needed. This focus will stand you in good stead for the period after December 20. Then you will have three long-term planets in stressful alignment and health will need more attention. This will be the case next year too.

But for most of the year, health looks good. However, you can make it even better. Give more attention to the following – the vulnerable areas of your Horoscope (the reflex points are shown in the chart overleaf):

- The colon, bladder and sexual organs. These are always important for Scorpio, as are safe sex and sexual moderation. Listen to your body and not your mind and you will know when enough is enough. A herbal colon cleanse every now and then would be good.
- The head, face and scalp. Regular scalp and face massage should be part of your regular routine. The plates in the skull tend to shift

Important foot reflexology points for the year ahead

Try to massage all of the foot on a regular basis – the top of the foot as well as the bottom – but pay extra attention to the points highlighted on the chart. When you massage, be aware of 'sore spots' as these need special attention. It's also a good idea to massage the ankles, and especially below them.

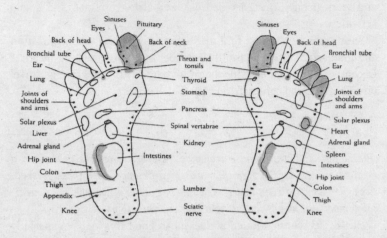

and need to be in right alignment – craniosacral therapy is also good for this.

- The adrenal glands are always important for Scorpio and the vital thing with the adrenals is to avoid anger and fear – the two emotions that stress them out.

- The musculature. You don't need to be a bodybuilder with bulging muscles, you just need good muscle tone to avoid knocking the spine and skeleton out of alignment, as this will cause all kinds of other problems. So vigorous physical exercise – according to your age and stage in life – is important.

- The heart is important between March 23 and July 1 and from December 18 onwards, Scorpio, and will be important next year too. The thing with the heart is to avoid worry and anxiety – we can define this as a lack of faith. Meditation will be a big help for this.

Mars, your health planet, is a relatively fast-moving planet and this year he moves through six of the signs and houses of your Horoscope. Thus there are many short-term health trends that are best discussed in the monthly reports.

In general, hot, spicy foods – things that heat up the body – are healing for you. Onions, garlic (the penicillin of the ancient world), jalapeños and cayenne pepper are healing foods. Hotter climates are better healthwise for you than colder ones. If you live in a cold climate make sure to bundle up in the winter. Heat is a good therapy for you and you benefit from saunas, steam rooms, hot baths and fire and candle-lighting ceremonies. (These bring in metaphysical fire, which is good.)

The fire element is weak this year. There will be periods where it gets stronger, but overall it is weak, and there will be periods where there is no fire in your chart. So keeping warm is even more important than usual.

Home and Family

This area of life becomes more important as the year progresses. Saturn enters your 4th house from March 23 to July 1 and then again (this time for the long term) on December 18. Jupiter enters your 4th house on December 20 and will be there for almost all of next year. So a move or renovation of the home can happen later this year, but is more likely in 2021.

When Saturn is in your 4th house by himself, the home and family seem like a burden and discipline. More family responsibilities are placed on you and you have to do your duty. These are not things you're able to avoid. A parent or parent figure seems more controlling than usual, and seems pessimistic. There is a greater tendency to depression. But things will lighten up when Jupiter enters the 4th house late in December. He lifts the gloom and injects a note of optimism and happiness. Where things looked bitter for a while, now they are bittersweet. Women of childbearing age will be more fertile after December 20 – and for the next two years. A pregnancy this year seems complicated though. There is more work involved. A pregnancy next year seems smoother.

Your family planet, Uranus, has been in your 7th house since March last year, and will remain there for years to come. This tends to show more socializing with the family and with people who are like family to you. A parent or parent figure seems very involved in your current relationship or with your love life in general. This parent probably means well, but can destabilize things.

With your family planet in your 7th house, you will be working to make the home more beautiful, more attractive. You're working to make it more of a social centre. You're having more parties at home and entertaining more from home. Probably you will redecorate, and perhaps multiple times. You're probably buying objects of beauty for the home too.

Saturn moving into your 4th house signals an upgrade of communication systems in the home, and investment in the latest communication equipment. It would not be a surprise if you held lectures or workshops in your home and made it more of an educational centre too. This will go on for the next two years, but you're feeling the beginnings of it this year.

Jupiter's move into your 4th house shows that you are spending more on the home and family – it seems like a good investment for you. It also indicates earning money from home, installing home offices and the like. Family support will be stronger – but there are challenges here. (More on the financial aspects below.)

The parents or parent figures in your life seem more restless this year. Moves could happen, perhaps multiple moves. One of them will be travelling around a lot and living in different places.

Siblings and sibling figures could be making important renovations or repairs this year – probably from June 28 onwards. They have an opportunity to move in March. Children or children figures in your life are having a stable family year. The same goes for grandchildren (if you have them) and for those who play that role in your life.

If you're planning major repairs or renovations, March 31 to May 13 is a good time. Redecorating can happen all year, but March 5 to April 3 is especially good.

Finance and Career

You're coming out of a two-year stretch of prosperity and financial expansion this year. By now most of your short-term goals should have been attained and you're more focused on your intellectual and mental development. The money house is basically empty this year; only short-term planets move through there. This tends to the status quo in finances. Last year was prosperous, and the year ahead will be too.

Your financial planet Jupiter spends most of the year in your 3rd house. This gives many messages. You spend more on intellectual pursuits – on books, magazines, courses, lectures and seminars – but you can also earn from these kinds of activities. This is a good year for teachers, writers, marketers, PR and advertising people. Jupiter travelling with Saturn for most of the year further reinforces this. These aspects are also good for trading – buying and selling.

Your financial planet will also be travelling with Pluto, the ruler of your Horoscope, for much of 2020, with varying degrees of exactness. This too shows prosperity. You spend on yourself. You invest in yourself. You cultivate the image of a prosperous person and people see you this way. This also signals that money and financial opportunity seek you out and there's nothing much that you need to do. Often this indicates financial windfalls. This is a very fortunate financial aspect.

Jupiter in the sign of Capricorn almost all year shows financial conservatism – sound financial judgement – another signal for prosperity. You're not worried by short-term fluctuations in investments but looking at their long-term worth. You have a good sense of this. This is an excellent year for setting up budget plans, savings and investment programmes. You have good financial discipline.

Though the year is prosperous, it's not about 'quick cash'. It's about attaining wealth in a step-by-step methodical kind of way. The financial planet in Capricorn favours conservative investments – investments in blue chip, stable, large cap companies listed on major stock exchanges.

Although this is a good financial year, it is not an especially strong career year. As we mentioned earlier, almost all the planets are below the horizon of your chart. Your 4th house of home and family becomes ever stronger this year while your 10th house of career is basically empty. Yet, because the North Node of the Moon (an abstract point) will be in your 10th house from May 6 onwards, there is a sense of fulfilment in the career. Perhaps you feel happy where you are in your career and can now focus on home, family and emotional issues. Also, a lot of your focus on the home, family and psychological infrastructure is career motivated. You have to get this part of life in order before you can attain your true career goals. You're in a preparation stage for the career.

Love and Social Life

This is an area that is both exciting and challenging at the same time. It is much easier for singles. It shows someone who is 'playing the field', experimenting in love and relationship. Eventually singles will learn what makes them happy. It is a trial-and-error process. Marriage is neither likely nor advisable for a while.

The good news for singles is that love is exciting and stimulating. There is never a dull moment. Love and romantic opportunities can happen at any time and any place – often when you least expect it or with people you least expected. You can be taking out the rubbish or doing some other mundane task and 'boom' – you meet someone. The only issue is the stability of these encounters. They can occur suddenly and dissolve just as suddenly. But no matter, there is always the next one.

For those of you who are married or in a serious relationship, this is a challenging time for love. I have seen relationships survive these kinds of aspects, but it was never a smooth ride. The commitment needs to be very intense. One needs to be willing to put a lot of work into the relationship. The spouse, partner or current love seems very restless and rebellious. He or she wants freedom and change. If the current relationship allows for this, it could work.

As we said earlier, there is more socializing from home and with family members. For singles, romantic opportunities can come through the family or family connections. Love opportunities could be close to home. An old flame from the past – or someone who has those personality traits – can come back into the picture. This can be another destabilizing factor in a current relationship. Generally these 'revisits' are for healing purposes. Old issues get resolved and you can both move on.

There are many short-term trends in love, because your love planet, Venus, moves so fast; romance can happen in many ways and through many people. This is just your nature. Your love needs and love attitudes also tend to change quickly. These depend on where Venus is at any given time and the aspects she receives. These are best dealt with in the monthly reports.

Four lunar eclipses this year will test the marriages or current relationships of siblings and sibling figures. They need not break up – good relationships tend to survive – but there is more disruption. If the relationship is essentially flawed, it is doubtful whether it will survive all these eclipses.

The marriage or current relationship of a parent or parent figure gets tested between March 23 and July 1. But things will ease up after December 20.

Children and children figures in your life have a quiet, stable kind of love year.

Self-improvement

The Scorpio mind is deep, deep, deep. No one goes deeper into any subject than Scorpio. Just memorizing facts and figures is not Scorpio's way. They have to really understand a subject, which is why they make such good researchers and intelligence people. They want to know what is behind the facts. This tendency is even stronger this year as your 3rd house is the strongest in your Horoscope. So take courses in subjects that interest you and go deeply into them. Take your time. It will pay off. This is a year for restocking your intellectual capital and making intellectual breakthroughs.

Saturn enters your 4th house for the long term in December. But before he does that he will make a brief foray there from March 23 to July 1. This, as we mentioned, brings added family responsibilities to you, which you can't avoid. Nor should you try. Take them on and you'll find that you have help in handling them. The other issue with Saturn in the 4th house is the emotional life. The 4th house has deeper meanings than just home and family. It rules your moods and emotions

– your psychological life – and this will be a focus for at least two years to come.

Saturn moving through the 4th house signals a need to put the emotional life in right order. It means learning to direct and manage the emotions so that they further your goals. This was the way things were always intended to be, but it needs to be done correctly. Directing and managing emotions is not the same as repressing them. Repression cannot go on for too long as eventually the negative feeling will be expressed and probably in a more destructive way than the situation demands. Nor will repression be good for your overall health. So negative feelings (many of them quite natural) need to be expressed in harmless ways. There are various ways to do this. Those of you working with a therapist can get release through talking through your feelings. But you can also write out your bad feelings when they arise, or speak them into some recording device. Hold nothing back. Express what it is you feel. No need for politeness here. This is between you and the recorder. When you are finished (and you'll know when to stop) tear up the paper or erase the recording. Don't reread or listen back again. It is out of your system and you can go forward with your life. When you release negative feelings like this, doors open in the mind and you can see solutions (or ways to proceed) for the problems you feel negative about. The point is you need not be a victim of your emotional states. If you are a meditator, your meditations will go much better than before.*

Neptune has been in your 5th house for many years now and, as we mentioned, your taste in entertainment and fun is becoming spiritual-ized and refined, as is your personal creativity. Those involved in the creative arts are really feeling it strongly.

---

* There are other methods too. These issues are discussed in my book *A Technique for Meditation*, and those who want to go into it more deeply can visit my blog at www.spiritual-stories.com.

Month-by-month Forecasts

January

Best Days Overall: 1, 9, 10, 18, 19, 27, 28
Most Stressful Days Overall: 5, 6, 12, 24, 25, 26
Best Days for Love: 5, 6, 13, 14, 18, 19, 27, 28
Best Days for Money: 5, 6, 14, 20, 21, 22, 23
Best Days for Career: 5, 6, 12, 14, 15, 24, 25

You begin your year near the midnight hour (figuratively speaking) of your year. In addition, 80 per cent – and sometimes 90 per cent – of the planets are below the horizon, the night side of the chart. So this is a period for dealing with the home, family and your emotional well-ness. Even your career planet, the Sun, will be in your 4th house from the 20th onwards. Home and family is the actual mission, the real career, this period (though sometimes this signals someone who pursues the career from home, too). This is a year of preparation for future career success. In order to attain your outer goals you need the right foundation. And this you are building in the year ahead.

You begin your year with the Eastern sector of self dominance, so you are still in a period of personal independence. Personal initiative matters. If you need to make changes for your happiness, make them early in the month however; by the 20th, the planetary power shifts to the social West and these changes will be more difficult to make.

A lunar eclipse on the 10th occurs in your 9th house and impacts on three other planets. So it is a powerful one. Its impact on Pluto, the ruler of your Horoscope, shows that you are personally affected by the eclipse. There can be a detox of the body and a re-evaluation of your image and presentation to the world. It also affects those of you who are students – either at college or pre-college level, bringing disruptions at school, changes of schools and changes in educational plans. Cars and communication equipment will get tested and can behave erratically. Siblings and sibling figures have personal dramas, and also need to redefine themselves in the coming months. The impact on Mercury reinforces the testing of cars and communication equipment, but also shows a testing of your high-tech gadgetry. The beloved is going through many changes anyway, but this eclipse brings financial changes. So take it nice and easy this eclipse period.

Health is good this month but needs more attention after the 20th. Your lowered energy is probably not pathology, but just the natural shift of the short-term planets. Overall health is good. Your health planet Mars will be in your money house from the 2nd onwards. Thus good health for you means good financial health. It also shows earning through work.

February

Best Days Overall: 6, 7, 14, 15, 23, 24, 25
Most Stressful Days Overall: 1, 2, 8, 9, 21, 22, 28, 29
Best Days for Love: 1, 2, 7, 8, 16, 17, 26, 27, 28, 29
Best Days for Money: 1, 2, 10, 11, 16, 17, 19, 20, 28, 29
Best Days for Career: 3, 4, 8, 9, 12, 13, 23, 24

Though health is good this month, it won't hurt to rest and relax more until the 19th. Overall energy is not up to its usual standard. You will see a dramatic improvement from the 19th onwards.

Mars has been in your money house since January 2 and he will remain there until the 16th. This shows money that comes from work – from productive service. It is not the aspect of a lottery winner. It also shows someone who spends more on health and health products and who can earn from this area as well. On the 16th Mars enters your 3rd house and the sign of Capricorn. Healthwise, the spine, knees, teeth and skeletal alignment become important. Good posture is vital. Finances are good this month but will get much better next month. Important financial developments are taking place.

Love has been complicated for a while, ever since Uranus moved into your 7th house. Until the 7th it seems very happy (relatively speaking). Your social grace is strong. A romantic opportunity presents itself between the 1st and the 3rd. Love is about fun until the 7th. You are attracted to spiritual-type people and to people who can show you a good time. On the 7th Venus moves into Aries and your 6th house – not her favourite position. She is weakened in this sign. Astrologers call it her 'detriment' and your love planet is far from her natural home.

Add to this she receives stressful aspects. So love is more challenging this period. There is a tendency to jump into relationships too quickly. You are a love-at-first-sight kind of person at the moment. And, you tend to meet these kinds of people. There are opportunities for an office romance – but these things are very complicated.

Venus has her solstice from the 8th to the 10th. She pauses in the heavens – occupies the same degree of latitude – and then changes direction. So a pause in your social life and then a change of direction is happening. This is nothing to be alarmed about. It is as natural as the sunrise.

On the 19th the Sun moves into your 5th house and you begin a yearly personal pleasure peak. It is time to have fun and to indulge the child within. You will find that you're getting on better with children too.

March

Best Days Overall: 4, 5, 12, 13, 22, 23
Most Stressful Days Overall: 1, 6, 7, 19, 20, 27, 28
Best Days for Love: 1, 8, 17, 18, 27, 28
Best Days for Money: 1, 8, 9, 14, 15, 17, 18, 27, 28
Best Days for Career: 4, 5, 6, 7, 12, 13, 24, 25

The Western, social sector of your chart grows ever more powerful this month. It has been dominant since January 20, so your focus is more on other people rather than yourself now. The cultivation of social skills is more important than personal initiative or professional skills. This is a time to let others have their way, so long as it isn't destructive. It is as if you take a vacation from yourself. Your good will come through the good graces of others.

The month ahead is very prosperous. Big paydays are happening. Jupiter, your financial planet, travels with Pluto, the ruler of your Horoscope, and there are windfalls and happy financial opportunities. Intellectual property is marketable and rises in value. The money people in your life are close to you and helpful. There is good fortune in trading – buying and selling – in sales, marketing and PR. Siblings and sibling figures in your life are also prospering and seem involved in your finances. Financial opportunities can come from neighbours as well.

Mars travels with Jupiter from the 15th to the 21st, indicating happy – and lucrative – job opportunities. The power in your 6th house of health and work from the 20th onwards also indicates job opportunities. If you hire others, you increase your workforce now.

Love is in the air, but it is highly unstable. Venus travels with Uranus from the 6th to the 9th, which can shake up an existing relationship. It can also bring a new and sudden relationship to you. Love will not be boring, that's for sure. More like a soap opera.

Your career planet, the Sun, travels with Neptune from the 6th to the 9th. Good intuition is important careerwise. Children and children figures are helping the career. The dream life will be more active at this time and is likely to shed light on career issues. There is a need these days (until the 20th) to enjoy your career path – to have fun as you work. Sometimes this signals entertaining a client or being entertained by someone involved in your career.

Health is good this month. You can enhance it further in the ways mentioned in the yearly report. Add to this back and knee massage too.

On the 20th the Sun enters your 6th house. A good work ethic will be noticed by superiors and will enhance the career. This transit reveals a focus on health. Hopefully this focus will involve healthy lifestyles and 'preventive medicine'. Sometimes when health is good a focus on this area shows a tendency to hypochondria – a tendency to magnify little things into big things. Be careful of this.

April

Best Days Overall: 1, 2, 9, 10, 18, 19, 28, 29
Most Stressful Days Overall: 3, 4, 15, 16, 23, 24, 30
Best Days for Love: 7, 8, 15, 16, 17, 23, 24, 25, 26
Best Days for Money: 6, 11, 12, 14, 24
Best Days for Career: 3, 4, 12, 23, 30

Health is more delicate this month. Saturn moved into stressful alignment with you on March 23 and Mars joined him on March 31. On the 19th of this month the Sun also moves into stressful alignment. So you need to watch your energy more. Those of you born early in the sign of Scorpio – October 23–25 – are going to feel this the strongest, but all of you will feel it to some degree. Your focus on health until the 19th will certainly help you after this date.

Prosperity is still very strong all month. Jupiter and Pluto are travelling together. Big paydays and happy financial opportunities are still happening. Prosperity will be even stronger after the 19th.

Love is the main headline this month. The social life is very active and there are many romantic opportunities for singles. You seem to get on with all kinds of people these days – the high and mighty, corporate types, creative types, spiritual types. The only issue, as has been the case for a while, is the stability of these things. Still, it is exciting while it's happening. There's no need to project too far into the future. Just enjoy things for what they are.

Career is becoming more important this month. On the 19th the upper half of the Horoscope, the day side, starts to become strong. Though it will never overpower the lower, night side, there are times when it will be equal in power. So, you, like many people these days, need to balance a successful career with a successful home and family life. You will bounce from one to the other. Your career planet, the Sun, will travel with Uranus from the 24th to the 26th. This shows some sudden career development – some sudden event. Perhaps a change is needed. The family seems supportive of the career, and the bosses in your life seem supportive of your family goals.

Your career planet will be in your 7th house from April 19. Thus, you further your career by social means. A lot of your socializing is career related. You mingle with people of power, people who can help you careerwise. Social contacts boost the career and open doors for you. It will be beneficial to attend the right kinds of gatherings and perhaps to host a few as well.

Mercury travels with Neptune on the 3rd and 4th, signalling a hyperactive, revelatory dream life over that period. Those of you involved in the creative arts will receive inspiration.

May

Best Days Overall: 6, 7, 15, 16, 25, 26
Most Stressful Days Overall: 1, 13, 14, 20, 21, 27, 28
Best Days for Love: 4, 5, 13, 14, 20, 21, 23, 24
Best Days for Money: 3, 8, 9, 12, 22
Best Days for Career: 1, 2, 3, 11, 23, 27, 28

Venus, your love planet, went 'out of bounds' on April 13 and will remain so all this month. You are way outside your normal sphere in both love and your spiritual life. It could be that singles are dating more 'exotic' people than normal, or that the search for love takes you to new places. You are exploring spiritual systems and practices that are outside the norm as well. You feel there are no answers in your normal sphere and thus have a need to go beyond. In unknown territory the social confidence is weakened – this is especially so after the 13th as Venus starts to retrograde. So enjoy your love life (it is exciting and adventurous) but don't make important decisions just yet – and especially not after the 13th.

Venus spends the month in your 8th house, thus sexual magnetism seems all important in love. But other things also seem important. There is a need for mental compatibility, for ease of communication too.

The planetary power is still in the Western, social sector this month. And, until the 20th, you're still in the midst of a yearly love and romantic peak. So the social life is dominant. Other people and their interests take precedence over your own. You might seem more dependent, but your good social skills will bring your good to you. It will happen through others. Continue to let others have their way, so long as it isn't destructive. Your way is probably not the most appropriate these days.

Health improves dramatically after the 20th. In the meantime you can enhance your health in the ways mentioned in the yearly report. Until the 13th calf and ankle massage will be beneficial. It is also important to maintain good emotional health. Keep your moods positive and constructive. After the 13th your health planet Mars moves into Pisces, your 5th house. This aspect favours foot reflexology or foot whirlpool treatments. If you feel under the weather soak in a natural spring, lake or river. If this is impractical, soak in the bathtub at home. Spiritual therapies will be powerful from the 13th onward, and if you feel under the weather a spiritual healer can help.

Prosperity is still very strong this month, but you seem indecisive about some of the opportunities. Pluto, your ruling planet, went retrograde on April 25 and will be moving backwards for many months. So it is time to reassess your personal goals. Self-confidence and self-esteem could be weaker than usual, but since it is a social period, this might be good. Too much self-will is not called for right now.

Your favourite 8th house becomes powerful after the 20th. So, you are involved in the things that Scorpio does best – personal transformation and reinvention, decluttering the life, the mind and the emotions.

June

Best Days Overall: 3, 4, 11, 12, 13, 21, 22, 28, 29
Most Stressful Days Overall: 9, 10, 16, 17, 18, 24
Best Days for Love: 1, 9, 10, 16, 17, 18, 19, 20
Best Days for Money: 5, 6, 8, 18, 27, 30
Best Days for Career: 1, 9, 10, 20, 21, 24

Retrograde activity spikes to the yearly maximum this month (it will do so again in September). From the 23rd to the 25th 60 per cent of the planets will be retrograde, and after the 25th it will still be 50 per cent. Events in the world slow down. What you read in the newspapers should be taken with a few grains of salt. The main impact on you is the retrograde of Venus, Jupiter and Pluto – three very important planets in your chart. Pluto is the ruler of your Horoscope and represents your personal desires. Venus rules your love life and Jupiter rules your finances. So all these areas are slowing down. Yet prosperity will still happen, albeit with delays and glitches. Jupiter is still travelling with Pluto this month. And the love life will improve after the 25th when Venus starts to move forward.

It is good to use these retrograde periods to review your goals and see where improvements can be made. It's very important to attain some degree of mental clarity about these things. Then, later on in the year, you'll be in a good position to move forward as the planets start moving forward again.

We have two eclipses this month. The first is a lunar eclipse on the 5th, and the second a solar eclipse on the 21st. Eclipses always bring change and disruption, but the changes can happen with a delayed reaction this time because of the retrogrades.

The lunar eclipse of the 5th occurs in Sagittarius, your money house. Thus important financial changes have to be made. Your financial thinking and planning haven't been realistic and corrections are necessary. But, as we mentioned, think things through thoroughly before you make the changes. Look at all the angles. Get as many facts as you can. This eclipse also affects Venus, the love planet, so love is getting tested too. It can also bring spiritual changes – changes in your practice, teachings and teachers. There are shakeups in a spiritual or charitable organization you belong to. The gurus or guru figures in your life have personal dramas. Mars, your health and work planet is also affected. Thus there can be job changes either with your present company or a new one. The conditions of work change or there can be disruptions in the workplace. There are changes in your health regime too. Every lunar eclipse impacts on college-level Scorpios, and this one is no different (and there will be more as the year continues). So there are changes in educational plans, perhaps changes of school and turmoil and disruption in your school. There are shakeups and crises in your place of worship and in the lives of worship leaders.

The solar eclipse of 21st also impacts on college-level students, your place of worship and the lives of worship leaders. It is almost, but not quite, a repeat of the lunar eclipse. It brings career changes, changes in the management of your company or industry and dramas in the lives of bosses, parents or parent figures.

July

Best Days Overall: 1, 9, 10, 19, 20, 27, 28
Most Stressful Days Overall: 6, 7, 8, 14, 15, 21, 22
Best Days for Love: 6, 7, 8, 14, 15, 16, 17, 25, 26
Best Days for Money: 2, 3, 4, 5, 14, 15, 23, 24, 29, 30, 31
Best Days for Career: 1, 9, 10, 20, 21, 22, 29

Another lunar eclipse, the third one this year, affects all students – college level and below. It occurs on the 5th and in your 3rd house. It will also have an impact on three other planets – Mercury, Jupiter and Mars – although it is more of a sideswipe than a direct hit.

Thus, students suffer disruptions at school. There are changes (once again) in educational plans. Cars and communication equipment get tested and could need repairs or replacement. Drive more carefully this period. Unnecessary travel – foreign or domestic – should be avoided, and rescheduled for a better time. There are shake-ups in your place of worship and personal dramas in the lives of worship leaders. Legal issues take a dramatic turn, one way or another. Your religious beliefs get tested and some will have to be discarded while others will be modified – fine-tuned. Siblings and sibling figures have to redefine themselves – their image, personality and appearance. The money people in your life make important financial changes. The impact on Mercury shows a minor testing of computers and high-tech equipment. The spouse, partner or current love has to make financial course corrections. You too need to make financial changes. There can be dramas at the workplace, job changes and changes in the conditions of work. The health regime will be changed in coming months too.

With Saturn moving away from his stressful aspect with you on the 1st, health is very much improved, although it will need some attention again on the 22nd. This is nothing serious – just the natural action of the short-term planets. The good news is that you are focused on health and things should go well for you. Health is enhanced in the ways mentioned in the yearly report. Scalp and face massage and physical exercise is especially beneficial. Maintain good muscle tone.

The upper, day side of your chart is as strong as it will ever be this year. On the 22nd the Sun, your career planet, moves into your 10th house of career. He is strong in this position. Not only is he in his own sign and house but he is at the top of your chart. You enter a yearly career peak, and it looks successful. (You've had stronger career periods in the past, and will do again in the future, but for the current year this is a peak.)

Much of what we've said above can happen with a delayed reaction. Retrograde activity is very strong. Half the planets are retrograde until the 12th; after then it is still 40 per cent. These are high percentages. Caution is still necessary in financial matters, as Jupiter is still retrograde. You will need to make some changes this month, but do your homework beforehand. You are still in a prosperous year, though things are slowing down.

August

Best Days Overall: 5, 6, 15, 16, 23, 24
Most Stressful Days Overall: 3, 4, 10, 11, 17, 18, 30, 31
Best Days for Love: 3, 4, 10, 11, 15, 16, 23, 24
Best Days for Money: 2, 11, 20, 25, 26, 27, 29
Best Days for Career: 8, 9, 17, 18, 19, 28

A successful – relatively speaking – month ahead, Scorpio. Though the night side of your Horoscope is still dominant, it is good to give more attention to the career. Probably you will shuttle back and forth between home and career, working to be successful at both.

Health will improve dramatically after the 22nd. Your financial planet, Jupiter, will be part of a very fortunate Grand Trine in the Earth signs. So very fortunate financial events are happening. Jupiter is still retrograde, however, so these developments need studying and fine-tuning. The month ahead is prosperous, but not as prosperous as it would be if Jupiter were moving forward.

Your love planet started to move forward on June 25 and will be forward for the rest of the year. So there is clarity in love. On the 7th Venus will move into your 9th house, where she receives challenging aspects. So you need to work harder to achieve your social and romantic goals. Perhaps there are some financial and personal disagreements between you and the beloved. You seem very distant with each other. Usually this signals psychological distance. You have opposite perspectives on life and things in general. If the differences can be bridged, this makes for the strongest type of partnership. The beloved seems more moody this month, more sensitive, more easily hurt. You, by contrast, are down-to-earth and practical. For singles, romantic opportunities happen through the family and family connections. Foreigners who live close to home seem alluring. The school and place of worship are

venues for romance too. Good philosophical and emotional compatibility seem very important.

Your 11th house becomes strong after the 22nd. This is a happy
period. The 11th house is a beneficent house: it is the place where
fondest hopes and wishes come true. Romance might be challenging,
but friendships are happy. Being involved with groups, trade and
professional organizations will help the career. It is a good period to
learn more about science, technology, astronomy and astrology. Many
people have their Horoscopes done under this kind of transit.

Your family planet Uranus starts to move backwards on the 15th. So
although home and family are a major focus, avoid making dramatic
changes here. Study the lie of the land. As the months progress (and
Uranus will be retrograde for a long time) other solutions will come to
you.

September

Best Days Overall: 1, 2, 3, 11, 12, 20, 21, 29, 30
Most Stressful Days Overall: 6, 7, 8, 14, 15, 26, 27
Best Days for Love: 2, 3, 6, 7, 8, 13, 14, 22, 23
Best Days for Money: 6, 7, 16, 17, 22, 23, 24, 25
Best Days for Career: 6, 7, 14, 15, 17, 26

Retrograde activity reaches its maximum level once again; between the
9th and the 12th 60 per cent of the planets are retrograde. Life moves
slowly. There is more gridlock personally and in the world at large.
(Babies born during this period will have many internal issues to work
out as they grow up and will tend to be 'late bloomers'.) This is a period
for learning patience. If there is something positive that can be done,
do it. If not, work on your issues in a spiritual way. Worldly doors seem
closed but the spiritual doors are always open – especially from the
22nd onwards.

With so many planets retrograde the cosmos is calling all of us to be
more perfect in all that we do. Avoid short cuts. Do things right. This
won't stop delays, but will minimize them.

Your love planet Venus moves into your 10th house on the 6th.
Generally this is good for love, signalling that it is high on your

priorities. Also, any planet at the top of your chart is going to operate more powerfully than usual. So your social grace is stronger than usual and you advance your career by social means. Likeability is perhaps more important than professional skills. The spouse, partner or current love seems very successful and is helpful in your career. Much of your socializing this month is career-related. Singles are attracted to people of power and prestige – and are having romantic opportunities with these kinds of people. The danger here is being involved in a relationship of convenience rather than of true love. This is the aspect of the office romance – romantic opportunities with bosses or superiors. Getting the family to accept your love seems a challenge.

Jupiter, your financial planet, will start moving forward on the 13th, which is a great plus for your finances. There is more clarity here now. Moreover, Jupiter receive very positive aspects until the 22nd so there is prosperity this month. Prosperity will happen even after the 22nd but there is more challenge involved. You'll have to work harder for your earnings than usual.

The month ahead is quite spiritual in nature – a good thing with all these retrogrades. On the 22nd the Sun moves into your spiritual 12th house (joining Mercury, there from the 5th onwards). So you can further your career through involvement with charities and altruistic activities. Spirit is guiding the career through dreams, hunches and, perhaps, through psychics, tarot readers, astrologers or spiritual channels. Another way to read this is that your spiritual growth and practice *is* the career – the actual mission this period.

October

Best Days Overall: 9, 10, 17, 18, 26, 27
Most Stressful Days Overall: 4, 5, 11, 12, 23, 24, 25, 31
Best Days for Love: 3, 4, 5, 21, 22, 31
Best Days for Money: 4, 5, 13, 14, 19, 20, 21, 23, 31
Best Days for Career: 6, 7, 11, 12, 15, 16, 25

The planetary power has been in the Eastern sector of self for a few months, and now it is at its maximum Eastern strength. You are in a period of personal independence. Other people are always important and should be shown respect, but you have the power to go your own way now. Your way is the best way these days. You have the power to make the changes you need to for your own happiness. You have to take responsibility for your happiness. It's up to you. The cosmic powers are supporting you.

Love is happy this month. There is still much instability here, but it is happier than in previous months. Venus will spend most of the month in your beneficent 11th house of friends. Further, your love planet is receiving very nice aspects from the other planets. She is part of a Grand Trine in the Earth signs. So, love opportunities for singles happen as you involve yourself in groups and group activities. Things that start as a friendship can lead to much more. Family seems supportive of love and your choices. Where last month you were attracted by people of power and prestige, this month you like a more egalitarian kind of relationship. You want friendship as much as passion. The only drawback in love, but it is easily correctable, is the tendency to be hyper-critical and perfectionistic. Venus is not very strong in Virgo. She becomes too intellectual and analytical. She means well. She looks for flaws so that she can correct them. But this can spoil romantic moments. So, as much as possible, avoid criticism – especially if it is destructive.

On the 28th Venus will move into your 12th house. Thus you will find spiritual-type people alluring – people involved in the fine arts, or spiritual channels, psychics, tarot readers and the like. Spiritual compatibility becomes important.

The month ahead is prosperous. Jupiter, your financial planet, is moving forward and receiving good aspects. The financial life moves forward.

The ruler of your Horoscope, Pluto, starts to move forward on the 4th. On the 23rd the Sun enters your own house and you begin a yearly personal pleasure peak. There is more personal clarity as to what you want and you have the power to get it. Happy career opportunities will come to you. You look successful and people see you this way. Bosses, parents and parent figures (one set of them at least) seem more devoted to you. You'll have to work harder with the family though.

November

Best Days Overall: 5, 6, 14, 15, 22, 23
Most Stressful Days Overall: 1, 7, 8, 20, 21, 27, 28
Best Days for Love: 1, 2, 3, 12, 21, 22, 27, 28
Best Days for Money: 2, 11, 16, 19
Best Days for Career: 5, 6, 7, 8, 14, 15, 24, 25

A happy and very prosperous month ahead. Enjoy! You're still in the midst of a yearly personal pleasure peak, so it is OK to indulge the body (so long as you don't overdo things). Show appreciation to it for the yeoman service it has given all these years. Also it is a good time to get the body and image into right shape now.

This is a period for having things your way. The cosmos supports you. Create your own happiness. Don't worry about what others will think, they will come around eventually.

Love is happy this month, but unstable. Venus moves into your sign on the 21st and stays there for the rest of the month. For singles this indicates that love is pursuing you. Just go about your daily business and it will find you. It is a time where you have love on your own terms. For those already in a relationship, this shows the devotion of the spouse, partner or current love. He or she puts your interest ahead of his or her own. You come first.

Health is excellent this month. Mars's continued presence in your 6th house shows that face and scalp massage and physical exercise are still important. Mars has been retrograde since September 9, but he will start to move forward on the 14th. So if you are making changes in the health regime or job situation, after the 14th will be a better time to do so than before.

We have our fourth and final lunar eclipse on the 30th. This one occurs in your 8th house making it a more serious kind of eclipse. Take it easy over this time and avoid stressful activities. The spouse, partner or current love needs to make dramatic financial changes. The money people in your life are having their marriages tested. There can be encounters with death – generally on the psychological level. These are love messages from above: 'Life is short and can end at any time. Get busy with your mission in life.' Once again students are affected (this

time it is college-level students). This has been the trend all year. There
are dramas in school and changes of educational plans. There are
dramas at your place of worship and in the lives of worship leaders.
Disruptions. Avoid foreign travel this period. If you must travel, schedule your trip around the eclipse period. Once again, your religious and
philosophical beliefs get tested. The cosmos is not leaving you alone
until you get this right.

December

Best Days Overall: 2, 3, 11, 12, 19, 20, 21, 29, 30, 31
Most Stressful Days Overall: 5, 6, 17, 18, 24, 25, 26
Best Days for Love: 2, 3, 11, 12, 22, 23, 24, 25, 26
Best Days for Money: 8, 13, 14, 16, 27
Best Days for Career: 5, 6, 13, 14, 24

The sixth and final eclipse of the year occurs in your money house on
the 14th. It is a solar eclipse and brings important financial changes.
These more or less coincide with the other financial changes that are
happening. Your financial planet changes signs on the 20th – an
important change. Jupiter moves out of Capricorn, your 3rd house,
into your 4th house of Aquarius. Where you've been pretty conservative in financial matters this past year, now you become more adventurous and experimental. You'll be spending more on the home and
family in the coming year but also earning from them too. Family and
family connections will be playing a big role in your financial life. This
transit favours the fortunate purchase or sale of a home. It also favours
the technological world – computers, software, makers of apps, new
inventions and the whole online world.

This eclipse – like every solar eclipse – brings career changes. There
can be shakeups in your company and industry. Bosses, parents or
parent figures can have life-changing personal dramas. The rules of
the game are changing. Neptune is impacted by this eclipse. Thus
children and children figures in your life are affected. They should
reduce their schedules and avoid stressful kinds of activities during
this period. They have a need to redefine themselves and this will
manifest as wardrobe and image changes in the coming months. A

parent or parent figure has to make corrections to their financial plans and thinking. He or she will be prospering in the coming year.

In spite of the eclipse, the month ahead looks prosperous. You are in the midst of a yearly financial peak until the 21st. Your financial intuition is good. The social connections are helpful and even an opportunity for a business partnership or joint venture is likely.

Love also seems happy this month. Venus remains in your sign until the 15th and this indicates (as we saw last month) that love pursues you. Just go about your daily business and it will find you. On the 15th Venus will enter your money house – a good signal for prosperity. The spouse, partner or current love is very active – and supportive – in your finances. For singles this shows an allurement to the wealthy. Material gifts turn you on. Love is expressed in material kinds of ways, through gifts and financial support. Love opportunities for singles happen as they pursue their financial goals and with people involved in their finances.

Health is good this month, but next year it will need more attention – there will be three long-term planets in stressful alignment with you.

Sagittarius

THE ARCHER

Birthdays from
23rd November to
20th December

Personality Profile

SAGITTARIUS AT A GLANCE

Element – Fire

Ruling Planet – Jupiter
  Career Planet – Mercury
  Love Planet – Mercury
  Money Planet – Saturn
  Planet of Health and Work – Venus
  Planet of Home and Family Life – Neptune
  Planet of Spirituality – Pluto

Colours – blue, dark blue

Colours that promote love, romance and social harmony – yellow,
  yellow-orange

Colours that promote earning power – black, indigo

Gems – carbuncle, turquoise

Metal – tin

Scents – carnation, jasmine, myrrh

Quality – mutable (= flexibility)

Qualities most needed for balance – attention to detail, administrative and organizational skills

Strongest virtues – generosity, honesty, broad-mindedness, tremendous vision

Deepest need – to expand mentally

Characteristics to avoid – over-optimism, exaggeration, being too generous with other people's money

Signs of greatest overall compatibility – Aries, Leo

Signs of greatest overall incompatibility – Gemini, Virgo, Pisces

Sign most helpful to career – Virgo

Sign most helpful for emotional support – Pisces

Sign most helpful financially – Capricorn

Sign best for marriage and/or partnerships – Gemini

Sign most helpful for creative projects – Aries

Best Sign to have fun with – Aries

Signs most helpful in spiritual matters – Leo, Scorpio

Best day of the week – Thursday

Understanding a Sagittarius

If you look at the symbol of the archer you will gain a good, intuitive understanding of a person born under this astrological sign. The development of archery was humanity's first refinement of the power to hunt and wage war. The ability to shoot an arrow far beyond the ordinary range of a spear extended humanity's horizons, wealth, personal will and power.

Today, instead of using bows and arrows we project our power with fuels and mighty engines, but the essential reason for using these new powers remains the same. These powers represent our ability to extend our personal sphere of influence – and this is what Sagittarius is all about. Sagittarians are always seeking to expand their horizons, to cover more territory and increase their range and scope. This applies to all aspects of their lives: economic, social and intellectual.

Sagittarians are noted for the development of the mind – the higher intellect – which understands philosophical and spiritual concepts. This mind represents the higher part of the psychic nature and is motivated not by self-centred considerations but by the light and grace of a Higher Power. Thus, Sagittarians love higher education of all kinds. They might be bored with formal schooling but they love to study on their own and in their own way. A love of foreign travel and interest in places far away from home are also noteworthy characteristics of the Sagittarian type.

If you give some thought to all these Sagittarian attributes you will see that they spring from the inner Sagittarian desire to develop. To travel more is to know more, to know more is to be more, to cultivate the higher mind is to grow and to reach more. All these traits tend to broaden the intellectual – and indirectly, the economic and material – horizons of the Sagittarian.

The generosity of the Sagittarian is legendary. There are many reasons for this. One is that Sagittarians seem to have an inborn consciousness of wealth. They feel that they are rich, that they are lucky, that they can attain any financial goal – and so they feel that they can afford to be generous. Sagittarians do not carry the burdens of want and limitation which stop most other people from giving generously. Another reason for their generosity is their religious and philosophical idealism, derived from the higher mind. This higher mind is by nature generous because it is unaffected by material circumstances. Still another reason is that the act of giving tends to enhance their emotional nature. Every act of giving seems to be enriching, and this is reward enough for the Sagittarian.

Finance

Sagittarians generally entice wealth. They either attract it or create it. They have the ideas, energy and talent to make their vision of paradise on Earth a reality. However, mere wealth is not enough. Sagittarians want luxury – earning a comfortable living seems small and insignificant to them.

In order for Sagittarians to attain their true earning potential they must develop better managerial and organizational skills. They must learn to set limits, to arrive at their goals through a series of attainable sub-goals or objectives. It is very rare that a person goes from rags to riches overnight. But a long-drawn-out process is difficult for Sagittarians. Like Leos, they want to achieve wealth and success quickly and impressively. They must be aware, however, that this over-optimism can lead to unrealistic financial ventures and disappointing losses. Of course, no zodiac sign can bounce back as quickly as Sagittarius, but only needless heartache will be caused by this attitude. Sagittarians need to maintain their vision – never letting it go – but they must also work towards it in practical and efficient ways.

Career and Public Image

Sagittarians are big thinkers. They want it all: money, fame, glamour, prestige, public acclaim and a place in history. They often go after all these goals. Some attain them, some do not – much depends on each individual's personal horoscope. But if Sagittarians want to attain public and professional status they must understand that these things are not conferred to enhance one's ego but as rewards for the amount of service that one does for the whole of humanity. If and when they figure out ways to serve more, Sagittarians can rise to the top.

The ego of the Sagittarian is gigantic – and perhaps rightly so. They have much to be proud of. If they want public acclaim, however, they will have to learn to tone down the ego a bit, to become more humble and self-effacing, without falling into the trap of self-denial and self-abasement. They must also learn to master the details of life, which can sometimes elude them.

At their jobs Sagittarians are hard workers who like to please their bosses and co-workers. They are dependable, trustworthy and enjoy a challenge. Sagittarians are friendly to work with and helpful to their colleagues. They usually contribute intelligent ideas or new methods that improve the work environment for everyone. Sagittarians always look for challenging positions and careers that develop their intellect, even if they have to work very hard in order to succeed. They also work well under the supervision of others, although by nature they would rather be the supervisors and increase their sphere of influence. Sagittarians excel at professions that allow them to be in contact with many different people and to travel to new and exciting locations.

Love and Relationships

Sagittarians love freedom for themselves and will readily grant it to their partners. They like their relationships to be fluid and ever-changing. Sagittarians tend to be fickle in love and to change their minds about their partners quite frequently.

Sagittarians feel threatened by a clearly defined, well-structured relationship, as they feel this limits their freedom. The Sagittarian tends to marry more than once in life.

Sagittarians in love are passionate, generous, open, benevolent and very active. They demonstrate their affections very openly. However, just like an Aries they tend to be egocentric in the way they relate to their partners. Sagittarians should develop the ability to see others' points of view, not just their own. They need to develop some objectivity and cool intellectual clarity in their relationships so that they can develop better two-way communication with their partners. Sagittarians tend to be overly idealistic about their partners and about love in general. A cool and rational attitude will help them to perceive reality more clearly and enable them to avoid disappointment.

Home and Domestic Life

Sagittarians tend to grant a lot of freedom to their family. They like big homes and many children and are one of the most fertile signs of the zodiac. However, when it comes to their children Sagittarians generally err on the side of allowing them too much freedom. Sometimes their children get the idea that there are no limits. However, allowing freedom in the home is basically a positive thing – so long as some measure of balance is maintained – for it enables all family members to develop as they should.

Horoscope for 2020

Major Trends

Though the year ahead is a major financial year – prosperity is very strong – it is not an especially strong career year. Money trumps status and prestige. In addition, all the long-term planets are on the night side of your chart this year. The day side, the upper half, will get a bit stronger as the year progresses, but will never dominate. The night side, the side of home, family and emotional issues, will always be the strongest. More on this later.

Last year you were your normal bubbly, enthusiastic Sagittarian self. Happy-go-lucky. This year you seem more serious about life. Your Sagittarian qualities are toned down. The focus on business and finance is the probable cause.

Neptune has been in your 4th house for many years and will be there for many more. Thus your home, family and emotional life are becoming more refined, more spiritualized. More details later.

Uranus moved into your 6th house of health and work last March and will remain there for many more years. There is great experimentation happening in your health regimes. You are ultra-experimental here. But health overall is good this year. It looks like there is much instability in the job situation however. More on this later.

Mars will spend over six months in your 5th house – from June 28 onwards. This is an unusually long time for Mars to stay in a house (usually he stays for only about six weeks or so). There is a love affair brewing for singles. Though there might be a love affair, marriage doesn't seem in the stars. There is admittedly nothing against it, but there's nothing especially supporting it. You don't seem very interested in committed kinds of relationships these days. More on this later.

Four lunar eclipses this year (twice as many as usual) impact on your 8th house. Thus you seem to be dealing with death and death issues. Perhaps surgery too. Generally these encounters are on the psychological level and are not literal. But by the time the year is over you will have a better understanding of death and less fear of it.

Your areas of greatest interest this year are finance; communication and intellectual interests (from March 23 to July 1 and from December 18 onwards); home and family; children, fun and creativity (from June 28 onwards); and health and work.

Your paths of greatest fulfilment this year are finance (until December 20); communication and intellectual activities (after December 20); sex, personal transformation and occult studies (until May 6); and religion, philosophy, higher learning and foreign travel (from May 6 onwards).

Health

(Please note that this is an astrological perspective on health and not a medical one. In days of yore there was no difference, both these perspectives were identical. Now there could be quite a difference. For a medical perspective, please consult your doctor or health practitioner.)

Health looks super this year. There is only one long-term planet – Neptune – in stressful alignment with you. Thus you have abundant energy and tend to good health. Sure, there will be periods in the year where health is less easy than usual, but these are temporary things caused by the planetary transits and not trends for the year. When they pass your naturally good health and energy return.

The times to rest and relax more are from February 19 to March 20, May 21 to June 21 and August 23 to September 22. We will discuss this in the monthly reports too.

Uranus is in your health house for the long term, as we mentioned. Thus you are in a cycle where you throw out all the rule books on health and learn how you personally function – learn, through trial, error and experimentation, what works for you. This is really every person's job in life. But for you it's happening now. You are a unique individual, wired up in a unique way. The law of averages doesn't really apply to you. You are not a statistic. Things that work for 'most' people might not work for you. Things that don't work for others could work for you. You have to learn this for yourself.

Uranus in the 6th house can sometimes lead to too much of a good thing. One can become a health faddist, pursuing every new diet or therapy merely because it is new. You need to do your homework as this can be quite expensive. Uranus in your 6th house also tends to show someone who gravitates to alternative therapies rather than orthodox medicine. However, the new cutting-edge technologies in orthodox medicine could also appeal to you.

Your health is good, but you can make it even better. Give more attention to the following, the vulnerable areas of your Horoscope (the reflex points are shown in the chart below):

Important foot reflexology points for the year ahead

Try to massage all of the foot on a regular basis – the top of the foot as well as the bottom – but pay extra attention to the points highlighted on the chart. When you massage, be aware of 'sore spots' as these need special attention. It's also a good idea to massage the ankles in particular, and below them.

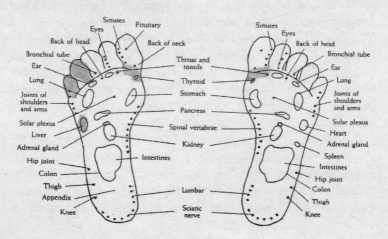

- The liver and thighs are always important areas for Sagittarius. Thighs should be regularly massaged; it should be part of your normal health regime. A herbal liver cleanse every now and then would be good, especially if you feel under the weather.
- The neck and throat. These too are always important for Sagittarius and, again, regular neck massage should be part of your health regime. Tension tends to collect there – especially if you feel stressed out – and needs to be released. Craniaosacral therapy is great for the neck.
- The ankles and calves have become important since March last year, but will continue to be so for the next seven years, approximately. So massage the ankles and calves regularly, and support the ankles well when exercising.

There are many short-term health trends for you, Sagittarius, because your health planet Venus is a fast-moving planet. This year she moves through 11 signs and houses of your Horoscope. So health needs can change depending on where Venus is and the aspects she receives. These are best dealt with in the monthly reports.

Venus is the generic planet of love and in your chart she is the ruler of your 11th house of friends. So there is always a strong social dimension to health. Good health for you means a healthy love and social life – harmony with friends. If problems arise in these areas your physical health can be affected. So, always strive to restore harmony as fast as you can.

Home and Family

Home and family has been important for many years now, with Neptune residing in your 4th house, and they will continue to be important for many more years. Many of the trends we've written about in past years are still very much in effect.

The home is a place of safety and comfort. This is a given. But for you it has become (and this will continue) more like a spiritual retreat. An ashram or a temple. I can easily imagine home altars being set up – either personally or with family members. I can imagine the walls covered with pictures of holy men or saints. I wouldn't be surprised if you hosted prayer meetings or meditation sessions in the home. Your home has (and will) become a portal to the spirit.

This is a good year to apply the principles of feng shui to the house. Keep in mind that there are other spiritual systems for this as well (Ayurveda and hermetic science, for instance). But it makes a difference when things are arranged properly in spiritually correct ways. The family as a whole, and a parent or parent figure in particular, seem much more spiritual. The attempt is to run family life in a spiritual kind of way.

Neptune is the planet of revelation. It sheds light – impersonal light – on everything it touches. This light often reveals hidden things, secrets, that are often unpleasant. Family secrets – good and bad – come to light. Thus, there can be scandals in the family. Despite this, you are getting on reasonably well with the family this year.

A move or renovations to the home could have happened in 2018. This year, however, a move is not likely. There's nothing against it, but nothing that specially favours it either. Next year or 2022 seem much better for a move than now.

Parents and parent figures are having a stable family year. Moves are not likely. Their marriage or current relationship also seems stable and solid. One of the parent figures will have many good job opportunities at the end of the year (and next year). Siblings and sibling figures in your life are taking on more responsibility and seem more serious about life. They prosper towards the end of the year. Their domestic life seems highly unstable and they can have multiple moves or undertake multiple house renovations this year and for years to come. They need to work on emotional stability. If they are of childbearing age they seem more fertile this year. Children and children figures in your life can endure many disruptions and repairs to the home, but a move is not likely. Grandchildren (if you have them) or those who play that role in your life can move this year, but it's a complicated matter and there are many glitches and delays involved.

If you're planning renovations or major repairs, May 13 to June 28 would be a good time. If you're decorating the home in a cosmetic kind of way – or buying art or other objects of beauty for the home – January 13 to February 7, August 7 to September 16 and November 21 to December 15 would be good periods to do this.

Finance and Career

Last year was prosperous and the year ahead is even more so. Your money house is easily the strongest in your Horoscope this year. It is not only strong quantitatively but qualitatively as well. A strong money house shows focus. It shows someone willing to face all the issues and challenges that arise. It shows passion and fervour – the Will to Wealth. This is generally more important than just 'easy' aspects.

But there are other signals of prosperity too. Your financial planet, Saturn, is powerful in his own sign and house, which signals strong earnings this year. In addition Jupiter, the ruler of your Horoscope, will be in your money house until December 20. While this is not Jupiter's best position, he is not very strong here, still it shows good fortune. Perhaps you are not that comfortable with this focus on finance and business, but prosperity is happening.

Jupiter in your money house shows that you spend on yourself – invest in yourself – take on the image of wealth and prosperity. Others see you as a 'money person' this year too. You will be richer at the end of the year than when you began. The Horoscope doesn't give numbers, but it shows increase.

By nature you are a risk taker. But these days you are much more conservative in financial matters and your financial judgement will be sound. These days it's not about gaining a 'quick buck' but about amassing wealth in steady, methodical, step-by-step ways. A business is favoured.

Those of you who invest will do well with conservative, blue-chip, traditional companies – companies that comprise major stock exchange listings. Sagittarians are generally not good with budgets – they tend to spend freely – but this year it will be good to set up budgets and disciplined savings and investment plans. You have the discipline to see them through.

Saturn in the sign of Capricorn favours commercial real estate, makers of office equipment, and companies that service the government or corporate world. Saturn's move into Aquarius from March 23 to July 1 and from December 18 onwards favours the world of technology: computers, online activities, online companies and companies involved with new inventions or innovations. Saturn is strong when he is in Aquarius too (by classical astrology he rules the sign).

Saturn's move into your 3rd house favours telecommunications, transportation and media companies. It favours companies involved with education and retailing. It favours trading – buying and selling.

Your money house will be strong all year, but by the end of the year, it will be less strong, and there will be less emphasis on finance. This I read as a good thing. Most financial goals (the short-term ones at least) will have been attained and you can shift your focus to other areas – to your intellectual pursuits and interests.

Career, as we said, is not prominent this year. Money is much more important. You don't care that much about status or prestige – just give me the cash, thank you. As we also mentioned, the lower half, the night side of your Horoscope is overwhelmingly stronger than the day side. Your 4th house of home and family is stronger than your 10th house of career. So this is a year of inner preparation – the behind-the-scenes actions – that will further the career later on. These actions shouldn't be despised. They are just as important as the outer career: they make the outer career possible.

Mercury, your career planet, is very fast moving and often erratic. During the year he will move through every area of your Horoscope, so there are many short-term career trends that depend on where Mercury is, his direction and the aspects he is receiving. These are best discussed in the monthly reports.

Love and Social Life

As we mentioned, this is not a very strong love or romance year. Your 7th house of love is empty, only short-term planets move through there. It doesn't seem like a major focus this year. This tends to the status quo. Those who are married will tend to stay married; singles will tend to stay single. The good news here is that this shows a basic contentment with things as they are and you have no compelling need to make changes. On the downside, if romantic problems occur, it is probably due to a lack of attention, a lack of focus. This will be a signal to start paying more attention here.

There is another issue in love this year. The ruler of your Horoscope,

Jupiter, is in his 'fall' – his weakest position. Thus your personal self-confidence and self-esteem are not up to their usual standards. This is not helpful in love. Also – and this is perhaps more important – you seem too serious this year, and perhaps more pessimistic than usual. You might feel older than your years. The normal Sagittarian ebullience and verve is not there. This can be off-putting to others. You can come across as cold, aloof, detached or unapproachable. Now, this is not who you are. But others can see you this way. And this can impede the love life. Happily, the solution is easy. Lighten up. Make it a priority to send love and warmth to others. This will turn everything around.

Marriage might not be in the stars for singles, but a love affair is. Mars will be in your 5th house of fun and creativity from June 28 onwards. This relationship is more about fun and entertainment rather than something committed.

Your love planet is Mercury – one of the fastest moving and erratic planets in the zodiac. Sometimes he speeds, sometimes he slows down, sometimes he stands still and sometimes he goes backwards. This pretty much describes your love life (and also the kind of partners you attract). There is always change. Romantic opportunity can come to you in a number of ways and through many different kinds of people and situations. Because Mercury will move through all the houses of your chart this year, there are many short-term trends in love that depend on where Mercury is and the kinds of aspects he receives. These are best dealt with in the monthly reports.

Siblings, sibling figures, parents, parent figures, children and children figures in your life are all having stable love years.

Self-improvement

Your spiritual planet, Pluto, has been in your money house of Capricorn for many years. (He will be there for many more years, too.) This shows a 'down-to-earth' kind of spirituality. Spirituality is seen as a practice that has to have practical – and especially financial – benefits. It shows much charitable giving and a powerful financial intuition. Intuition, as our regular readers know, is the short cut to wealth. You are always a generous person, but these days even more so than usual. There is a spiritual agenda happening in your finances. You've been exploring and learning about the spiritual dimensions of wealth. You already understand much about this – Sagittarius has an inborn understanding. But there is always more to learn and one can always go deeper into things.

The spiritual concept of wealth is often at odds with the materialistic concept of it. And this conflict is especially strong in you. In finance you are very down-to-earth this year – conservative. You have a business-like attitude to it. But spiritual affluence cares nothing about material conditions, how much money you have in the bank, the size of your portfolio, or what your financial statement says. Spiritual affluence comes from above and works with the resources of the Universe, not your own. It is never about how much you have, but about how much spirit has – and spirit has it all.

Here's another interesting fact about spiritual affluence. It is always where you are. Always everywhere. It is an interior activity. It is about connecting to the principle and allowing it to operate through you as it wills. Moreover, it is there in its fullness whenever you make contact with it. That is, you have access to 'all the affluence there is'. In theory, you have access to as much affluence as Bill Gates, Warren Buffett or Jeff Bezos. Affluence gives itself fully and equally to all. The only difference is a person's capacity to receive, their capacity to take more of what is given.

We're saying deep and wonderful things here, but Sagittarius will understand. For those who want to go deeper into this, my blog – www.spiritual-stories.com – has more information.

Neptune's presence in your 4th house shows that your spiritual practice will not only help you financially but also in your family and emotional life. Family issues need a spiritual understanding to be resolved. And spirit is very willing if you call on it.

Your emotional sensitivities are much greater than usual – and more than those of an average person. Thus you can be easily hurt. Much of the time others don't even mean to do this – you just feel things more. So, it is best to be around positive and uplifting kinds of people. This is so for family members as well. They too seem more sensitive emotionally.

Month-by-month Forecasts

January

Best Days Overall: 2, 3, 12, 20, 21, 29, 30, 31
Most Stressful Days Overall: 1, 7, 8, 14, 27, 28
Best Days for Love: 5, 6, 7, 8, 13, 14, 15, 18, 19, 25, 26, 27, 28
Best Days for Money: 5, 6, 14, 22, 23
Best Days for Career: 5, 6, 14, 15, 25, 26

The planetary power is mostly in the East this month. Not only that, but dynamic Mars moves into your own house on the 2nd and stays there for the rest of the month. You're really in high spirits now. Personal independence would be strong even without the presence of Mars. But now personal independence is on steroids. There are good and bad points about this. The good points are that happiness is up to you. You are the master of your fate this month. Your personal initiative and skills matter. You don't really need the approval of others to get what you want and you have lots of energy and dynamism. The bad points come from too much of a good thing. You can be seen as 'spoiling for a fight'. This can lead to arguments or even physical conflict. You could be in too much of a rush and this can lead to accidents. So be bold by all means, but in a mindful way.

A lunar eclipse on the 10th occurs in your 8th house, which makes it a dangerous kind of eclipse. It not only occurs in the 8th house but impacts on the ruler of that house – a double effect. So, stay out of harm's way during this period and spend it quietly at home. Perhaps the gym would be a good place to hang out. There can be encounters with death or near-death experiences, although usually these are on the psychological level. The cosmos wants you to get a better understanding of death. The spouse, partner or current love will need to make very dramatic financial changes (and this will be the case all year). The eclipse's impact on Saturn, your financial planet, also shows important financial changes for you personally. The impact on Pluto brings spiritual changes – changes of practice, attitudes, teachings and teachers. There are disruptions in spiritual or charitable organizations you're involved with. Those you see as guru figures are having personal dramas. This eclipse also affects Mercury, so love is being tested and there are career changes. There are personal dramas in the lives of bosses, parents and parent figures and perhaps shakeups in the management of your company or industry. A pretty strong eclipse all round! Though it is difficult to see this while all the excitement is happening, these changes will be good.

You begin your year in the midst of a yearly financial peak. The eclipse might shake things up, but it won't stop your prosperity. It will be a prosperous month ahead.

Health is good this month. Most of the planets are kind to you. But you can make health even better by giving more attention to the ankles and calves (massage them regularly) until the 13th and to the feet after that date. You get excellent results from spiritual healing after the 13th, and especially from the 26th to the 28th.

February

Best Days Overall: 8, 9, 16, 17, 26, 27
Most Stressful Days Overall: 3, 4, 5, 10, 11, 23, 24, 25
Best Days for Love: 3, 4, 5, 6, 7, 8, 14, 15, 16, 17, 23, 24, 25, 26, 27
Best Days for Money: 1, 2, 10, 11, 18, 19, 20, 28, 29
Best Days for Career: 6, 7, 10, 11, 14, 15, 23, 24

Mars remains in your sign until the 16th, so review our discussion of this in January.

The planetary power is shifting this month. On the 16th Mars will leave your sign. On the 3rd Mercury moves to the West, and on the 19th the Sun will also move westward. So the social Western sector of your chart is getting ever stronger. Personal independence is much less than last month, so it is time to start cultivating your social skills. Since both sectors are more or less equal this month, the trick is to balance your personal interests with those of others. Sometimes you have your way, sometimes you let others have their way.

Your money house is very strong this month. The only house that rivals it in power is your 4th house of home and family. These are the two major interests this month. So the month ahead should be prosperous. You might be more speculative than usual, but this should be kept in check. Well-hedged, well-thought out risks can pay off, but casino-type risks should be avoided.

This is a month for focusing on the home and family, with career put on the back burner for a while. Even your career planet, Mercury, will be in your 4th house from the 3rd onwards. Thus your home, family and emotional wellness is the real career, the real mission this month. It also shows that this is a time for working on your career by the methods of night, rather than by overt, direct action. Before you go to sleep visualize where you want to be careerwise. Get into the mood of it. Feel yourself there. Then let go. When the planets start to shift to the upper half of your chart you will be more able to work on things more directly.

Health needs some attention this month, especially from the 19th onwards. There is nothing serious afoot (overall your health is good this year), but this is a period of lowered energy. Enhance the health by spiritual means until the 7th, and if you feel under the weather see a spiritual healer. On the 7th, as your health planet Venus moves into your 5th house, you benefit from scalp and face massage and physical exercise. Having fun is excellent therapy from the 7th onwards.

Love is close to home this month. Your love planet Mercury spends most of the month (from the 3rd onwards) in your 4th house, indicating that you are socializing more with the family and from home. Family and family connections are playing a role in your love life – perhaps by making introductions. You are attracted to spiritual people and to those who are emotionally sensitive. Emotional sharing is a big turn on in love at the moment. On the 17th Mercury goes into retrograde motion and love can slow down. Perhaps there is some hesitancy on your part or on the part of the current love interest. A good time to review the love life.

March

Best Days Overall: 6, 7, 14, 15, 24, 25
Most Stressful Days Overall: 2, 3, 8, 9, 22, 23, 29, 30
Best Days for Love: 2, 3, 8, 10, 11, 17, 18, 22, 23, 27, 28, 29, 30
Best Days for Money: 1, 8, 9, 17, 18, 27, 28, 29
Best Days for Career: 8, 9, 10, 11, 22, 23

Your 4th house of home and family is still very strong, so keep your focus there. Since your career planet, Mercury, is retrograde until the 10th, there is not much going on careerwise so you might as well focus on the home. This is a great month for those of you involved in psychological therapies. There will be great progress. But even if you're not in any 'official' therapy, nature will arrange things so that many past issues will be resolved. Nature will bring up the memories – and often they seem haphazard, with no rhyme or reason to them – and by looking at them from your present state of emotional evolution, they lose their grip on you. The dream life will be very active this month too. (It might be more interesting than everyday life.) This too is part of nature's therapeutics.

Finance is still very strong this month. Your money house is chock-full of planets for most of the month. This shows focus, and by the spiritual law we get what we focus on. On the 23rd Saturn, your financial planet will leave the money house and move into Aquarius, your 3rd house. Mars also leaves the money house, on the 31st.

Saturn's move is not the full-blown transit just yet; it's merely a temporary flirtation with your 3rd house of communication. It basically announces how finance will be next year. So, you will be a little less conservative. You will have a good feeling for the high-tech sector. Online activities are favoured. You profit from trading – buying and selling – and from good use of the media. Whatever you are doing, good marketing, advertising and PR are important. People need to know about your product or service. You will spend more on this, but will also earn from it.

Jupiter will travel with Pluto, your spiritual planet, all month. This shows various things. Financial intuition will be super. You will be even more generous than usual (Sagittarians are famous for their generosity), and you will have spiritual-type breakthroughs and super-natural kinds of experiences.

On the 20th the Sun will move into your 5th house and you begin a yearly personal pleasure peak. Health will be much improved. You are getting on with the children and children figures in your life (this is especially so from the 15th to the 21st as Mars and Jupiter travel together). The 15th to the 21st would also favour speculations, but keep in mind that these should be calculated and well hedged – not casino-type gambles.

You can enhance your already good health with scalp and face massage and physical exercise until the 5th. Afterwards give more attention to the neck and throat.

April

Best Days Overall: 3, 4, 11, 12, 20, 21, 22
Most Stressful Days Overall: 5, 6, 18, 19, 25, 26
Best Days for Love: 1, 2, 7, 8, 10, 11, 15, 16, 17, 20, 21, 25, 26, 30
Best Days for Money: 6, 7, 13, 14, 15, 24, 25
Best Days for Career: 1, 2, 5, 6, 10, 11, 20, 21, 30

Like last month the month ahead is very spiritual. Jupiter and Pluto are travelling together all month. So, the financial intuition is super. Like last month this is a time for spiritual breakthroughs and supernatural experiences.

Health is good this month, and you are strongly focused here from the 19th onwards. Hopefully this focus will be about healthy lifestyles and preventive strategies. Sometimes, especially when health is good, this focus can lead to hypochondria and a tendency to magnify little things into big things.

I doubt if there are too many unemployed Sagittarians these days. But if you are one, the month ahead brings happy job opportunities. Some can even be in foreign countries or with foreign companies. Even if you are already employed, there are opportunities for second jobs and overtime. If you employ others there are many qualified applicants. And probably you will expand the workforce.

You are still in a yearly personal pleasure peak until the 19th. It is time to enjoy life and explore its many raptures. Travel for pleasure is likely until the 19th. Mars and Saturn travel together at the beginning of the month, which can bring luck in speculations and either spending or earning from children or children figures. Money is earned in happy ways those days. You spend more on happy things too.

Love is complicated from the 11th to the 27th. You will have to work harder on your relationship, and there seems to be some conflict. Before the 11th Mercury, your love planet, is in your 4th house, indicating that you are still socializing more at home and with the family. Spiritual and emotional compatibility are very important. After the 11th, Mercury enters your 5th house and love comes more about having fun. You don't seem too serious about romance. You just want fun (and you could be attracting these kinds of people). Love opportunities happen in the normal ways – at parties, resorts and places of entertainment. On the 27th Mercury will enter your 6th house and you become more serious. Love goes better then. If you are single there are happy romantic opportunities. The workplace becomes a venue for romance. Romantic opportunities can also happen as you pursue your health goals or with people involved in your health. Your health planet, Venus, will be in your 7th house from the 3rd onwards, which reinforces what we've just said. You are attracted to health professionals or co-workers.

May

Best Days Overall: 1, 8, 9, 18, 19, 27, 28
Most Stressful Days Overall: 2, 3, 15, 16, 23, 24, 29, 30
Best Days for Love: 2, 3, 4, 5, 12, 13, 14, 23, 24
Best Days for Money: 3, 4, 12, 13, 14, 22
Best Days for Career: 2, 3, 12, 13, 23, 24, 29, 30

Your financial planet Saturn will start to retrograde on the 11th and will remain so for many months. This won't stop earnings, but slows things down a bit. More due diligence is needed before making important investments or purchases. Time to take a 'wait and see' attitude to finance. Prosperity is still intact.

The planetary power is mostly in the West now and this month – after the 13th – the Western, social sector becomes even stronger. You are in a social period. On the 20th, as the Sun enters your 7th house, you begin a yearly love and social peak. Love looks happy. If you are single there are many romantic opportunities. You are meeting new people – foreigners perhaps, or mentor or religious types. Health professionals are still alluring. Your love planet is moving speedily this month. You cover much territory and have good confidence. If you are in a relationship, there is more romance within the relationship and more going out, more socializing.

Mars moves into your 4th house on the 13th, signalling an excellent time for doing repairs or construction work in the home. Family members can be more aggressive and hot tempered at this time, so be more patient with them.

Health needs more attention from the 20th onwards. As always, make sure to get enough rest. Don't burn the candle at both ends. Enhance your health in the ways mentioned in the yearly report, but also through arm and shoulder massage. Breathing exercises are good too. So is fresh air. Your health planet, Venus, goes retrograde on the 13th so study health changes – changes of diet or therapies – more carefully after this date.

Venus went 'out of bounds' on April 3 and will be this way all month. So in health issues you're exploring things outside your normal sphere. It could also be that your job is taking you outside your normal boundaries.

Mercury, your love planet, will also be 'out of bounds' from the 17th to the end of the month. So in love, too, you are outside your normal sphere, and perhaps are attracted to people outside your usual circles.

Pluto, your spiritual planet, went retrograde on April 25 and will be retrograde for many more months. Thus in spiritual matters you are backtracking and reviewing things. Your intuition needs to be verified these days.

June

Best Days Overall: 5, 6, 14, 15, 24, 30
Most Stressful Days Overall: 11, 12, 13, 19, 20, 26, 27
Best Days for Love: 1, 3, 4, 9, 10, 11, 12, 19, 20, 21, 22
Best Days for Money: 2, 7, 8, 9, 18, 19, 27
Best Days for Career: 3, 4, 11, 12, 21, 22, 26, 27

Venus moves back 'in bounds' after the 1st for the rest of the month. So in health matters and work you are back in your normal sphere.

Mercury remains 'out of bounds' until the 9th. So, for the beginning of June at least, like last month you are looking for love outside your normal circles. Perhaps your current love interest is outside your usual sphere. But this changes after the 9th when your love planet moves back in bounds.

We have two eclipses this month, and planetary retrograde activity spikes to its maximum level for the year. From the 23rd to the 25th 60 per cent of the planets are retrograde. After the 25th the percentage drops slightly to 50 per cent, which is still very high. Babies born this period will need a lot of internal development and are apt to be late bloomers in life.

The lunar eclipse of the 5th affects you very strongly, so take a nice, easy, relaxed schedule then. It occurs in your own sign. Thus you will be forced (over the next few months) to redefine yourself – your image, personality and self-concept. This will manifest as wardrobe and image changes over the coming months. This lunar eclipse brings confrontations with death and perhaps some near-death kinds of experiences – another reason to take it easy. The spouse, partner or current love is forced to make dramatic financial changes, usually because of financial disruptions. This eclipse impacts on both Mars and Venus. So, children and children figures are affected. They too should take it easy over this period. They also need to redefine themselves. They should avoid foreign travel at this period. A parent or parent figure is also forced to make important financial changes. The impact on Venus indicates job changes and changes in your health regime. Friendships can be tested and there are dramas in the lives of friends.

The solar eclipse of the 21st occurs in your 8th house, bringing more confrontations with death – though usually on the psychological level. Perhaps surgery is recommended. Once again the beloved is forced to make financial changes. Their financial strategy and thinking hasn't been realistic and needs another correction. College-level students are affected by this eclipse too. There are changes in educational plans and disruptions in schools. There are shakeups in your place of worship and dramas in the lives of worship leaders.

July

Best Days Overall: 2, 3, 11, 12, 21, 22, 29, 30
Most Stressful Days Overall: 9, 10, 16, 17, 23, 24
Best Days for Love: 1, 6, 7, 8, 9, 10, 16, 17, 19, 20, 25, 26, 27, 28
Best Days for Money: 4, 5, 14, 15, 23, 24, 31
Best Days for Career: 1, 9, 10, 19, 20, 23, 24, 27, 28

Your financial planet moves back into Capricorn on the 2nd: your money house is full of planets once again so it is a prosperous month, but earnings come more slowly with many delays. It's very important to take more care with all the little details of finance; if you're mailing an important payment make sure the addresses are correct, and that the payment is made out properly. Double-check bank details of online payments. Taking care of the details can be tedious but you will minimize delays.

We have another lunar eclipse on the 5th, the third one this year. (Usually there are only two.) It occurs in your money house and shows a need to make important financial changes. However, with all these planetary retrogrades going on, you need more research and thought before making any alterations. The spouse, partner or current love also has to make financial changes, and the same advice applies: give it more study. There will be personal dramas in the lives of the money people in your life. As with all lunar eclipses, there can be (generally psychological) encounters with death or near-death experiences. This eclipse impacts, but not too directly, three other planets – Mercury, Jupiter and Saturn. The impact on Saturn only reinforces the financial changes detailed above. The impact on Jupiter is a personal impact.

You could have a physical detox or a need to redefine or reinvent yourself. The impact on Mercury shows that love gets tested and there are career changes. Parents, parent figures and bosses have personal dramas.

The night side of your Horoscope is the strongest side this year, but the upper half is as strong now as it will ever be in the year ahead. So home and family – your emotional wellness – is still the priority, but now you can start shifting some energy to the career. Dawn, figuratively speaking, is breaking in your year, although you might not want to get out of bed.

Health is good this month. You can enhance it further through arm and shoulder massage and through breathing exercises. Good health for you means a healthy love and social life. So if, God forbid, problems arise, restore harmony in these areas as quickly as possible.

Love is complicated this month. Mercury is retrograde until the 12th and is receiving difficult aspects. You have to work harder on this department.

August

Best Days Overall: 8, 9, 17, 18, 25, 26, 27
Most Stressful Days Overall: 5, 6, 13, 14, 19, 20
Best Days for Love: 3, 4, 8, 13, 14, 15, 16, 17, 18, 23, 24, 28, 29
Best Days for Money: 1, 2, 11, 20, 28, 29
Best Days for Career: 8, 17, 18, 19, 20, 28, 29

Your 10th house of career becomes strong from the 22nd onwards, signalling focus on the career. However, this career push will not be as strong as at times in your past – or even compared to what it will be in future years. It's a sort of half-hearted focus. Most of the power in the chart is below the horizon. So, some career progress will be made, but you are capable of much more.

Still, the month ahead looks happy. Your 9th house – your favourite – became powerful on July 22 and is still strong until the 22nd, so foreign lands call to you. You are probably travelling (it doesn't take much to get you on a plane, any excuse will do). You are doing what you most love to do. College-level students will do well this period.

There is focus on education and thus success is more likely. After the 22nd there is career-related travel.

The love life is much better this month. Mercury, your love planet, is moving speedily forward. You have confidence and cover a lot of territory. Mercury will have much better aspects after the 5th than before that date, when he moves into Leo, your 9th house, and stays there until the 20th. Thus there are love opportunities in foreign lands and perhaps with foreigners. Singles will also find romantic opportunity at college or university functions or at your place of worship. You are attracted to people you can learn from. There is a need for good philosophical compatibility too. On the 20th Mercury moves into your 10th house of career. This shows that you find romantic or social opportunities as you pursue your career goals or with people involved in your career. You mingle with people of power and prestige and can further the career by social means. Much of your socializing will be career related.

Health is excellent until the 22nd. After that make sure to get enough rest. Health is basically good, but this is not one of your best periods for health. Until the 7th, enhance the health through arm and shoulder massage – make sure you release tension in the shoulders. After the 7th detox regimes will work well. Good emotional health is very important. Keep the moods positive and constructive. Diet becomes important after the 7th too.

All the planets involved with your finances are retrograde this month. So things might be slower than usual but your prosperity is still good.

September

Best Days Overall: 4, 5, 14, 15, 22, 23
Most Stressful Days Overall: 1, 2, 3, 9, 10, 16, 17, 29, 30
Best Days for Love: 2, 3, 9, 10, 13, 14, 18, 19, 22, 23, 26, 27
Best Days for Money: 6, 7, 8, 16, 17, 24, 25
Best Days for Career: 9, 16, 17, 18, 19, 26, 27

Retrograde activity once again spikes to a yearly high this month. Between the 9th and the 12th 60 per cent of the planets are retrograde, while before and after that period it is 50 per cent. Retrograde activity will gradually decline over the next few months, however. You probably will not be able to prevent all glitches and delays, but you can minimize them by being more perfect in all that you do. Slow and correct is much better than fast and slipshod.

Mars makes one of his rare retrogrades from the 9th onwards. This impacts on children and children figures in your life. They lack direction. They seem aimless. A parent or parent figure needs to adopt more of a 'wait-and-see' attitude to finance. He or she should avoid major purchases or investments from the 9th onwards.

You're still in a yearly career peak until the 22nd. You might as well focus here as your family planet, Neptune, is still retrograde and only time will resolve family issues.

Health still needs watching until the 22nd. You are basically in good health but this is not one of your best periods in terms of energy. Until the 6th enhance the health through right diet and good emotional health. After the 6th chest massage is beneficial. Give the heart more energy by avoiding worry and anxiety.

When the planetary power moved into your 10th house on August 22, there was a shift from the social Western sector to the independent Eastern sector of your chart. This will become even more pronounced next month and in the coming months. You are entering a period of greater personal independence. Others are important, but your way is the best way now. It will be easier to make the changes that need to be made for your happiness.

Finances are slowly but surely moving forward this month. Gridlock is ending. Jupiter, in your money house, moves forward on the 13th, and your financial planet, Saturn, will move forward on the 29th. Financial clarity is returning.

Love is happy – especially until the 5th. Your love planet is part of a Grand Trine in the Earth signs. Love is high on your agenda and you are focused here. Just go about your career goals and love will find you. On the 5th Mercury moves into romantic Libra, a positive for romance. The only problem is that he is making stressful aspects to other planets. Love will be active but challenging. On the 27th Mercury moves into your 12th house, and you become attracted to spiritual and artistic types. Spiritual compatibility becomes important.

October

Best Days Overall: 1, 2, 11, 12, 19, 20, 28, 29, 30
Most Stressful Days Overall: 6, 7, 13, 14, 26, 27
Best Days for Love: 3, 6, 7, 9, 10, 17, 18, 21, 22, 26
Best Days for Money: 4, 5, 13, 14, 21, 22, 23, 31
Best Days for Career: 9, 10, 13, 14, 17, 18, 26

Venus, your health and work planet, moves into your career house on the 2nd. Your good work ethic impresses your superiors. This transit is also a good signal for health. Health is high on your priorities. Venus is not particularly strong in the sign of Virgo, but because she is at the top of your chart she is positionally strong, terrestrially strong. Health will be good this month. You can enhance it even more through abdominal massage.

The month ahead is not especially romantic, but is nevertheless social. Your 11th house of friends is very strong and you are involved with friends, groups and group activities. The power in the 11th house is another indicator for a happy month.

A parent or parent figure is having a banner financial month. The other parent or parent figure is prospering but more slowly, with the financial planet still retrograde all month.

When Pluto starts moving forward on the 4th, finances are gung ho. A prosperous month. All the planets involved with finance will be moving forward. There is clarity on this subject and the moves you make will be good. Your approach to finance is conservative and long term – just as it has been all year.

It is interesting that Pluto, your spiritual planet, moves forward shortly before your spiritual 12th house becomes powerful. All systems are go in your spiritual life from the 23rd onwards and you will be making good progress here. The Sun's move into your 12th house suggests that you benefit from the mystical traditions of your native religion. There's no need to explore exotic systems for enlightenment; your own native religion has a strong mystical side.

Your love planet, Mercury, will go retrograde on the 14th, complicating romance. Singles will still date, but less than usual.

Social confidence is not up to its usual standard. A current relationship seems to go backwards instead of forwards. There are romantic meetings in spiritual-type settings, but there's no rush here. Let love develop as it will. Take a wait-and-see attitude to things. Charity events are also conducive to romantic meetings.

Venus's move into your independent Eastern sector cements the power in the East. It is now the dominant sector and will become even more so in the coming months. It is time to have your way in life. Time to take the initiative. You don't need to wait for others to approve your moves. Your personal happiness is now in your hands.

November

Best Days Overall: 7, 8, 16, 25, 26
Most Stressful Days Overall: 2, 3, 4, 10, 22, 23, 30
Best Days for Love: 2, 3, 4, 12, 13, 14, 21, 22, 23, 30
Best Days for Money: 2, 11, 18, 19
Best Days for Career: 3, 4, 10, 13, 14, 22, 23

Basically a happy and spiritually fulfilling month, Sagittarius – even a lunar eclipse on the 30th will do little to block your happiness. It will just introduce some excitement.

Jupiter is travelling with both Pluto and Saturn – your spiritual and financial planets. Thus there are spiritual breakthroughs and prosperity this month. The financial intuition is firing on all cylinders and financial goals are attained rather easily.

The month ahead is spiritual for other reasons too. Your 12th house is even stronger than it was last month. This is a great month for studying sacred literature and for spiritual practices. The dream life will be active and revelatory.

The Sun's entry into your own sign on the 21st initiates a yearly personal pleasure peak. There will likely be foreign travel (the opportunities will surely come). College-level students will do well in their studies. There is good fortune in legal matters – you get the best-case scenario. This is a good time to indulge the body (so long as you don't overdo it) and to get the body and image into the shape you want.

The pace of life will quicken this month too – and the fast pace is what you like. By the end of the month 90 per cent of the planets will be moving forward.

The lunar eclipse of the 30th – the fourth and final lunar eclipse of the year – occurs in your 7th house of love. So a current relationship will get tested. Business partnerships will also likely get tested. Once again the spouse, partner or current love will have to make financial changes. There can be encounters with death or near-death kinds of experiences. Aunts or uncles also make important financial changes.

Health is good this month, but take steps to reduce your schedule a few days before and after the eclipse (sensitive people feel an eclipse up to two weeks before it happens). Health can be enhanced through hip massage until the 21st and through detox regimes afterwards. Spiritual healing will be powerful after the 21st.

Love becomes happier after the 11th. On the 3rd your love planet starts to move forward, and on the 11th he moves away from his stressful aspect with you. Love happens in spiritual venues after the 11th. Get right spiritually, and love will just naturally happen.

December

Best Days Overall: 5, 6, 13, 14, 22, 23
Most Stressful Days Overall: 1, 7, 8, 19, 20, 21, 27, 28
Best Days for Love: 1, 2, 3, 11, 12, 22, 23, 27, 28
Best Days for Money: 8, 9, 15, 16, 17, 27
Best Days for Career: 5, 6, 7, 8, 13, 14, 24

Though this is a happy and healthy month, a solar eclipse on the 14th (the final eclipse of the year) occurs in your own sign, so take things easy at this time. Often with this kind of eclipse you need to fend off some bad-mouthing or slanders from others. They attempt to define you in ways that are not correct. The best defence against this is to define yourself for yourself. It won't be a good idea to travel over that period either. If you must, schedule things around the eclipse period. College-level students are particularly affected. They can change schools or educational plans. Sometimes the school that you wanted rejects you but a better one accepts you. There are disruptions at school, in your place of worship and in the lives of professors and worship leaders. This eclipse impacts on Neptune, your family planet. So a parent or parent figure has a personal drama. Family members are more temperamental this period too. There can be a need for repairs in the home as well. The dream life will probably be active at this time, but shouldn't be given too much weight.

The eclipse adds some spice and excitement to the month, but your basic happiness is undimmed. You look good (though you need to be careful of your weight). Your love planet, Mercury, is in your sign until the 21st, and Venus will enter your sign on the 15th. So, you are attracting the opposite sex. Love is pursuing you rather than the other way around. You are having love on your terms and there is little you need to do to attract it. If you are in a relationship, the spouse, partner or current love is very devoted. You come first. Mercury will be 'out of bounds' from the 13th onwards, suggesting that in love issues you are attracted to people outside your normal sphere. Sometimes this shows that the beloved is operating outside his or her usual sphere.

The month ahead is also very prosperous. Two important planets will leave the money house this month (Jupiter and Saturn), but two other planets move in to replace them. On the 21st you begin a yearly financial peak, which extends into next month too. But the focus on finance will lessen next year. You are more interested in intellectual development this month and next year. It is a good aspect for students below college level as they are more focused on their studies. When financial goals are achieved – at least in the short term – it is natural to want to develop the mind.

This month 90 per cent of the planets are in forward motion, so the pace of events quickens – just as you like it. You make faster progress towards your goals.

Capricorn

𑀊

THE GOAT

Birthdays from
21st December to
19th January

Personality Profile

CAPRICORN AT A GLANCE

Element – Earth

Ruling Planet – Saturn
   Career Planet – Venus
   Love Planet – Moon
   Money Planet – Uranus
   Planet of Communications – Neptune
   Planet of Health and Work – Mercury
   Planet of Home and Family Life – Mars
   Planet of Spirituality – Jupiter

Colours – black, indigo

Colours that promote love, romance and social harmony – puce, silver

Colour that promotes earning power – ultramarine blue

Gem – black onyx

Metal – lead

Scents – magnolia, pine, sweet pea, wintergreen

KAY 1/13/51,
CHRIS 12/25/75
ED 1/12/70

Quality – cardinal (= activity)

Qualities most needed for balance – warmth, spontaneity, a sense of fun

Strongest virtues – sense of duty, organization, perseverance, patience, ability to take the long-term view

Deepest needs – to manage, take charge and administrate

Characteristics to avoid – pessimism, depression, undue materialism and undue conservatism

Signs of greatest overall compatibility – Taurus, Virgo

Signs of greatest overall incompatibility – Aries, Cancer, Libra

Sign most helpful to career – Libra

Sign most helpful for emotional support – Aries

Sign most helpful financially – Aquarius

Sign best for marriage and/or partnerships – Cancer

Sign most helpful for creative projects – Taurus

Best Sign to have fun with – Taurus

Signs most helpful in spiritual matters – Virgo, Sagittarius

Best day of the week – Saturday

Understanding a Capricorn

The virtues of Capricorns are such that there will always be people for and against them. Many admire them, many dislike them. Why? It seems to be because of Capricorn's power urges. A well-developed Capricorn has his or her eyes set on the heights of power, prestige and authority. In the sign of Capricorn, ambition is not a fatal flaw, but rather the highest virtue.

Capricorns are not frightened by the resentment their authority may sometimes breed. In Capricorn's cool, calculated, organized mind all the dangers are already factored into the equation – the unpopularity, the animosity, the misunderstandings, even the outright slander – and a plan is always in place for dealing with these things in the most efficient way. To the Capricorn, situations that would terrify an ordinary mind are merely problems to be managed, bumps on the road to ever-growing power, effectiveness and prestige.

Some people attribute pessimism to the Capricorn sign, but this is a bit deceptive. It is true that Capricorns like to take into account the negative side of things. It is also true that they love to imagine the worst possible scenario in every undertaking. Other people might find such analyses depressing, but Capricorns only do these things so that they can formulate a way out – an escape route.

Capricorns will argue with success. They will show you that you are not doing as well as you think you are. Capricorns do this to themselves as well as to others. They do not mean to discourage you but rather to root out any impediments to your greater success. A Capricorn boss or supervisor feels that no matter how good the performance there is always room for improvement. This explains why Capricorn supervisors are difficult to handle and even infuriating at times. Their actions are, however, quite often effective – they can get their subordinates to improve and become better at their jobs.

Capricorn is a born manager and administrator. Leo is better at being king or queen, but Capricorn is better at being prime minister – the person actually wielding power.

Capricorn is interested in the virtues that last, in the things that will stand the test of time and trials of circumstance. Temporary fads and fashions mean little to a Capricorn – except as things to be used for profit or power. Capricorns apply this attitude to business, love, to their thinking and even to their philosophy and religion.

Finance

Capricorns generally attain wealth and they usually earn it. They are willing to work long and hard for what they want. They are quite amenable to foregoing a short-term gain in favour of long-term benefits. Financially, they come into their own later in life.

However, if Capricorns are to attain their financial goals they must shed some of their strong conservatism. Perhaps this is the least desirable trait of the Capricorn. They can resist anything new merely because it is new and untried. They are afraid of experimentation. Capricorns need to be willing to take a few risks. They should be more eager to market new products or explore different managerial techniques. Otherwise, progress will leave them behind. If necessary, Capricorns must be ready to change with the times, to discard old methods that no longer work.

Very often this experimentation will mean that Capricorns have to break with existing authority. They might even consider changing their present position or starting their own ventures. If so, they should be willing to accept all the risks and just get on with it. Only then will a Capricorn be on the road to highest financial gains.

Career and Public Image

A Capricorn's ambition and quest for power are evident. It is perhaps the most ambitious sign of the zodiac – and usually the most successful in a worldly sense. However, there are lessons Capricorns need to learn in order to fulfil their highest aspirations.

Intelligence, hard work, cool efficiency and organization will take them a certain distance, but will not carry them to the very top. Capricorns need to cultivate their social graces, to develop a social style, along with charm and an ability to get along with people. They need to bring beauty into their lives and to cultivate the right social contacts. They must learn to wield power gracefully, so that people love them for it – a very delicate art. They also need to learn how to bring people together in order to fulfil certain objectives. In short, Capricorns require some of the gifts – the social graces – of Libra to get to the top.

Once they have learned this, Capricorns will be successful in their careers. They are ambitious hard workers who are not afraid of putting in the required time and effort. Capricorns take their time in getting the job done – in order to do it well – and they like moving up the corporate ladder slowly but surely. Being so driven by success, Capricorns are generally liked by their bosses, who respect and trust them.

Love and Relationships

Like Scorpio and Pisces, Capricorn is a difficult sign to get to know. They are deep, introverted and like to keep their own counsel. Capricorns do not like to reveal their innermost thoughts. If you are in love with a Capricorn, be patient and take your time. Little by little you will get to understand him or her.

Capricorns have a deep romantic nature, but they do not show it straightaway. They are cool, matter of fact and not especially emotional. They will often show their love in practical ways.

It takes time for a Capricorn – male or female – to fall in love. They are not the love-at-first-sight kind. If a Capricorn is involved with a Leo or Aries, these Fire types will be totally mystified – to them the Capricorn will seem cold, unfeeling, unaffectionate and not very spontaneous. Of course none of this is true; it is just that Capricorn likes to take things slowly. They like to be sure of their ground before making any demonstrations of love or commitment.

Even in love affairs Capricorns are deliberate. They need more time to make decisions than is true of the other signs of the zodiac, but given this time they become just as passionate. Capricorns like a relationship to be structured, committed, well regulated, well defined, predictable and even routine. They prefer partners who are nurturers, and they in turn like to nurture their partners. This is their basic psychology. Whether such a relationship is good for them is another issue altogether. Capricorns have enough routine in their lives as it is. They might be better off in relationships that are a bit more stimulating, changeable and fluctuating.

Home and Domestic Life

The home of a Capricorn – as with a Virgo – is going to be tidy and well organized. Capricorns tend to manage their families in the same way they manage their businesses. Capricorns are often so career-driven that they find little time for the home and family. They should try to get more actively involved in their family and domestic life. Capricorns do, however, take their children very seriously and are very proud parents – particularly should their children grow up to become respected members of society.

Horoscope for 2020

Major Trends

Your 1st house is where the power is this year, Capricorn. You are personally more independent, self-willed and self-motivated. And though you are enjoying all the pleasures of the senses, you are not likely to gain too much weight. It looks like you binge, then diet, binge, then diet – and so forth and so on. A great year for getting the body and image in shape.

Jupiter is in your sign now, and you are in a prosperity period. This will get even stronger as the year progresses. More on this later.

Now that Uranus has left your 4th house for good (and won't return for approximately eighty-four years) things at home, and the emotional life in general, are much calmer. Uranus is now in your 5th house for the next seven or so years, and those of you involved in the creative arts or entertainment are having an exciting time. Rarely have you been this original and innovative. You're not capable of copying anyone. Your work is original. More patience will be needed with children and children figures in your life, though – they seem unusually rebellious and difficult to handle. More on this later.

Four lunar eclipses this year (twice as many as usual) shake up the love life and test current relationships. More details below.

Mars will spend over six months in your 4th house of home and family, from June 28 onwards (an unusually long time for Mars to be in a house). This can temporarily ignite passions in the home and family. However it is a very good transit for doing major renovations or repairs to the home. Some of you might want to build a house during that period. More on this later.

Capricorns are always ambitious but the year ahead is not a very strong career year. It's more about preparation for future career pushes. All the long-term planets are below the horizon of your chart – on the night side. So the activities of night are more interesting than the activities of day. Details to come.

Your most important areas of interest this year are the body and image; finance (from March 23 to July 1 and from December 18 onwards); communication and intellectual interests; home and family (from June 28 onwards); and children, fun and creativity.

Your paths of greatest fulfilment this year are the body and image (until December 20); finance (after December 20); love, romance and social activities (until May 6); and sex, personal transformation and occult studies (from May 6 onwards).

Health

(Please note that this is an astrological perspective on health and not a medical one. In days of yore there was no difference, both these perspectives were identical. Now there could be quite a difference. For a medical perspective, please consult your doctor or health practitioner.)

Health should be good this year. Usually Saturn in someone's sign – which you've had for two years now – is not a great health signal. But because Saturn is a friendly planet to you – the ruler of the Horoscope – you are comfortable with his presence. There are no long-term planets in stressful alignment with you this year, and your 6th house of health is basically empty – only short-term planets will move through there. These are all positives for health. You need not focus much here as there is nothing wrong. You tend to be disease resistant. Sure, there will be periods in the year where health and energy are less easy than usual. These are only temporary, caused by the planetary transits, not trends for the year ahead. When the stressful transits pass your normal health and energy return.

Good though your health is you can make it even better. Give more attention to the following – the vulnerable areas of your Horoscope (the reflex points are shown in the chart overleaf):

- The spine, knees, teeth, skin and overall skeletal alignment are always important areas for you, Capricorn. Regular back and knee massage should be part of your regular health regime. Regular visits to a chiropractor or osteopath would also be a good idea. It is very important to keep the vertebrae in right alignment. Good posture is more important for you than for other signs, and so I like therapies such as Alexander Technique, yoga and Pilates. All of these help the posture. Therapies such as Rolfing or Feldenkrais are also good for the spine. Good dental hygiene is always important, and you should give the knees more support when exercising.

- The lungs, arms, shoulders and respiratory system. These also are always important for Capricorn as Mercury, your health planet, rules these areas. Arms and shoulders should be regularly massaged. Tension tends to collect in the shoulders and needs to be released.

Important foot reflexology points for the year ahead

Try to massage all of the foot on a regular basis – the top of the foot as well as the bottom – but pay extra attention to the points highlighted on the chart. When you massage, be aware of 'sore spots' as these need special attention. It's also a good idea to massage the ankles and below them.

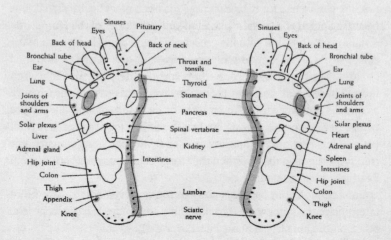

A lunar eclipse on November 30 occurs in your 6th house of health, showing that you'll be making important changes to the health regime after that date. Sometimes such an eclipse shows a health scare, but since health is good this year, it is not likely to be more than that.

With fast and often erratic Mercury as your health planet, your needs in health constantly change. Also you tend to respond better to certain therapies at different times. These are the short-term trends in health that are best covered in the monthly reports.

Normally when Jupiter is in someone's 1st house – which is the situation this year – people tend to put on weight. Women of child-bearing age tend to be more fertile as well. But Capricorns tend to slimness. They tend to be personally more 'Spartan'. This tendency is even stronger this year as both Pluto and Saturn are also in your sign. So you might put on some pounds (this comes from enjoying the good life) but then you'll diet to lose them. This, as we mentioned earlier, is a constant see-saw this year.

Pregnancies for women of childbearing age seem complicated.

With so many planets in your 1st house (it is easily the strongest in your Horoscope this year), self-esteem and self-confidence should be good. But you need to be careful of overdoing a good thing. The South Node of the Moon will also be in your 1st house – this denotes a feeling of deficiency. You might be overcompensating because of this. Real self-confidence is quiet and natural. It's not bombastic. Saturn in your own sign counsels 'shine but silently' – keep a lower profile.

Home and Family

After seven years of instability in the home, family crises and perhaps even family break-ups, things are much calmer now Uranus has moved on – especially until June 28. Many of you have moved multiple times over the past seven years. Some have made multiple renovations to the home. You have kept upgrading the home the way you upgrade your software or computer. You are much calmer on the emotional level now too. Family members seem more stable as well.

Enjoy the calm while it lasts. On June 28 Mars will move into your 4th house and spice things up. This can bring conflicts with a parent or parent figure – you will have to work harder on your relationship. This parent figure is having some emotionally rough times. But other family members (or those who play that role in your life) also seem more passionate, angry perhaps, at the moment. They seem easily 'triggered' to anger. So, you will have to work harder on your relationship with them too.

Mars in the 4th house often signals construction or serious repairs happening to the home. The home should be safeguarded against fires too. Make sure the electrical wiring is safe and keep your smoke detectors in good working order. Keep sharp objects out of the reach of children too.

Mars in the 4th house would indicate that you're installing athletic or exercise equipment in the home. The home is as much a gym as a home. Home security seems a priority as well. Probably security systems are being installed.

Moves are not likely this year, but renovations are very likely to happen.

Mars, your family planet, is a relatively fast-moving planet. This year he will move through six signs and houses of your chart, so there are many short-term family trends that depend on where Mars is and the kind of aspects he receives. These are best dealt with in the monthly reports.

Renovations and major repairs are best done in the latter half of the year – from June 28 onwards. If you're repainting, redecorating or buying objects of beauty for the home – February 7 to March 5, September 6 to October 2 and December 15 onwards are good times.

A parent or parent figure has dramas in the home and emotional upsets this year, but a move is not likely. Siblings and sibling figures are spiritual and idealistic these days. Perhaps they are dealing with scandals and unpleasant revelations. A move is not likely either, but they can be redecorating from April 3 to August 7.

Children and children figures are more difficult to handle, as we mentioned earlier. They are more rebellious and self-willed. If you want them to do something, they need a good reason for it. You have to explain the 'whys' behind your request. They don't respond well to authoritarianism. They can be living in different places for long periods of time but an actual move is not likely.

Grandchildren (if you have them), or those who play that role in your life, will have a stable family year. However, if they are of childbearing age, they are more fertile than usual.

Finance and Career

Ever since your financial planet, Uranus, moved into Taurus in March last year, you've been in a new financial era – and a prosperous one. Uranus is receiving beautiful aspects for most of the year; Jupiter, the planet of abundance, is making especially nice aspects. So earnings are increasing. This will be the case all year, but early in the year earnings come more easily than later in the year. Late in the year, as both Saturn and Jupiter move into Aquarius, there's more work involved – but prosperity is still happening.

But the year ahead is not just about increased earnings. The quality of the earnings is much improved too. Your financial planet in your 5th house of fun, creativity and children (and for many more years to come) shows 'happy money' – money that is earned in happy, enjoyable ways. Money is also spent on happy things – on leisure and fun activities. You're enjoying your wealth more.

The financial planet in the 5th house indicates that you spend more on your children or the children figures in your life. But they can also be a source of income – much depends on their age and stage in life. Older children can actually be financially supportive. Younger ones are a strong motivating force for earnings and often they have ideas that lead to profits – 'out of the mouth of babes'.

The 5th house is a speculative kind of house, but Capricorns are not usually speculators. Further, the financial planet in conservative Taurus is not a very speculative transit. So you might indulge in a little bit of speculation, but you're not likely to go overboard.

The financial planet in the 5th house signals a good affinity for the entertainment and music industries. Also for companies that cater to the youth market. Utilities and power companies are also interesting – especially those that are involved in technology.

Uranus as your financial planet tends to instability in finance. Earnings can be erratic. And this was the case over the past seven years. But here in the sign of Taurus earnings are less volatile, much more stable than they have been.

Saturn, the ruler of your Horoscope, will move into the money house from March 23 to July 1 – a brief flirtation – and then again, for the long term, on December 18. This too is a positive for finance – it shows focus and good fortune. You adopt the image of a money person and people see you that way. You're taking more personal control over finances – not delegating things to others. On December 20, Jupiter also moves into your money house and will be there through most of 2021. Jupiter's move into the 2nd house is a classic signal for prosperity. (Also keep in mind that Jupiter will be much stronger in Aquarius than he was in Capricorn – he is more comfortable there.)

This is not an especially strong career year. All the long-term planets are below the horizon – on the night side of the chart. So you are preparing for career success later on. It is a much stronger financial year than a career year. This is a year for building the psychological infrastructure, carrying out the behind-the-scenes activity, so necessary for career success.

Your career planet, Venus, is a fast-moving planet. So career issues will depend on where Venus is at any given time and the aspects she receives. These are short-term trends and are best dealt with in the monthly reports.

Love and Social Life

Your 7th house of love is not prominent this year. It is basically empty and only short-term planets will move through there. Also, as we've mentioned, most of the long-term planets are in the Eastern sector of self – of personal independence. The Western, social sector will strengthen as the year progresses, but only briefly. This is not a strong romantic or love year. Usually this shows contentment and stability in love. Singles tend to remain single, those who are married tend to remain married. But this year we have an unusual number of eclipses – six this year (two more than normal). Moreover, five of the six will impact on the love life. Two eclipses – one solar and one lunar – will actually occur in your 7th house. And since the Moon is your love planet, the four lunar eclipses this year also affect the love life. There will be many shakeups in the love life, many disruptions, many crises this year. The good news is that good relationships – those that are fundamentally sound – will survive. It is the flawed ones that are likely to dissolve.

Often these love testings are not happening because of the relationship per se, but because of personal dramas in the life of the beloved or that of friends. Love is a rocky ride this year. Fasten your seat belts.

The Moon is the fastest of all the planets. Where the other fast-moving planets need a year to move through your entire chart, the Moon will do so every month. So there are many short-term – very short-term – trends in love that can only be covered in the monthly reports.

In general, you have stronger social magnetism when the Moon is waxing (growing) than when she is waning (getting smaller). The waxing Moon increases your enthusiasm for love as well. The New and Full Moons tend to be strong love days (if the aspects are good). Also the Moon's perigee (when she is at her closest distance to earth) will increase social magnetism and energy.

With the Moon as your love planet, mood is everything in love. You (and the people you attract) can be very moody about it. In a good mood, love is magical and perfect; in a bad mood love can turn to hate. It is vital to keep your moods positive and constructive.

The strength in your Eastern sector of self makes you more independent – a good thing. However, in love independence is not that good. You might feel that you will do whatever you want, regardless of the feelings of your partner. So while independence is a good thing, avoid disrespecting others.

For the past two years your ruling planet Saturn has been in your own sign and this remains the case for much of the year ahead. Thus you are more of a Capricorn than usual. All the Capricorn strengths and weaknesses are greatly magnified. Thus your business and management ability is at all-time highs. (This is a very good position for business.) But – and we have written of this in previous years' reports – you can come across as too cold, too aloof, too bossy to others. You might not even realize that you're doing it. It just comes out. This can cause problems in love. So, as was advised in previous reports, make it a project to send love and warmth to others. It will take conscious practice.

Love might be complicated, but the overall social life is very good. You attract friends. Opportunities for friendship seek you out. They will find you with little effort on your part. Just go about your daily business.

Love affairs are also likely for singles. But these are just entertainment – they don't seem to lead anywhere.

Self-improvement

Capricorns are down-to-earth, practical people. They are not known for their spirituality. They feel that 'duty' and 'responsibility' on the earthly plane is the highest form of spirituality. (They have a point here.) But of late, over the past few years, spirituality has been more important. In 2016 and 2017 Saturn was in your spiritual 12th house, indicating a great focus here, while in 2019 Jupiter, your spiritual planet, spent the year in your 12th house, showing even more interest and great interior growth. This year, Jupiter is in your own sign. So much of what has been learned recently is 'showing' – it is more manifest. The lessons are being applied to the physical body. You have more power over it. You are seeing how it can be moulded and shaped by spiritual means. People are seeing you as more spiritual.

Your spiritual planet in your own sign points to a practical kind of spirituality. It has to work in the world – improve your life and circumstances. Often it would indicate a liking for traditional orthodox religion. Capricorns like this anyway. They like the rules, regulations, rites, rituals, pomp and ceremony of traditional religion. This year even more so. This would be a good year to explore the mystical side of your native religion. (Every religion has its mystical side.)

Neptune has been in your 3rd house for many years now. This shows a spiritualization – a refinement – of the intellect and thought process. Your taste in reading is becoming ever more refined. You now favour spiritual types of books and magazines. You are more attracted to spiritual lectures, courses and seminars. Just plain everyday reading is not very alluring.

Your spiritual planet Jupiter will move into Aquarius, your 2nd house, on December 20. This strengthens Jupiter's influence. He is much stronger in Aquarius than in Capricorn (his 'fall'). This transit also favours a practical spirituality. You will be developing your financial intuition – and it will be a lot stronger. This will go on well into next year too. Financial guidance will come in dreams or through psychics, tarot readers, spiritual channels or ministers. This transit also favours astrology – especially its esoteric side. It is a valid spiritual path.

Month-by-month Forecasts

January

Best Days Overall: 5, 6, 14, 22, 23
Most Stressful Days Overall: 2, 3, 9, 10, 16, 29, 30, 31
Best Days for Love: 5, 6, 9, 10, 13, 14, 15, 18, 19, 24, 25, 27, 28
Best Days for Money: 4, 5, 6, 13, 14, 22, 23, 24, 25, 26
Best Days for Career: 13, 14, 16, 18, 19, 27, 28

You begin your year with the Eastern sector of your Horoscope overwhelmingly powerful; 80 per cent – sometime 90 per cent – of the planets are in the East. In addition, your 1st house of self is unusually strong, while your 7th house of love and social activities is basically empty. We have a clear message. The focus this month is on yourself and your personal interests. Happiness is up to you. You have more independence now, and can and should make the changes in your life that need to be made. Other people are important (as you learn on the 10th with a lunar eclipse), but your way is the best way. You are master of your destiny these days.

The lunar eclipse of the 10th occurs in your 7th house and, of course, impacts on your love planet, the Moon. So it is a powerful eclipse both for you and your spouse, partner or current love. He or she can be having personal dramas. This could be the reason for the testing of the relationship. But it could also come from too much self-absorption – you might be overdoing a good thing lately, overdoing personal independence. The eclipse will force you to give a bit more attention to others. This eclipse also impacts on Saturn, the ruler of your chart, which can bring a detox of the body and a need to redefine yourself. In the coming months (and probably all year) you will be changing your look and your image. Take it easy and reduce your schedule a bit over this period. This eclipse also impacts on Pluto, which can affect your high-tech gadgetry. Take precautions before the eclipse – back up your important files and be sure your anti-hacking and anti-virus software is up to date. Mercury is also affected by this eclipse, so job changes and changes in the health regime are also happening. Avoid foreign travel during this period.

Health is good this month, but reduce your schedule during the eclipse period, for a few days before and after the event. You can enhance your health even more by paying attention to the spine, knees, teeth and bones until the 16th, and to the ankles and calves after then.

On the 20th the Sun enters your money house and you begin a yearly financial peak. The month ahead is prosperous and you will feel it even before the 20th. From the 21st to the 23rd there can be important financial changes, some financial disruption, but it is only temporary. There is some financial disagreement with the spouse, partner or current love.

February

Best Days Overall: 1, 2, 10, 11, 18, 19, 20, 28, 29
Most Stressful Days Overall: 6, 7, 12, 13, 26, 27
Best Days for Love: 3, 4, 6, 7, 8, 12, 13, 16, 17, 23, 24, 26, 27
Best Days for Money: 1, 2, 9, 10, 11, 18, 19, 20, 21, 22, 28, 29
Best Days for Career: 7, 8, 12, 13, 16, 17, 26, 27

Your personal independence is even stronger than last month. On the 16th Mars enters your sign and stays for the rest of the month. This has some good points. You have more energy. You are courageous. You don't back away from conflict. You excel at exercise regimes and sports. The danger (like most dangers) is of pushing things too far. You can be overly combative. Perhaps too hasty. It does not help the love life.

You're still in the midst of a yearly financial peak. Your financial planet Uranus is moving forward as well (he started moving forward on January 11). So the financial judgement is good and things are advancing. The Sun in your money house until the 19th signals good access to outside money – either through banks or external investors. This is a good period in which to pay down debt. It is also good for tax planning and, if you are of appropriate age, for estate planning.

Health is excellent this month. You have superabundant energy, and with this all kinds of doors open up for you. Things that seemed impossible are now eminently doable. You can enhance the health even more through ankle and calf massage until the 3rd and through foot massage after then. Spiritual healing also becomes powerful after the 3rd. Your health planet will go retrograde on the 17th so avoid making important health decisions after that date. (It won't be a good time for taking scans or tests after then either – they could be faulty or inaccurate.)

Love doesn't seem a major issue this month. Your 7th house is basically empty, with only the Moon moving through there on the 6th and 7th. This tends to the status quo. Your social grace and social energy will be stronger from the 1st to the 9th and from the 23rd to the 28th – as the Moon waxes. The Full Moon of the 10th is almost a 'Super Full Moon' – it occurs with the Moon near perigee, her closest distance to earth. This should be an especially good love and social day.

The upper half of your Horoscope is bereft of planets this month, and after the 16th there will be no planets in the day side of your Horoscope either. This is *not* a strong career period! The focus should be on the home, family and emotional wellness. It is a preparatory period for career developments that will happen later this year and in future years. Even your career planet, Venus, will be in your 4th house of home and family from the 7th onwards. This is another indication to focus on the home and family. Venus will have her solstice from the 8th to the 10th. She pauses in the heavens (in latitude) and then changes direction. So a pause and a change of career direction is likely. It is basically a good thing – a natural event.

March

Best Days Overall: 1, 8, 9, 17, 18, 27, 28
Most Stressful Days Overall: 4, 5, 10, 11, 24, 25
Best Days for Love: 4, 5, 8, 12, 13, 17, 18, 24, 25, 27, 28
Best Days for Money: 1, 8, 9, 16, 17, 18, 19, 20, 26, 27, 28
Best Days for Career: 8, 10, 11, 17, 18, 27, 28

Mercury is still retrograde until the 10th, so (like last month) avoid making important health decisions until after the 10th and forward motion résumés. Job seekers (and employers) should avoid making and accepting offers of employment until after the 10th as well.

Saturn, the ruler of your Horoscope and a very important planet in your chart, moves into your money house on the 23rd. This is a wonderful financial transit. It shows personal focus on finance and, by the spiritual law, we get what we focus on. It shows a more personal involvement with finance. You're not delegating things to others. You spend on yourself and have the image of prosperity. People see you this way. Your personal appearance and overall demeanour is a big factor in earnings. Venus will travel with your financial planet from the 6th to the 9th and this brings increased earnings. They can come from speculation or from a pay rise (official or unofficial). Bosses, parents and parent figures are favourable to your financial goals.

Health will need more attention from the 20th onwards. There is nothing serious afoot, just lower than usual energy. If you feel tired, just rest. Rest is the panacea for health issues this month. You can also enhance the health through foot massage – from the 1st to the 3rd and from the 16th onwards – and through spiritual-healing techniques during that same period. From the 4th to the 16th enhance the health with ankle and calf massage. Don't let the normal financial ups and downs of life impact on your health.

Jupiter travels with Pluto all month, which indicates the prosperity of friends. They are doing very well. It is also likely that you buy some good high-tech equipment. Children or children figures in your life of the appropriate age have a good romantic month.

Highly unusually, the upper half of your chart is still bereft of planets; power is concentrated in the 4th house of home and family. So continue to focus on the home and emotional wellness. Career can be downplayed now and perhaps left on autopilot.

The Sun travelling with Neptune on the 8th and 9th brings an active dream life. Dreams can bring financial guidance for the spouse, partner or current love.

Your 7th house of love is still empty this month with only the Moon moving through there on the 4th and 5th. So love is stable. Social energy and social grace will be strongest from the 1st to the 9th and from the 24th to the 31st. The Full Moon of the 9th occurs very near the Moon's perigee point and should be a powerful love and social day.

April

Best Days Overall: 5, 6, 13, 14, 23, 24
Most Stressful Days Overall: 1, 2, 7, 8, 20, 21, 22, 28, 29
Best Days for Love: 1, 2, 3, 4, 7, 8, 12, 15, 16, 17, 23, 25, 26, 28, 29
Best Days for Money: 5, 6, 13, 14, 15, 16, 17, 23, 24
Best Days for Career: 7, 8, 15, 16, 17, 25, 26

Jupiter will be travelling with Pluto all month (both in your own sign). So friends are prospering greatly and seem well disposed to you (perhaps you are involved in this). You're making spiritual-type friends these days. And, as we mentioned last month, you're buying high-tech gadgetry and equipment.

Health still needs some attention, but you will see a great improvement after the 19th. You can enhance the health with more rest until the 19th. Until the 11th health is enhanced by spiritual means and through foot massage. Spiritual healing is especially effective on the 3rd and 4th. After the 11th scalp and face massage will be beneficial. Physical exercise and good emotional health are also important. After the 27th neck and throat massage will be effective.

Saturn moved into your money house on March 23; Mars moved in on March 31 and both will spend this month there. Mars in the money house makes you more risk-taking and speculative, but Saturn's presence will rein you in a bit (a good thing). So, well-hedged, well-thought out speculations can work, but casino-type gambles should be avoided.

Mars, your family planet, in the money house indicates good family support – and it seems mutual. You spend more on the home and family but can earn from here as well. Family connections also seem important financially. The Sun will travel with your financial planet from the 24th to the 26th and this should be a good financial period. You will have opportunities to either borrow money or pay down debt – depending on your need. You and the spouse, partner or current love seem in financial harmony.

On the 19th the Sun enters your 5th house and you begin one of your yearly personal pleasure peaks. Enjoy your life! Make time for fun and leisure! Let go of your Capricorn seriousness for a while – you'll get back to it soon enough.

Love is a bit more active than usual this month. While your 7th house is mostly empty, the Moon will visit it twice this month (usually it's only once). Your social grace and social enthusiasm will be strongest from the 1st to the 8th and from the 23rd to the 30th as the Moon waxes. The Full Moon of the 8th occurs very near the Moon's perigee (her closest distance to earth) and this should be a strong love and social day. It will also be a strong career day.

May

Best Days Overall: 2, 3, 10, 11, 20, 21, 29, 30
Most Stressful Days Overall: 4, 5, 18, 19, 25, 26
Best Days for Love: 2, 3, 4, 5, 11, 13, 14, 23, 24, 25, 26
Best Days for Money: 2, 3, 10, 12, 13, 14, 20, 22
Best Days for Career: 4, 5, 13, 14, 23, 24

Venus has been 'out of bounds' since April 3, and will remain so for the entire month ahead. Thus in career matters you are venturing outside your normal sphere. It could be that career assignments take you outside your normal comfort zone. Children, children figures, parents and parent figures also seem outside their normal boundaries.

Mercury will also be 'out of bounds' from the 17th onwards. This means that in health matters, and in your job, you are going outside your normal boundaries. It could be – as we saw in the career – that work responsibilities are taking you away from your normal modes of working. Job seekers might be looking outside their normal circles for opportunities as well.

Health is excellent this month. Until the 29th there are no planets in stressful alignment with you. Only the Moon (and then only occasionally) will make short-term stressful aspects. You have naturally high energy and this is the best defence against disease. If you like, you can enhance the health still further through neck and throat massage until the 12th, and by having fun. After the 12th arm and shoulder massage and breathing exercises will be beneficial.

You're still in one of your yearly personal pleasure peaks until the 20th so enjoy your life and let go of worry and stress. You'll achieve more by doing what you love than by hard work. The urge to work and to be more serious will return from after the 20th. Indeed, this will be a good period to tackle those boring, mundane, detailed tasks that you keep putting off. You have more energy for these things now. And although your health is very good this month, it will be a good time to kick-start a healthy lifestyle drive.

Job seekers have many good opportunities this month. And even those who are employed have opportunities for overtime and to take on second jobs.

Venus will go retrograde on the 13th, which is a relatively rare event. (It only happens once in two years.) Children and children figures can lack direction these days. They just need time to gain clarity on things. Career issues also seem unclear and only time will straighten things out. So you may as well have fun and focus on your emotional wellness.

Love will become more important after the 29th as Mercury moves into your 7th house. Singles will be attracted to religious and highly educated kinds of people – also to health professionals or people involved in their health.

June

Best Days Overall: 7, 8, 16, 17, 18, 26, 27
Most Stressful Days Overall: 1, 14, 15, 21, 22
Best Days for Love: 1, 9, 10, 19, 20, 21, 22
Best Days for Money: 7, 8, 9, 10, 16, 17, 18, 26, 27
Best Days for Career: 1, 9, 10, 19, 20

In a way it is good that your 7th house of love becomes powerful this month, as it is very important to focus here now. Two eclipses this month impact on the love life, so there is much turbulence.

The lunar eclipse of 5th occurs in your 12th house of spirituality. Every lunar eclipse impacts on your relationships and this one is no different. The relationship gets tested. Usually long-suppressed emotions, dirty laundry, surface for resolution. Often there are personal dramas in the life of the beloved which can be the root cause of the problem. The beloved can be experiencing job changes or health challenges. Friends are making important financial changes. For you this eclipse also brings spiritual changes – changes in your practice, teachings or teachers. There are upheavals and disruptions in spiritual or charitable organizations that you're involved with. There are personal dramas in the lives of gurus or guru figures. This eclipse impacts pretty directly on both Mars and Mercury. So there can be family dramas or repairs needed to the home. The impact on Mercury brings changes to your health regime and upheavals in your place of worship or school. College-level students change their educational plans.

The solar eclipse of the 21st affects you strongly as well – perhaps more strongly than the previous one. All of you will feel this, but those of you born early in the sign of Capricorn (December 21–22) will be most affected. It occurs in your 7th house of love and again tests the current relationship. The beloved is forced to make dramatic financial changes; perhaps there is some financial crisis that forces this. You are once again confronting death and issues to do with death – albeit generally on the psychological level. You can experience a 'close call' – a near-death kind of experience. You can read of some grisly crime or the passing of someone you know. Often there are dreams of death.

These are love letters from above. Life is short and can end at any time. Get busy with the work you were born to do.

You should reduce your schedule from the 21st onwards, but especially around the eclipse periods. Health needs attention after the 21st – and especially after the 28th. Rest is probably the best cure for any problem, but your health can also be enhanced with right diet, abdominal massage and good emotional and social health. Meditation will be a big help here.

July

Best Days Overall: 4, 5, 14, 15, 23, 24, 31
Most Stressful Days Overall: 11, 12, 19, 20, 25, 26
Best Days for Love: 1, 6, 7, 8, 9, 10, 16, 17, 19, 20, 21, 22, 25, 26, 29
Best Days for Money: 4, 5, 6, 7, 8, 14, 15, 23, 24, 31
Best Days for Career: 6, 7, 8, 16, 17, 23, 24, 25, 26

The planetary power is now moving to the social West. This began last month on the 28th as Mars moved to the West. Your 7th house of love is also very strong and you are still in the midst of a yearly love and social peak. So the month ahead is social. Let go of your personal will for a while. Let others have their way, so long as it isn't destructive. Allow your good to come to you through the grace of others. Cultivate your social skills.

Like last month, the social focus is good – necessary. Another lunar eclipse on the 5th rocks the love life. Once again the current relationship is tested. If the relationship is fundamentally sound, it might be a rocky period but your relationship will survive. It is the unsound relationships that are in danger. This eclipse occurs in your own sign, so take it easy over this period. There's no need for stressful kinds of activities. Things that must be done should be done, but anything else can be rescheduled.

Since the eclipse occurs in your sign there can be a detox of the body (this is not disease, though it can feel that way). The body expels effete material. It will also precipitate a redefinition of the self – your self-concept and image. This is basically healthy. We are growing and evolving beings. It is good every now and then to redefine ourselves. But here the eclipse forces the issue and it will result in wardrobe and image changes in the coming months. Mercury, Jupiter and Mars all get sideswiped by this eclipse. There can be disturbances at work and changes in the health regime. There can be more family dramas and repairs in the home. And, once again, there can be spiritual changes.

Health needs attention being paid to it until the 22nd – and especially around the eclipse period. As always, make sure to get enough rest. Enhance the health in the ways mentioned last month – eat right, keep the moods positive and constructive, massage the abdomen regularly and do your best to maintain good social health (not so easy).

Saturn moves back into your own sign on the 2nd. Finance doesn't seem a big issue this month. Finances will go much easier until the 22nd than afterwards, however. After the 22nd you'll have to work harder to achieve your financial goals.

The Sun's move into your 8th house on the 22nd is a good financial transit for the beloved. He or she is in a yearly financial peak. You and the beloved need to work out your financial differences. There seems to be some conflict here.

August

Best Days Overall: 1, 2, 10, 11, 19, 20, 28, 29
Most Stressful Days Overall: 8, 9, 15, 16, 21, 22
Best Days for Love: 3, 4, 8, 9, 15, 16, 18, 19, 23, 24, 28
Best Days for Money: 1, 2, 3, 4, 10, 11, 19, 20, 28, 29, 30, 31
Best Days for Career: 3, 4, 15, 16, 21, 22, 23, 24

Your 8th house is strong until the 22nd, so this is a month for detox regimes and decluttering your life. The 8th house of transformation is where we eliminate what doesn't belong in the organism – materially, physically, psychologically and mentally. Purgation is always the prelude to renewal. So go through your possessions and get rid of what you don't need or use. Sell it or give it to charity. Use meditation to get rid of mental and emotional patterns that are not useful any more. You will feel like a different person afterwards.

This is a good month for either making or paying down debt – according to your need. It is good for tax planning and, if you are of appropriate age, estate planning. It is also a sexually active kind of month. Whatever your age or stage in life, the libido is stronger than usual.

Health is good this month and will get even better after the 22nd, when there will be a Grand Trine in the Earth signs (your native element). This is comfortable for you. Your already strong management and organizational skills are even stronger than normal. Finances will go much better and easier too. There is good prosperity from the 22nd onwards. Financial conflicts with the spouse, partner or current love are resolved after the 2nd. The only issue moneywise this month is the retrograde of your financial planet Uranus, which begins on the 15th. This will slow things down, but won't stop earnings. There will be many happy financial opportunities after the 22nd but they need some diligent study. Don't rush into anything.

Health is enhanced through detox regimes after the 5th. Massage the reflex to the heart (shown on the chart in the yearly report). Chest massage will also be beneficial.

Venus moves into your 7th house on the 7th and will be there the rest of the month. For singles this shows a relationship, but it doesn't seem that serious. This transit also shows that you are mixing with people of power and prestige, people above you in status. The career is enhanced by social means; a lot of your socializing is career-related now.

Your social grace and magnetism are strongest from the 1st to the 3rd and from the 19th onwards – as your love planet waxes. The Full Moon of the 11th and the New Moon of the 27th are other good love and social days.

September

Best Days Overall: 6, 7, 8, 16, 17, 24, 25
Most Stressful Days Overall: 4, 5, 11, 12, 18, 19
Best Days for Love: 2, 3, 6, 7, 11, 12, 13, 14, 17, 22, 23, 26
Best Days for Money: 6, 7, 16, 17, 24, 25, 26, 27
Best Days for Career: 2, 3, 13, 14, 18, 19, 22, 23

The upper, day side of your Horoscope is as strong as it will ever be this year. But still the lower half, the night side, is dominant. So, though you are in the 'midday' of your year, you still seem half asleep. Yet, with Mars, your home and family planet, going retrograde on the 9th, it might be a good idea to focus more on the career and outer activities. Your 10th house of career becomes strong after the 22nd, so do your best. You've had better career years in your life and will have better ones in the future, but this is the peak for this year.

Retrograde activity hits its maximum level this month (as it did back in June too). From the 9th to the 12th 60 per cent of the planets are moving backwards. The pace of life is slow. Not much happening in the world or in your life. The career, though, seems unaffected.

This is a month for dealing with death, near-death issues and perhaps surgery. The ruler of your 8th house, the Sun, will be at the top of the chart – his most powerful position. Your career planet, Venus, will be in the 8th house from the 6th onwards, and so these near-death issues seem to involve bosses, parents and parent figures – authority figures in your life. Your job, your mission, is to be there for them.

Health is excellent until the 22nd but afterwards will need more watching. Until the 5th enhance the health with abdominal massage and earth-based treatments. Mud pack are good, as is soaking in waters with a high mineral content. After the 5th pay more attention to the kidneys and hips. Massage the kidney reflex (see the chart in the yearly report) and the hips regularly. After the 27th safe sex and sexual moderation are important. Detox regimes will also be effective.

Venus leaves your 7th house on the 6th and that house will be empty from then on. Only the Moon will move through there on the 11th and 12th. Love should be stable this month. Social grace and magnetism will be strongest on the 1st and 2nd and from the 17th to the 30th. The New Moon of the 17th occurs near her perigee – so it is a strong New Moon. It should be a good social and love day.

October

Best Days Overall: 4, 5, 13, 14, 21, 23, 31
Most Stressful Days Overall: 1, 2, 9, 10, 15, 16, 28, 29, 30
Best Days for Love: 3, 6, 7, 9, 10, 15, 16, 21, 22, 25
Best Days for Money: 4, 5, 13, 14, 21, 23, 24, 25, 31
Best Days for Career: 3, 15, 16, 21, 22

Your home and family planet, Mars, is retrograde all month, while your 10th house of career is strong: though you might not feel like it, it's better to focus on the career this month. Home and family issues need time to resolve. There are still many planets retrograde this month – not as many as last month but still a sizeable percentage (40 per cent after the 14th). But career doesn't seem affected. Your career planet, Venus, is moving speedily this month, travelling through three signs and houses. This shows confidence and fast progress. Until the 2nd she is in the 8th house, bringing dramas, near-death experiences and perhaps surgery into the lives of bosses, parents, parent figures or leaders in your industry. On the 2nd she moves into your 9th house, bringing career-related travel and educational opportunities related to the career. On the 28th she moves on into your 10th career house – her own sign and house – where she is powerful on your behalf.

Venus makes very nice aspects to Pluto on the 21st and 22nd. Thus friends are succeeding and are helpful in the career. Technology seems important careerwise as well. Thus there is career progress this month. The doors might be shut in other areas of life, but not in the career.

Mars, your family planet, is in your 4th house – his own sign and house – all month, and has been since June 28. So if you're renovating the home and doing extensive repairs there could be delays involved with this.

Though the month ahead is not particularly romantic – it is a stable kind of month romantically – the social life in general is good, active. Pluto, your planet of friends, starts to move forward on the 4th and on the 23rd the Sun moves into your 11th house. So there is more involvement with friends, groups and group activities. There can be dramas in the lives of friends too, but you are there for them. Friends seem very devoted to you.

Health needs some attention until the 23rd. As always, the most important thing is to get enough rest, to maintain high energy levels. Health is enhanced through detox regimes, through safe sex, sexual moderation and a focus on the colon, bladder and sexual organs. A herbal colonic might be just the ticket if you feel under the weather.

Your health planet Mercury goes retrograde on the 14th so avoid making major health changes after that date. The same is true for job offers. Study the details closely – things are not as they seem.

There will be a dramatic improvement in health and energy after the 23rd.

November

Best Days Overall: 1, 10, 18, 19, 27, 28
Most Stressful Days Overall: 5, 6, 12, 25, 26
Best Days for Love: 2, 3, 5, 6, 12, 14, 15, 21, 22, 24, 25
Best Days for Money: 1, 2, 9, 10, 11, 17, 18, 19, 20, 21, 27
Best Days for Career: 2, 3, 12, 21, 22

Venus has her solstice from October 29 until November 2. She pauses in the heavens (she occupies the same degree of latitude) this period, and then she reverses direction – in latitude. So a brief respite in the career is happening and then a change of direction. Children and children figures experience this in a more personal way. There is a brief pause in their personal affairs and then a change of direction.

Retrograde activity having reached a crescendo in June and September, this month almost disappears. After the 14th 80 per cent of the planets are moving forward, and by the end of the month 90 per cent are going forward. The pace of life quickens. Gridlock is released. Progress starts to happen in the world and in your personal affairs.

Our fourth and final lunar eclipse this year occurs on the 30th. Once again the love life gets shaken up and tested. (You've been dealing with this all year.) This eclipse occurs in your 6th house. Thus there are job changes afoot – this could be within your present company or with another one. There are changes in the conditions of work as well. There can be disruptions at the workplace. If you employ others there can be staff turnover now (and in the coming months). There are changes in your health regime too (probably also in coming months). The spouse, partner or current love experiences spiritual changes – changes in his or her practice, teachings or teachers. There are shake-ups in spiritual or charitable organizations that he or she is involved with. Children and children figures need a financial course correction, and parents and parent figures should drive more carefully. Their cars and communication equipment gets tested.

In spite of the eclipse, health is good this month. Your health planet starts to move forward on the 3rd so there is clarity in this area. Until the 3rd enhance the health through hip massage. A herbal kidney cleanse would also be good if you feel under the weather. After the 3rd detox regimes will be effective. And, as we mentioned last month, safe sex and sexual moderation are important.

Your social grace is strongest from the 15th to the 30th, as your love planet waxes. The New Moon of the 15th occurs very near the Moon's perigee and thus will be a particularly powerful love and social day.

December

Best Days Overall: 7, 8, 15, 16, 24, 25, 26
Most Stressful Days Overall: 2, 3, 9, 10, 22, 23, 29, 30, 31
Best Days for Love: 2, 3, 5, 6, 11, 12, 13, 14, 22, 23, 24, 29, 30, 31
Best Days for Money: 7, 8, 15, 16, 17, 18, 24, 25, 27
Best Days for Career: 2, 3, 9, 10, 11, 12, 22, 23

As the year ends, the cosmos, like us, is preparing for the new. The chess pieces are being moved and the trends for 2021 will be very different from this past year.

Saturn, the ruler of your Horoscope will make his final move out of your sign and enters Aquarius, your money house, on the 18th. Jupiter, which has been in your sign all year, also makes a major move into Aquarius on the 20th, and will be there for almost all of 2021. Next year looks to be a very prosperous year.

A solar eclipse on the 14th (the sixth eclipse of the year) occurs in your 12th house of spirituality. This is the announcement of spiritual changes to come due to Jupiter's move, and it brings changes in your spiritual practice, attitudes, teachings and perhaps teachers. There are disruptions and crises in spiritual or charitable organizations you're involved with. There are dramas in the lives of gurus and guru figures. Friends need to change their financial plans. The spouse, partner or current love has job changes and changes in the health regime. And, since the eclipsed planet, the Sun, is ruler of your 8th house, there can be encounters with death or near-death kinds of experiences. (These are generally psychological encounters, rather than literal deaths.) These encounters, as our regular readers know, are love messages from above – 'Life is too short to delay your focus on your mission. Be about the business for which you were born.'

The past year has been spiritual and the month ahead is spiritual – especially until the 21st. So this is a good month for the study of sacred literature, meditation and getting involved in idealistic and charitable causes. There will be spiritual breakthroughs for those who desire them.

On the 21st the Sun enters your own sign and you begin a yearly personal pleasure peak. This is a good time to indulge the body (within limits) and get it into the shape that you want. It is also good for weight loss and detox regimes.

Earnings are a slower than usual as your financial planet Uranus is still retrograde. But in spite of this, earnings will increase – it just happens slower.

Health is good this month. You can enhance it further with spiritual-healing methods until the 21st. After the 21st enhance the health in the ways mentioned in the yearly report.

Aquarius

~~~

THE WATER-BEARER

Birthdays from
20th January to
18th February

Personality Profile

AQUARIUS AT A GLANCE

Element – Air

Ruling Planet – Uranus
   Career Planet – Pluto
   Love Planet – Sun
   Money Planet – Neptune
   Planet of Health and Work – Moon
   Planet of Home and Family Life – Venus
   Planet of Spirituality – Saturn

Colours – electric blue, grey, ultramarine blue

Colours that promote love, romance and social harmony – gold, orange

Colour that promotes earning power – aqua

Gems – black pearl, obsidian, opal, sapphire

Metal – lead

Scents – azalea, gardenia

DEVIN 2/16/94

Quality – fixed (= stability)

Qualities most needed for balance – warmth, feeling and emotion

Strongest virtues – great intellectual power, the ability to communicate and to form and understand abstract concepts, love for the new and avant-garde

Deepest needs – to know and to bring in the new

Characteristics to avoid – coldness, rebelliousness for its own sake, fixed ideas

Signs of greatest overall compatibility – Gemini, Libra

Signs of greatest overall incompatibility – Taurus, Leo, Scorpio

Sign most helpful to career – Scorpio

Sign most helpful for emotional support – Taurus

Sign most helpful financially – Pisces

Sign best for marriage and/or partnerships – Leo

Sign most helpful for creative projects – Gemini

Best Sign to have fun with – Gemini

Signs most helpful in spiritual matters – Libra, Capricorn

Best day of the week – Saturday

Understanding an Aquarius

In the Aquarius-born, intellectual faculties are perhaps the most highly developed of any sign in the zodiac. Aquarians are clear, scientific thinkers. They have the ability to think abstractly and to formulate laws, theories and clear concepts from masses of observed facts. Geminis might be very good at gathering information, but Aquarians take this a step further, excelling at interpreting the information gathered.

Practical people – men and women of the world – mistakenly consider abstract thinking as impractical. It is true that the realm of abstract thought takes us out of the physical world, but the discoveries made in this realm generally end up having tremendous practical consequences. All real scientific inventions and breakthroughs come from this abstract realm.

Aquarians, more so than most, are ideally suited to explore these abstract dimensions. Those who have explored these regions know that there is little feeling or emotion there. In fact, emotions are a hindrance to functioning in these dimensions; thus Aquarians seem – at times – cold and emotionless to others. It is not that Aquarians haven't got feelings and deep emotions, it is just that too much feeling clouds their ability to think and invent. The concept of 'too much feeling' cannot be tolerated or even understood by some of the other signs. Nevertheless, this Aquarian objectivity is ideal for science, communication and friendship.

Aquarians are very friendly people, but they do not make a big show about it. They do the right thing by their friends, even if sometimes they do it without passion or excitement.

Aquarians have a deep passion for clear thinking. Second in importance, but related, is their passion for breaking with the establishment and traditional authority. Aquarians delight in this, because for them rebellion is like a great game or challenge. Very often they will rebel strictly for the fun of rebelling, regardless of whether the authority they defy is right or wrong. Right or wrong has little to do with the rebellious actions of an Aquarian, because to a true Aquarian authority and power must be challenged as a matter of principle.

Where Capricorn or Taurus will err on the side of tradition and the status quo, an Aquarian will err on the side of the new. Without this virtue it is doubtful whether any progress would be made in the world. The conservative-minded would obstruct progress. Originality and invention imply an ability to break barriers; every new discovery represents the toppling of an impediment to thought. Aquarians are very interested in breaking barriers and making walls tumble – scientifically, socially and politically. Other zodiac signs, such as Capricorn, also have scientific talents. But Aquarians are particularly excellent in the social sciences and humanities.

Finance

In financial matters Aquarians tend to be idealistic and humanitarian – to the point of self-sacrifice. They are usually generous contributors to social and political causes. When they contribute it differs from when a Capricorn or Taurus contributes. A Capricorn or Taurus may expect some favour or return for a gift; an Aquarian contributes selflessly.

Aquarians tend to be as cool and rational about money as they are about most things in life. Money is something they need and they set about acquiring it scientifically. No need for fuss; they get on with it in the most rational and scientific ways available.

Money to the Aquarian is especially nice for what it can do, not for the status it may bring (as is the case for other signs). Aquarians are neither big spenders nor penny-pinchers and use their finances in practical ways, for example to facilitate progress for themselves, their families, or even for strangers.

However, if Aquarians want to reach their fullest financial potential they will have to explore their intuitive nature. If they follow only their financial theories – or what they believe to be theoretically correct – they may suffer some losses and disappointments. Instead, Aquarians should call on their intuition, which knows without thinking. For Aquarians, intuition is the short-cut to financial success.

Career and Public Image

Aquarians like to be perceived not only as the breakers of barriers but also as the transformers of society and the world. They long to be seen in this light and to play this role. They also look up to and respect other people in this position and even expect their superiors to act this way.

Aquarians prefer jobs that have a bit of idealism attached to them – careers with a philosophical basis. Aquarians need to be creative at work, to have access to new techniques and methods. They like to keep busy and enjoy getting down to business straightaway, without wasting any time. They are often the quickest workers and usually have suggestions for improvements that will benefit their employers. Aquarians are also very helpful with their co-workers and welcome responsibility, preferring this to having to take orders from others.

If Aquarians want to reach their highest career goals they have to develop more emotional sensitivity, depth of feeling and passion. They need to learn to narrow their focus on the essentials and concentrate more on the job in hand. Aquarians need 'a fire in the belly' – a consuming passion and desire – in order to rise to the very top. Once this passion exists they will succeed easily in whatever they attempt.

Love and Relationships

Aquarians are good at friendships, but a bit weak when it comes to love. Of course they fall in love, but their lovers always get the impression that they are more best friends than paramours.

Like Capricorns, they are cool customers. They are not prone to displays of passion or to outward demonstrations of their affections. In fact, they feel uncomfortable when their other half hugs and touches them too much. This does not mean that they do not love their partners. They do, only they show it in other ways. Curiously enough, in relationships they tend to attract the very things that they feel uncomfortable with. They seem to attract hot, passionate, romantic, demonstrative people. Perhaps they know instinctively that these people have qualities they lack and so seek them out. In any event, these relationships do seem to work; Aquarian coolness calming the more passionate partner while the fires of passion warm the cold-blooded Aquarius.

The qualities Aquarians need to develop in their love life are warmth, generosity, passion and fun. Aquarians love relationships of the mind. Here they excel. If the intellectual factor is missing in a relationship an Aquarian will soon become bored or feel unfulfilled.

Home and Domestic Life

In family and domestic matters Aquarians can have a tendency to be too non-conformist, changeable and unstable. They are as willing to break the barriers of family constraints as they are those of other areas of life.

Even so, Aquarians are very sociable people. They like to have a nice home where they can entertain family and friends. Their house is usually decorated in a modern style and full of state-of-the-art appliances and gadgets – an environment Aquarians find absolutely necessary.

If their home life is to be healthy and fulfilling Aquarians need to inject it with a quality of stability – yes, even some conservatism. They need at least one area of life to be enduring and steady; this area is usually their home and family life.

Venus, the generic planet of love, rules the Aquarian's 4th solar house of home and family, which means that when it comes to the family and child-rearing, theories, cool thinking and intellect are not always enough. Aquarians need to bring love into the equation in order to have a great domestic life.

Horoscope for 2020

Major Trends

Spirituality has been a major interest for many years now, but this year even more so. Your 12th house of spirituality is easily the most powerful in your chart. So the year ahead is all about your spiritual growth and development. Your focus here will lead to career development and success as well. More on this later.

Finances, too, are following a long-term – many years – trend. Neptune, your financial planet, has been occupying your money house for many years. He is very powerful in his own sign and house and this is good for earnings. The year ahead is prosperous. More on this later.

Your 4th house of home and family has recently become prominent – since March of last year. Uranus, the ruler of your Horoscope, entered your 4th house then and he will remain there for the next seven or so years. There's a lot of upheaval going on there and the family situation needs your attention. Details later.

This is not one of your best love and social years. It's not a bad year – there's just a lack of interest. Your 7th house is empty with only short-term planets passing through there. Thus it is pretty much a status quo kind of year for love. More on this later.

Aquarians are not conservative people. They are innovators, inventors, rebels and non-conformists. But since Uranus moved into Taurus last year you seem more mellow, more conservative than usual.

This year we will have six eclipses instead of the more normal four. Not only that, but we will have double the number of lunar eclipses this year. Usually there are two; this year there are four. Five of the six eclipses impact on your health and job situation, so there are many changes going on in these areas this year. More on this later.

Your 3rd house of communication and intellectual interests will become powerful from June 28 onwards. Mars, the ruler of your 3rd house will spend an unusually long time here – four times the length of his usual stay. So this is great for students. There is focus on their studies and focus leads to success. It is also good for writers, teachers, bloggers, journalists, and advertising, marketing and sales people – people who earn through their communication skills. However, a word of caution: there will be a tendency to get into arguments and verbal spats.

Your important areas of interest this year are the body and image (from March 23 to July 1 and December 18 onwards); finance; communication and intellectual interests (June 28 onwards); home and family; and spirituality.

Your paths of greatest fulfilment will be health and work (until May 6); love, romance and social activities (from May 6 onwards); spirituality (until December 20); and the body and image (after December 20).

Health

(Please note that this is an astrological perspective on health and not a medical one. In days of yore there was no difference, both these perspectives were identical. But now there could be quite a difference. For a medical perspective, please consult your doctor or health practitioner.)

Health will be basically good this year. There is one (sometimes two) long-term planets in stressful aspect with you, but generally this is not enough to cause serious problems. Sure, there will be periods where health and energy are less easy than usual. These are the temporary stresses caused by the transiting planets. They are not trends for the year. When they pass your normally good health and energy return. Health will be much more delicate next year.

Good though your health is you can make it even better. Give special attention to the following – the vulnerable areas of your Horoscope (the reflex points are shown in the chart below):

Important foot reflexology points for the year ahead

Try to massage all of the foot on a regular basis – the top of the foot as well as the bottom – but pay extra attention to the points highlighted on the chart. When you massage, be aware of 'sore spots' as these need special attention. It's also a good idea to massage the ankles especially, and below them.

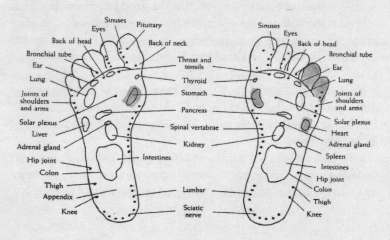

- The ankles and calves – always important for Aquarius, and ankle and calf massage should be part of your regular health regime.
- The stomach and breasts. These are also always important for Aquarius as the Moon, your health planet, rules these areas and the reflex points are shown above. (Our chart only shows the soles of the feet, but in your case the upper part of the foot is also important. Make sure to massage it regularly.) Health problems for Aquarius can often be alleviated with simple dietary changes. *What* you eat is important and should be checked with a professional, but *how* you eat is just as important. The act of eating should be elevated from mere animal appetite to an act of worship and thanksgiving. Grace (in your own words) should be said before and after meals. Food should be blessed, and meals taken in a calm and relaxed way. These practices will not only elevate the energy vibration of the food but also the energy vibration of your body and digestive system. You will get the best from the food you eat and it will digest better. This is why almost every religion has rituals for eating.
- The heart gained in significance since March last year, and will be important for the next couple of years. The important thing here is to let go of worry and anxiety. There is a consensus among spiritual healers that these are the root causes of heart problems. Meditation will be a big help here.

The Moon is your health planet. She is the fastest moving of all the planets and moves through your entire Horoscope every month. So there are many short-term health trends that depend on where the Moon is and the kind of aspects she receives. These are best dealt with in the monthly reports.

In general, you will feel more energetic when the Moon waxes (grows) than when she wanes. The waxing Moon is good for therapies where you add things to the body. The waning Moon is good for detoxing and cleanses.

As we mentioned earlier, five of the six eclipses this year will impact on health. So there can be a few health scares (and the good thing about these is that they force necessary changes to the health regime).

But, overall, health looks good and these things will likely be nothing more than scares.

With the Moon as your health planet, good health for you means good emotional health. It is very important to maintain positive moods and emotions. This will be more challenging this year but meditation will be a big help. It is also important for your health to maintain harmony within the family – another challenging area.

Home and Family

Your 4th house of home and family has become a major focus since March of last year, and will remain important – and tempestuous – for the next seven years or so. Uranus, the planet of revolutionary and sudden change, is now in your 4th house.

The family circle will go through many crises. There will be upheavals in the family and perhaps breakups or near breakups. The marriage of a parent or parent figure is being severely tested. You are very devoted to the family and putting much attention here, but will it be enough?

Family members have extreme and sudden mood swings. You don't know from one moment to the next where you stand or where they stand. You too can have sudden and inexplicable mood shifts.

By the time Uranus finishes his sojourn in your 4th house, your family and domestic situation will be totally different. Understand that Uranus is not there to punish. He is there in answer to your prayers and desires. You (or family members) have desired a better situation, and in order to have this shakeups are necessary.

With Uranus in the 4th house you can have multiple moves this year and in future years. Often we also see multiple renovations to the home – a never-ending process. Every time you think you have things 'just right' a new idea comes to you and you upgrade again. This goes on and on.

There will also be many technology upgrades to the home this year. You are installing high-tech gadgetry and equipment. In the future we can see 'smart appliances' and perhaps a totally 'smart' home. Everything is connected to the internet.

Aquarians of childbearing age are more fertile this year – but especially after December 20. Fertility is higher next year too.

There are always many short term home and family trends in your Horoscope, because Venus, your family planet, moves quickly. This year she will move through eleven signs and houses in your chart, so many family events will depend on where Venus is at any given time and the kinds of aspects she receives. These are best dealt with in the monthly reports.

One of the parents or parent figures in your life is very restless and freedom-loving these days. He or she will be moving around a lot and perhaps staying in different places for long periods of time. But a formal move isn't likely. The other parent or parent figure could move at the end of this year, but more probably next year. This is not a smooth transaction. There are many delays and glitches involved with it.

Siblings and sibling figures are having many family dramas this year, but a move is not likely. Children and children figures are having a stable family year. Grandchildren (if you have them) and those who play that role in your life could move this year, but it's a challenging kind of action. If they are of childbearing age they are more fertile for the next two years.

Renovations will probably go on all year, but February 16 to March 31 is an excellent time for such work. If you're redecorating or beautifying the home in cosmetic kinds of ways – or buying objects of beauty for the home – March 5 to April 3 is a good time.

Finance and Career

The year ahead looks prosperous. Your money house has been prominent for many years and will continue to be so. This shows focus, and by the spiritual law we get what we focus on. Also, your financial planet is receiving beneficial aspects from the long-term planets – another positive for finance. On December 20, Jupiter, the planet of abundance, will move into your own sign, signalling a two-year cycle of prosperity. You will end the year in better financial shape than when you began.

Neptune is your financial planet and, as we have mentioned in many previous reports, he is the most spiritual of all the planets. He is, in a sense, 'other worldly'. He is not concerned with any material condition or circumstance, for he knows he can create new circumstances.

Because he is so otherworldly he operates by his own law and, if you're not careful, this can lead to financial scandals. It is good to be otherworldly in a positive way, but be aware of this terrestrial world too.

The financial intuition is very strong these days – just as it has been for many years. In fact your intuition is being trained in financial matters.

On a worldly level, Neptune rules water utilities, water bottlers and companies involved with water – shipping, shipbuilders, fisheries and the like. Neptune also rules oil, natural gas (especially from offshore drilling), retirement homes, hospices, alcohol and certain pharmaceuticals – the makers of mood enhancers and anaesthetics. You have a good feeling for all these industries. Moreover, people from these industries can play an important role in your finances.

With spiritual Neptune in your money house for so many years, many of you are attracted to 'spiritually correct' ways of earning. You like idealistic kinds of enterprises – things that benefit the whole planet. Often this shows working for a charity or a not-for-profit enterprise. Those of you concerned with the environment will find opportunities with companies that are involved with this, and there are many these days. Others will get involved in marketing spiritual books, seminars or lectures (or perhaps will give them). Neptune also rules film, photography and the fine arts. There are money-making opportunities here too and you would enjoy them.

We see this same idealism in the career as well. Your career planet, Pluto, has been in your spiritual 12th house since 2008 and will be there for many years to come. So just being successful and making money is not enough for you. You need work that is meaningful and soul-satisfying. The career looks very successful this year, as Jupiter will be travelling with your career planet most of the year. So you are elevated in your professional and social status this year.

Your main career challenge this year is something that many people face, but with you it is more intense. You need to balance a successful home and domestic life with a successful career. There's a lot of juggling going on. Both the demands of the family and the demands of the career are very strong. Now you will lean one way and now another. Everyone finds their own solution to this.

Love and Social Life

The love and romantic life is not prominent this year. For a start, most of the long-term planets are in the Eastern sector of self – of personal independence. While the Western, social sector will strengthen as the year unfolds, it will never overpower the Eastern sector. At its strongest (and this will only be for brief periods) it will equal the Eastern sector. So, you are more independent this year. More self-sufficient. You chart your own course. You have less need of others than usual. This is a wonderful trait but is not that good for love. Secondly, your 7th house of love is basically empty this year, while your 1st house of the self gets steadily stronger as the year progresses. Only short-term planets will move through the 7th house. So romance seems to be on the back burner. In spite of this, the Moon's North Node (an abstract point) will move into your 7th house on May 6 and stay there for the rest of the year. So, while it is good to be independent and self-sufficient, it is also good to socialize and cultivate friendships. I read this as a social year tending to the status quo. Singles will tend to stay single, and those who are married will tend to stay married.

Aquarians are more into friendships than love. In fact love is just a 'friendship with benefits'. Love is just friendship on a deeper level. This area will be active this year.

Your planet of friends, Jupiter, will travel with your career planet. This shows that a lot of your socializing is career-related. You are meeting important, influential people and interacting with them. These are not romantic meetings, but more about professional affinities. The friendships of the 11th house are different from the friendships of the 7th house. The 7th house shows friendships of the heart – you just love these people, regardless of status, position or wealth. The friendships of the 11th house are more platonic – they are friendships of the mind, friendships based on common interests. These latter are what's happening this year.

Since Jupiter will spend almost all year in your 12th house of spirituality, you are meeting spiritual kinds of people. Perhaps they are corporate types, but they are spiritual. These connections further your spiritual path as well as your career.

On December 20 Jupiter will enter your own sign. This shows that friends are very devoted to you and that you attract friends easily. They seek you out rather than vice versa.

Self-improvement

The year ahead is a spiritual kind of year. As we've mentioned, your 12th house is easily the strongest in your Horoscope. Get right spiritually, get a good connection with the Divine within and most areas of life – finance, career, friendships – will just fall into place. Even the romantic life is impacted by the spiritual life. Saturn, your spiritual planet, will move into your sign twice this year. (Once a brief foray from March 23 to July 1, and then for the long term from December 18 onwards.) Thus Saturn will start to impact on your Sun. Those of you born early in the sign of Aquarius (January 20–23) are going to feel this the strongest. Keep in mind that the Sun is your love planet. So there is a need for spiritual compatibility with the spouse, partner or current love – and this will get tested during those periods.

Most of you have worldly types of careers, but the real message here is that your spiritual practice, your spiritual growth *is* the actual career, the actual mission, these days. This has been the case for many years, but it is much more intense now.

Your dream life has been active and prophetic for many years, and now even more so than ever. (When we study this chart we wonder why a person would even bother waking up – the dream life is so much more interesting than the mundane world!) Pay attention to your dreams – they are giving financial and career guidance this year. Career and financial guidance will also come from psychics, astrologers, tarot readers, spiritual channels or gurus. You are making these kinds of friends this year too.

With the 12th house so strong, you live in the supernatural realm. It becomes just as real as the natural realm – maybe even more real. You have all kinds of supernatural-type experiences – synchronicities and ESP. Your spiritual abilities grow and expand.

There will be many spiritual breakthroughs this year – more than you've had for the past few years. When these happen it is a most joyous thing. The whole outlook on a given situation (and on life) changes for the better.

Your grasp of the spiritual dimension of wealth is growing year by year. Your ability to access it is also growing. You will have many 'miracle money' moments. After a while they will become common-place – you start to take them for granted (to the amazement of those around you). It becomes natural for spirit to supply you.

You have been a generous giver for years now. And this trend contin-ues in the year ahead. Tithing is an excellent practice, and many of you are already doing this. If not, it is good to get into it. I consider tithing as a form of financial therapy. It opens the doors to the supernatural supply.*

Month-by-month Forecasts

January

Best Days Overall: 7, 8, 16, 24, 25, 26
Most Stressful Days Overall: 5, 6, 12, 18, 19
Best Days for Love: 5, 6, 12, 13, 14, 15, 18, 19, 24, 25, 27, 28
Best Days for Money: 1, 5, 6, 9, 10, 14, 18, 19, 22, 23, 27, 28
Best Days for Career: 6, 14, 15, 18, 19, 23

You begin your year with the 80 per cent of the planetary power (and sometimes 90 per cent) in the independent East of your chart. This sector will dominate all year, but not as strongly as now. Happiness is up to you. You can – and should – have your way. Other people are always important, and should be treated with respect, but your way is the best way for you. You are not dependent on others. Make the changes now that bring about your happiness: if you are happy, there is that much less misery on the planet.

The month ahead is *very* spiritual. Your 12th house of spirituality is easily the strongest in the Horoscope, with at least half the planets there or moving through there. So, this is a month for spiritual

---

* For those who want to go deeper into the spiritual laws of affluence I recommend my blog – www.spiritual-stories.com – for more information.

breakthroughs. You will have all kinds of synchronistic and supernatural kinds of experiences. The invisible world is close to you and letting you know it's around.

The first of four lunar eclipses occurs on the 10th and impacts strongly on health. It occurs in your 6th house of health and the Moon is the ruler of that house. So, although health is good, you will be making important changes to the health regime in the coming months. The eclipse can also bring job changes (an unstable area this year) and disruptions at the workplace. Those who employ others can have employee turnover now. Children and children figures in your life are forced to make important financial corrections. Aunts and uncles have personal life-changing kinds of dramas.

Since this eclipse affects three other planets, it is powerful. It impacts on Saturn, your spiritual planet, Pluto, your career planet, and Mercury, ruler of children and personal transformation. So spiritual changes are likely. Since the spiritual life is so active I would say these changes come from new personal revelations that change your practice and teachings. These are good changes. The impact on Pluto affects the career. There are dramas in your company, industry and their hierarchies. There are personal dramas in the lives of bosses, parents and parent figures. New rules are enacted that can change your career approach.

On the 20th the Sun enters your own sign and you begin a yearly personal pleasure peak. Love seems very happy. You have it on your terms. If you are in a relationship, the beloved is very attentive and eager to please. If you are single, love opportunities are seeking you out. All you need to do is show up.

February

Best Days Overall: 3, 4, 5, 12, 13, 21, 22
Most Stressful Days Overall: 1, 2, 8, 9, 14, 15, 28, 29
Best Days for Love: 3, 4, 7, 8, 9, 12, 13, 16, 17, 23, 24, 26, 27
Best Days for Money: 1, 2, 6, 7, 10, 11, 14, 15, 19, 20, 23, 24, 25, 28, 29
Best Days for Career: 2, 10, 11, 20, 29

You're still in the midst of a yearly personal pleasure peak. So enjoy the pleasures of the body and senses. Pamper the body. Show gratitude for the yeoman service it has given you all your life.

Love is still very happy this month. Love and love opportunities are seeking you out. Social invitations also come. You look great. You have a sense of style and star quality. Your personal appearance shines. On the 19th the love planet moves into your money house, indicating that the spouse, partner or current love is supportive financially. It can also show opportunities for business kinds of partnerships or joint ventures.

Until the 19th singles need not do much to attract love. After the 19th love and romantic opportunities come as you pursue your financial goals or with people involved in your finances. Wealth attracts you, but by itself it is not enough. There needs to be spiritual compatibility as well. However, if your finances are in order love should go well.

The month ahead is prosperous. With the Sun entering the money house on the 19th you begin a yearly financial peak. Earnings will increase. The financial intuition, always good, becomes super this period (and next month it is even better).

There are two houses of power this month – the money house and your house of spirituality. Finance and spirituality are the major foci this month. One goes with the other. Your spiritual understanding will benefit finance and good finance will benefit spiritual understanding.

Mars moves into your spiritual 12th house on the 16th, bringing an urge to express spiritual ideals in action, to express them in a physical kind of way through spiritual or charitable activism. It is not enough to just have insights and spiritual breakthroughs. This transit also favours spiritual kinds of exercise, such as yoga or tai chi.

Health is still excellent this month. There is only one long-term planet in stressful alignment with you; all the other planets are either in harmonious aspect or leaving you alone. You can enhance the health even further in the ways discussed in the yearly report.

All the planets are moving forward this month, which is highly unusual. So, after your birthday, it is an excellent time to launch new products or start new projects. The 23rd to the 28th – the waxing Moon phase – would be the very best time for this. You can also expect fast progress towards your goals.

March

Best Days Overall: 2, 3, 10, 11, 19, 20, 29, 30
Most Stressful Days Overall: 1, 6, 7, 12, 13, 27, 28
Best Days for Love: 4, 5, 6, 7, 8, 12, 13, 17, 18, 24, 25, 27, 28
Best Days for Money: 1, 4, 5, 8, 9, 12, 13, 17, 18, 22, 23, 24, 25,
    27, 28
Best Days for Career: 1, 9, 12, 13, 18, 28

Personal independence is still very strong this month, but is beginning to lessen slightly. Continue to exercise personal initiative and to take responsibility for your happiness. There's no one else to blame for unhappiness. Make the changes that need to be made.

Saturn temporarily moves into your sign on the 23rd, but this is only a prelude – an announcement – of things to come. He is merely flirting with your sign now. The transit has both good points and negative points. On the positive side, it brings a more serious attitude to life. It is good for losing weight. Since Saturn is your spiritual planet, it shows a more spiritual kind of period. You're expressing your spirituality in the body, in your persona and image. People see you as a spiritual person. It shows that you have the power (and the knowledge will come to you) to shape and mould the body by spiritual means. Your management and organizational skills are much stronger too. On the negative side, this transit can bring lower energy. One feels one's physical limits very strongly. There is a tendency to pessimism and people tend to feel older than their years. (This is the case for young people too.) Also it can impact on the love life. People around you can feel that you are cold, aloof and distant. Perhaps subconsciously you are erecting barriers. There is a simple solution. Make it a project to send love and warmth to others.

Though the career is not a major focus this month – the night side, the lower half of your Horoscope is easily the most prominent – there is career success happening. Perhaps it is behind the scenes. Jupiter is travelling with your career planet Pluto all month. Friends seem involved in this. Career-related travel can happen too.

You are still in the midst of a yearly financial peak until the 20th so the month ahead is prosperous. The Sun travels with Neptune, your financial planet, on the 8th and 9th, which will boost earnings. It enhances the financial intuition and social contacts seem very helpful. There is an opportunity for a business partnership or joint venture.

Health is still good. Energy might be a little lower because of Saturn's move into your sign, but this is not enough by itself to cause problems. Enhance the health in the ways mentioned in the yearly report.

Love happens as you pursue your financial goals until the 20th. After then, romantic opportunities occur at school or in educational functions – at lectures, seminars or workshops. Love can be found in the neighbourhood, and perhaps with neighbours.

April

Best Days Overall: 7, 8, 15, 16, 17, 25, 26
Most Stressful Days Overall: 3, 4, 9, 10, 23, 24, 30
Best Days for Love: 3, 4, 7, 8, 12, 15, 16, 17, 23, 25, 26, 30
Best Days for Money: 1, 2, 6, 9, 10, 14, 18, 19, 24, 28, 29
Best Days for Career: 6, 9, 10, 14, 24

Mars entered your sign on March 31 and he will remain there all this month, so you are more energetic – more independent and self-willed than usual. You have courage and are not likely to back away from controversy or conflict. You get things done quickly. Though your spiritual life is still prominent, this month you are a doer – an activist. Since Mars rules your 3rd house, it shows that your communication skills – always good – are even better than usual. It is a wonderful transit for students, teachers, writers, and sales and marketing people. The intellectual abilities are stronger than usual. But, there is a downside here too. It is great to be courageous and to stand your ground, but Mars can make you overly combative. You can speak too forcefully and this can create conflict. In addition, hastiness and impatience can lead to accidents or injury. So get things done, but in a mindful way.

The power this month – until the 19th – is in your 3rd house of communication and intellectual interests. This reinforces what we said above. This is a month to catch up on your reading and to take courses in subjects that interest you. It is also good for teaching subjects where you have expertise.

Jupiter is still travelling with your career planet, Pluto, all month. So wonderful career developments are happening. This also shows the prosperity of bosses, parents and parent figures.

Career, however, is not really the focus this month. On the 19th you enter the 'midnight' of your year. The Sun enters your 4th house. This is a time for being involved in internal matters, the activities of night. It is a time to focus on the home, family and your emotional wellness. Even career goals should be handled in a more 'interior' way, through meditation and visualization. Work to get in the 'mood' of your career goals. Feel that they have been attained. Then, when the planets shift to the upper half of your chart – the day side – you can implement this in a physical kind of way.

Health needs more attention after the 19th. Make sure you get enough rest; this is always the first line of defence. Then enhance the health in the ways mentioned in the yearly report.

Love is close to home this month. Until the 19th it is in your neighbourhood and perhaps with neighbours. After then it is at home. A romantic evening at home is preferable to a night out on the town. The Sun, your love planet, travels with Uranus, the ruler of your Horoscope, between the 24th and 26th, indicating a romantic meeting. In general you are socializing more from home and with the family.

May

Best Days Overall: 4, 5, 13, 14, 23, 24
Most Stressful Days Overall: 1, 6, 7, 20, 21, 27, 28
Best Days for Love: 1, 2, 3, 4, 5, 11, 13, 14, 23, 24, 27, 28
Best Days for Money: 3, 6, 7, 12, 15, 16, 22, 25, 26
Best Days for Career: 3, 6, 7, 11, 12, 21, 22

Your personal independence is getting weaker this month. It is still strong, but not in the way it has been in previous months. Mars leaves your sign on 13th and the planetary power in the Western social sector reaches its maximum for the year. So while your personal interests are still important, it is good now to cultivate your social skills.

Mars in your money house from the 13th shows a more risk-taking approach to finance. Your intuition is good so this approach could work out. It also shows that money comes from your intellectual and communication skills. It favours writing, teaching, sales and marketing. It favours good use of the media. The danger with Mars in the money house is the allure of 'quick money', which leaves you vulnerable to all sorts of scammers who prey on this tendency. So be careful about this.

You are probably spending more on books, magazines and communication equipment at the moment, but you can also earn from these things.

Wonderful career developments are still happening this month, as Jupiter is still travelling with your career planet Pluto. But Pluto is now retrograde so much of this won't be seen until later on. With your 4th house still very strong, keep your focus on the home and family.

Your love planet is in the 4th house until the 20th, so love is found close to home. Family and family connections are playing a big role in love. Perhaps they are playing Cupid. There is still more socializing at home and with the family. You are attracted to people with strong family values and those with whom you can have emotional as well as physical intimacy. Often with this transit one tends to live in the past when it comes to love. There is a tendency to want to re-experience past highs. There's nothing wrong with this per se, but you can lose the 'now' moment. Now is always the best time for love. Now is what is happening. Old experiences are merely dreams. Sometimes old flames come back into the picture with this transit. Sometimes it is the actual person, sometimes it is someone who resembles the old flame. There is good in this as old issues (traumas or misunderstandings) can be resolved.

On the 19th the Sun moves into your 5th house of fun, creativity and children. Love becomes 'unserious'. Love is about fun and entertainment, not necessarily commitment. You are attracted to people who can show you a good time.

June

Best Days Overall: 1, 9, 10, 19, 20
Most Stressful Days Overall: 3, 4, 16, 17, 18, 24, 28, 29
Best Days for Love: 1, 9, 10, 19, 20, 21, 24
Best Days for Money: 3, 4, 8, 11, 12, 13, 18, 21, 22, 27, 28, 29
Best Days for Career: 3, 4, 8, 18, 27, 28, 29

Retrograde activity reaches its peak for the year this month, with 60 per cent of the planets retrograde from the 23rd to the 25th. After the 25th half the planets are retrograde, which is still a high percentage. So, the pace of life slows down. There's nothing much happening in the world, so you may as well take a holiday or otherwise enjoy your life. You are in the midst of a yearly personal pleasure peak until the 21st.

There is another issue here too. We have two powerful eclipses this month. These force change, but with all the retrograde activity, these changes need more thought, more study, more due diligence.

Both eclipses impact on the job and work situation and on the health regime. The lunar eclipse of the 5th occurs in your 11th house, so friendships get tested. There are personal dramas – often life-changing ones – in the lives of friends. There are disruptions in professional or trade organizations you're involved with. High-tech equipment will be temperamental and will often need repair or replacement. Make sure important files are backed up and that your anti-hacking/anti-virus software is up to date. Aunts and uncles have personal dramas. If you employ others there can be employee turnover. Parents and parent figures are forced to make important financial changes. Since this eclipse also affects Mars and Venus (pretty directly), there can be a crisis in the home and with family members. Repairs might be needed to the home. Cars and communication equipment will get tested and it is a good idea to drive more carefully than usual during this time.

The solar eclipse of the 21st occurs in your 6th house, bringing more disruptions at the workplace and job changes. These can be within your present company or with another one. There are changes in your health regime too, manifested in the coming months. Children and children figures in your life can be having a financial crisis and need to make adjustments. Every solar eclipse impacts on your love life and current relationship, and this one is no different. Good relationships will survive a solar eclipse (you get them twice a year) but the flawed ones – the unsound ones – are in jeopardy. The beloved can experience personal dramas; he or she is making important spiritual changes – changes in practice, teachings and teachers. There are upheavals and disruptions in charitable or spiritual organizations that the beloved is involved with.

July

Best Days Overall: 6, 7, 8, 16, 17, 25, 26
Most Stressful Days Overall: 1, 14, 15, 21, 22, 27, 28
Best Days for Love: 1, 6, 7, 8, 9, 10, 16, 17, 20, 21, 22, 25, 26, 29
Best Days for Money: 1, 4, 5, 9, 10, 14, 15, 19, 20, 23, 24, 27, 28, 31
Best Days for Career: 1, 5, 15, 24, 27, 28

Another lunar eclipse on the 5th impacts on the job and the health regime. This is the third lunar eclipse of the year and there will be another one in November. Sometimes there are health scares, but since your overall health is excellent, it is not likely to be anything more than a scare. By the way, with so many retrogrades and eclipses happening, medical test results should be taken with large pinches of salt. If there is some negative result, have the test redone at a later time. Get a second opinion.

This eclipse occurs in your 12th house of spirituality, signalling important spiritual changes for you. I feel these are happening as a result of some breakthrough – causing changes naturally. It would indicate disruptions and upheavals in a spiritual or charitable organization you're involved with. There are personal dramas in the lives of gurus or guru figures. Friends are forced to make important financial changes. Aunts and uncles have their marriages or relationships tested. Once again there are job changes and disruptions at work.

Since your 6th house of work is very strong, there is little to fear from any job change. You have excellent aspects for work. This eclipse sideswipes three other planets – happily these are not direct hits, but the impact on Mercury affects children and children figures in your life. They have personal dramas – but nothing too serious. The spouse, partner or current love needs a course correction in finance. There are dramas (again, nothing serious) in the lives of friends and minor disturbances in trade or professional organizations you're involved with. High-tech equipment is more temperamental. Cars and communication equipment also get tested. Drive more carefully this period.

Mars moved into your 3rd house on June 28. He is powerful here in his own sign and house, thus your communication skills and intellectual faculties are in top form. This is an excellent transit for students, teachers, writers, sales and marketing people. The skills are enhanced. Mars will have his solstice from the 7th to the 16th. He occupies the same degree of latitude over that period, and so he seems to pause in the heavens. Then he will change direction (in latitude). So it is good to take a little mental vacation at this time. Let the mind lie fallow for a while; it will get recharged in due course.

On the 22nd the Sun, your love planet, moves into the 7th house of love. He is very strong in this position, in his own sign and house. You begin a yearly love and social peak. True, you need to work harder on love – you and the beloved are not in agreement. Compromises are necessary. But the social life becomes active.

August

Best Days Overall: 3, 4, 13, 14, 21, 22, 30, 31
Most Stressful Days Overall: 10, 11, 17, 18, 23, 24
Best Days for Love: 3, 4, 8, 9, 15, 16, 17, 18, 19, 23, 24, 28
Best Days for Money: 2, 5, 6, 11, 15, 16, 20, 23, 24, 29
Best Days for Career: 2, 11, 20, 23, 24, 29

A conflict with the beloved on the 1st and 2nd is a short-term problem and passes quickly; love will improve after the 2nd. You're still in the midst of a yearly love and social peak this month. The Eastern sector of self is still the most powerful, but the planets in the West (the social sector) are in their maximum Western position. So, the month ahead (and this was true last month too) is about balance – you need to balance your interests and desires with those of others. You're still very independent, but you have to take others into consideration.

A conflict with children or children figures in your life on the 9th and 10th also passes quickly. Again, a short-term issue.

Love is about fun, games and entertainment until the 22nd. You're attracted to people who can show you a good time. It is not especially conducive to marriage or commitment. Love is just another form of entertainment at the moment – like going to the movies or theatre.

On the 22nd the Sun moves into Virgo, your 8th house, and love becomes more serious. There is a greater harmony between you and the beloved. The social life sparkles. There are romantic meetings for singles. But there are also some complications. There could be a tendency to perfectionism and to destructive criticism. If this is not on your part, it could be in the people you attract. Too much analysis can destroy the romantic feelings. On the other hand, you show love through practical service to the beloved and this is how you feel loved.

Aquarians are intellectuals. They are idea people. But this month, after the 22nd, we have many planets in the Earth signs (60 per cent of them, and a Grand Trine in the Earth element to boot). So your ideas and visionary thoughts are not much appreciated. People, and the world at large, are interested in practical matters. Marketers need to stress the practicality of their product or service. They need to sell the steak, not the sizzle. People will also tend to be more conservative.

Health needs more attention until the 22nd. As always, make sure you get enough rest. Enhance the health in the ways mentioned in the yearly report. Also, from the 7th onwards, give more attention to the hips, neck, throat and kidneys. Hip, neck and throat massage will enhance health.

September

Best Days Overall: 9, 10, 18, 19, 26, 27
Most Stressful Days Overall: 6, 7, 8, 14, 15, 20, 21
Best Days for Love: 2, 3, 6, 7, 13, 14, 15, 17, 22, 23, 26
Best Days for Money: 1, 2, 3, 6, 7, 11, 12, 16, 17, 20, 21, 24, 25, 29, 30
Best Days for Career: 6, 7, 16, 17, 20, 21, 24, 25

Retrograde activity once again surges to a yearly high this month. From the 9th to the 12th 60 per cent of the planets are retrograde. Before and after this period the figure is 50 per cent. So, progress is slower this month. Delays and glitches are unavoidable – however, you can minimize this by being more perfect in all that you do. Again, medical tests may not be very reliable now, so get them redone at a later time or get a second opinion. Babies born at this time are likely to be late bloomers in life. They will have many internal things to work out.

The Earth element is still very strong until the 22nd. So keep in mind our discussion of this last month. Focus on practical issues. Keep your sales and marketing efforts practical.

Health is excellent. Energy is high. You can enhance the health further in the ways mentioned in the yearly report. Until the 6th you can enhance the health with hip, neck and throat massage. A herbal kidney cleanse might also be in order if you feel under the weather.

Love looks happy and all the retrograde activity doesn't seem to impact on love. You still need to be careful about destructive criticism and ultra-perfectionism though, until the 22nd. After that date, you (and the beloved) are less exacting and more romantic. Venus enters your 7th house of love on the 6th, signalling more socializing at home and with the family. There can be a romantic liaison with a family connection or with someone introduced by the family. Foreigners are highly alluring too. Often this aspect shows someone who falls in love with the professor or worship leader. There are romantic opportunities at religious and college functions. These trends are especially pronounced after the 22nd. Mere sexual chemistry is not enough. You also want people you can learn from, people with whom there is philosophical compatibility. A foreign trip can lead to romance this period too. The social circle will expand.

The power in your 9th house from the 22nd onwards shows an interest – a focus – on higher education, religion, theology and foreign travel. Often this brings theological and philosophical breakthroughs for those interested in these things.

Finance is a bit stressful this month. Your financial planet Neptune has been retrograde for many months and this month receives stressful aspects. So you need to work harder to achieve your financial goals. You will see improvement after the 22nd. In the meantime, take a 'wait and see' attitude to finance. And don't enter into any major commitment without proper due diligence (more than usual).

October

Best Days Overall: 6, 7, 15, 16, 23, 24, 25
Most Stressful Days Overall: 4, 5, 11, 12, 17, 18, 31
Best Days for Love: 3, 6, 7, 11, 12, 15, 16, 21, 22, 25
Best Days for Money: 1, 5, 9, 10, 13, 14, 17, 18, 21, 23, 26, 27, 31
Best Days for Career: 4, 5, 13, 14, 17, 18, 21, 23, 31

Retrograde activity will diminish slightly this month, but there is still a substantial amount. Next month will be a different story, but in the meantime strive to be perfect in all that you do. Slower, but more perfect, is better than quick and slipshod.

With your 9th house powerful since September 22, college-level students are having a good month. There is much focus on their studies and much success. Those students below college level are having more problems. Mars went retrograde on September 9 and will be retrograde all this month. So there is indecision on educational matters and a lack of clarity. For writers, the retrograde of Mars is a good thing. It is good for writing and blogging, but not so good for releasing these things into the world. Wait until next month for that.

Venus, your family planet, moves into Virgo on the 2nd. There is more harmony with the family now, though they seem more critical and perfectionist. Venus's move into Virgo creates another Grand

Trine in Earth. So if you want to market things, stress the practical aspects – the bottom-line aspects – of your product or service. Avoid the 'dream' aspects.

Your career planet Pluto starts moving forward on the 4th after many months of retrograde motion. There is now more clarity in your career and you can see your way forward. On the 23rd, the Sun enters your 10th house and you begin a yearly career peak. This is far from the strongest career peak you've known (most of the planets are still below the horizon of your chart – in the night side of the chart), but it is your strongest career period of the year. So progress is being made. In future years you will have much stronger career peaks. Pursue career goals by social means, through attending or hosting the right kinds of gatherings or parties. Likeability plays a huge role in the career. Two people of equal professional talents can vie for a position, but the more likeable one will get the promotion. So keep this in mind. Your social grace is an important career asset.

Love is happy this month. Until the 23rd love can be found in foreign countries, with foreigners, or at school or your place of worship. After the 23rd most of your socializing is career related. You hobnob with the high and mighty, with people of power and status. There are opportunities for office romances, but you don't seem to enjoy this. If you are already in a relationship, the spouse, partner or current love seems very successful this month. He or she is helping your career. On the other hand, you and the beloved seem very distant with each other. There is a need to bridge your differences.

November

Best Days Overall: 2, 3, 4, 12, 20, 21, 30
Most Stressful Days Overall: 1, 7, 8, 14, 15, 27, 28
Best Days for Love: 2, 3, 5, 6, 7, 8, 12, 14, 15, 21, 22, 24, 25
Best Days for Money: 2, 5, 6, 11, 14, 15, 19, 22, 23
Best Days for Career: 2, 11, 14, 15, 19

Health needed attention ever since the Sun entered Scorpio on October 23, and this remains the situation until the 21st of this month. So, as always, make sure you get enough rest. Don't allow yourself to get overtired. A lunar eclipse on the 30th – the fourth lunar eclipse of the year – impacts on your health so relax and take it easy over that time.

This lunar eclipse occurs in your 5th house, affecting children and children figures in your life. They are having personal dramas. They will need to redefine themselves in the coming months and this will lead to wardrobe and image changes. Our image is only a reflection of our self-concept. When that changes, the image changes. Those of you involved in the creative arts will be making changes to your creativity – taking a new path and new approach to it. Aunts and uncles are experiencing spiritual changes. Friends are having their relationships tested. And, once again, you have job changes, changes in the conditions of work and disruptions in the workplace. Parents and parent figures need financial course corrections. The same holds true for you as well: Neptune, your financial planet, is impacted by this eclipse.

The good news is that these necessary changes will happen easier and faster than earlier in the year. Retrograde activity has almost disappeared. By the time this eclipse occurs, 90 per cent of the planets will be moving forward. The pace of events in the world and in your life will quicken. The gridlock has been broken.

Career is going very well this month. You're still in the midst of a yearly career peak until the 21st but, more importantly, Jupiter is travelling with your career planet Pluto and both are moving forward. So there is success this month. Very positive career developments are happening. Mercury will move into your 10th house on the 11th and stays there for the rest of the month. So, children and children figures are successful and helping your career. This transit would also show that you're enjoying your career path more. It is more fun. On the 21st, Venus will move into your 10th house and stay there for the rest of the month. This shows that the family is also supportive of the career. Perhaps they see your success as a 'family project'.

Be more patient with children and children figures in your life on the 16th and 17th. You seem in conflict. They should be more mindful of the physical plane those days, and avoid stressful activities.

December

Best Days Overall: 1, 9, 10, 17, 18, 27, 28
Most Stressful Days Overall: 5, 6, 11, 12, 24, 25, 26
Best Days for Love: 2, 3, 5, 6, 11, 12, 13, 14, 22, 23, 24
Best Days for Money: 2, 3, 8, 11, 12, 16, 19, 20, 21, 27, 29, 30
Best Days for Career: 8, 11, 12, 16, 25, 26

In spite of the eclipse which occurs on the 14th, the month ahead is happy. Your favourite house, the 11th house, is powerful until the 21st, so you are involved in what you most love to do – spending time with friends, groups, group activities and networking. The 11th house is a beneficent house so these activities are pleasant and successful.

The solar eclipse of the 14th occurs in this 11th house and announces a shift in this area for next year. Your planet of friends, Jupiter, makes a major move from your 12th house of spirituality into your 1st house on the 20th. This month, and for almost all of next year, you are a 'Super Aquarius' – involved with friends, groups, group activities, networking and technology. Science is always interesting to you, but these days even more so than usual, and this will be the situation in 2021 as well.

The eclipse will test certain friendships – especially the flawed ones. But rest assured you will have plenty of friends – and good ones. They will seek you out. Children and children figures experience some social upheaval. If they are in a relationship, it gets tested. Your current relationship will also get tested. The good ones survive these things. It is the flawed ones that are in danger. Since this eclipse impacts on Neptune, your financial planet, you need to make important financial changes. The events of the eclipse will reveal where your financial thinking and planning were unrealistic.

Saturn will move into your sign on the 18th – a major transit. He will remain in your sign for at least two more years. Health will need more attention next year. On the other hand, you will be shown how you can shape and mould the body by spiritual means. Jupiter in your own sign from the 20th onwards (and for next year) can make you put on the pounds. But Saturn also in your sign will keep this in check. We get a picture of someone who binges and then diets. You alternate between the two extremes.

Finances will improve after the 21st. Neptune is now moving forward, and after the 21st will receive helpful aspects. In the meantime, you just have to work harder to achieve your financial goals.

Love is happy this month, in spite of the eclipse. The eclipse merely creates some excitement and drama. Singles will find love opportunities online, or as they involve themselves in groups or group activities. This month you want friendship as well as love, and it favours relationships that are more like 'friends with benefits'.

Pisces

THE FISH

Birthdays from
19th February to
20th March

Personality Profile

PISCES AT A GLANCE

Element – Water

Ruling Planet – Neptune
  Career Planet – Jupiter
  Love Planet – Mercury
  Money Planet – Mars
  Planet of Health and Work – Sun
  Planet of Home and Family Life – Mercury
  Planet of Love Affairs, Creativity and Children – Moon

Colours – aqua, blue-green

Colours that promote love, romance and social harmony – earth tones, yellow, yellow-orange

Colours that promote earning power – red, scarlet

Gem – white diamond

Metal – tin

Scent – lotus

ERICA 2/23 3/17
ALEX 3/4 3/9 5
ELIZA 3/14 02

Quality – mutable (= flexibility)

Qualities most needed for balance – structure and the ability to handle form

Strongest virtues – psychic power, sensitivity, self-sacrifice, altruism

Deepest needs – spiritual illumination, liberation

Characteristics to avoid – escapism, keeping bad company, negative moods

Signs of greatest overall compatibility – Cancer, Scorpio

Signs of greatest overall incompatibility – Gemini, Virgo, Sagittarius

Sign most helpful to career – Sagittarius

Sign most helpful for emotional support – Gemini

Sign most helpful financially – Aries

Sign best for marriage and/or partnerships – Virgo

Sign most helpful for creative projects – Cancer

Best Sign to have fun with – Cancer

Signs most helpful in spiritual matters – Scorpio, Aquarius

Best day of the week – Thursday

Understanding a Pisces

If Pisces have one outstanding quality it is their belief in the invisible, spiritual and psychic side of things. This side of things is as real to them as the hard earth beneath their feet – so real, in fact, that they will often ignore the visible, tangible aspects of reality in order to focus on the invisible and so-called intangible ones.

Of all the signs of the zodiac, the intuitive and emotional faculties of the Pisces are the most highly developed. They are committed to living by their intuition and this can at times be infuriating to other people – especially those who are materially, scientifically or technically orientated. If you think that money, status and worldly success are the only goals in life, then you will never understand a Pisces.

Pisces have intellect, but to them intellect is only a means by which they can rationalize what they know intuitively. To an Aquarius or a Gemini the intellect is a tool with which to gain knowledge. To a well-developed Pisces it is a tool by which to express knowledge.

Pisces feel like fish in an infinite ocean of thought and feeling. This ocean has many depths, currents and undercurrents. They long for purer waters where the denizens are good, true and beautiful, but they are sometimes pulled to the lower, murkier depths. Pisces know that they do not generate thoughts but only tune in to thoughts that already exist; this is why they seek the purer waters. This ability to tune in to higher thoughts inspires them artistically and musically.

Since Pisces is so spiritually orientated – though many Pisces in the corporate world may hide this fact – we will deal with this aspect in greater detail, for otherwise it is difficult to understand the true Pisces personality.

There are four basic attitudes of the spirit. One is outright scepticism – the attitude of secular humanists. The second is an intellectual or emotional belief, where one worships a far-distant God-figure – the attitude of most modern church-going people. The third is not only belief but direct personal spiritual experience – this is the attitude of some 'born-again' religious people. The fourth is actual unity with the divinity, an intermingling with the spiritual world – this is the attitude of yoga. This fourth attitude is the deepest urge of a Pisces, and a Pisces is uniquely qualified to pursue and perform this work.

Consciously or unconsciously, Pisces seek this union with the spiritual world. The belief in a greater reality makes Pisces very tolerant and understanding of others – perhaps even too tolerant. There are instances in their lives when they should say 'enough is enough' and be ready to defend their position and put up a fight. However, because of their qualities it takes a good deal to get them into that frame of mind.

Pisces basically want and aspire to be 'saints'. They do so in their own way and according to their own rules. Others should not try to impose their concept of saintliness on a Pisces, because he or she always tries to find it for him- or herself.

Finance

Money is generally not that important to Pisces. Of course they need it as much as anyone else, and many of them attain great wealth. But money is not generally a primary objective. Doing good, feeling good about oneself, peace of mind, the relief of pain and suffering – these are the things that matter most to a Pisces.

Pisces earn money intuitively and instinctively. They follow their hunches rather than their logic. They tend to be generous and perhaps overly charitable. Almost any kind of misfortune is enough to move a Pisces to give. Although this is one of their greatest virtues, Pisces should be more careful with their finances. They should try to be more choosy about the people to whom they lend money, so that they are not being taken advantage of. If they give money to charities they should follow it up to see that their contributions are put to good use. Even when Pisces are not rich, they still like to spend money on helping others. In this case they should really be careful, however: they must learn to say no sometimes and help themselves first.

Perhaps the biggest financial stumbling block for the Pisces is general passivity – a *laissez faire* attitude. In general Pisces like to go with the flow of events. When it comes to financial matters, especially, they need to be more aggressive. They need to make things happen, to create their own wealth. A passive attitude will only cause loss and missed opportunity. Worrying about financial security will not provide that security. Pisces need to go after what they want tenaciously.

Career and Public Image

Pisces like to be perceived by the public as people of spiritual or material wealth, of generosity and philanthropy. They look up to big-hearted, philanthropic types. They admire people engaged in large-scale undertakings and eventually would like to head up these big enterprises themselves. In short, they like to be connected with big organizations that are doing things in a big way.

If Pisces are to realize their full career and professional potential they need to travel more, educate themselves more and learn more about the actual world. In other words, they need some of the unflagging optimism of Sagittarius in order to reach the top.

Because of all their caring and generous characteristics, Pisces often choose professions through which they can help and touch the lives of other people. That is why many Pisces become doctors, nurses, social workers or teachers. Sometimes it takes a while before Pisces realize what they really want to do in their professional lives, but once they find a career that lets them manifest their interests and virtues they will excel at it.

Love and Relationships

It is not surprising that someone as 'otherworldly' as the Pisces would like a partner who is practical and down to earth. Pisces prefer a partner who is on top of all the details of life, because they dislike details. Pisces seek this quality in both their romantic and professional partners. More than anything else this gives Pisces a feeling of being grounded, of being in touch with reality.

As expected, these kinds of relationships – though necessary – are sure to have many ups and downs. Misunderstandings will take place because the two attitudes are poles apart. If you are in love with a Pisces you will experience these fluctuations and will need a lot of patience to see things stabilize. Pisces are moody, intuitive, affectionate and difficult to get to know. Only time and the right attitude will yield Pisces' deepest secrets. However, when in love with a Pisces you will find that riding the waves is worth it because they are good, sensitive people who need and like to give love and affection.

When in love, Pisces like to fantasize. For them fantasy is 90 per cent of the fun of a relationship. They tend to idealize their partner, which can be good and bad at the same time. It is bad in that it is difficult for anyone to live up to the high ideals their Pisces lover sets.

Home and Domestic Life

In their family and domestic life Pisces have to resist the tendency to relate only by feelings and moods. It is unrealistic to expect that your partner and other family members will be as intuitive as you are. There is a need for more verbal communication between a Pisces and his or her family. A cool, unemotional exchange of ideas and opinions will benefit everyone.

Some Pisces tend to like mobility and moving around. For them too much stability feels like a restriction on their freedom. They hate to be locked in one location for ever.

The sign of Gemini sits on the cusp of Pisces' 4th solar house of home and family. This shows that Pisces likes and needs a home environment that promotes intellectual and mental interests. They tend to treat their neighbours as family – or extended family. Some Pisceans can have a dual attitude towards the home and family – on the one hand they like the emotional support of the family, but on the other they dislike the obligations, restrictions and duties involved with it. For Pisces, finding a balance is the key to a happy family life.

Horoscope for 2020

Major Trends

You're just coming out of a very strong career year in 2019; major goals (the short-term ones at least) have been attained and now you can shift your focus to other things – friends, groups and group activities. The fruits of career success are in the people you get to meet and socialize with due to your success. Success puts you in a new social sphere. More on this later.

Your 11th house of friends, groups and group activities is the strongest overall in your chart this year. So, while your social life will not be especially romantic, it is satisfying and very active.

Neptune, your ruling planet, has been in your own sign for many years now, and will be there for many more to come. So the spiritual life has been more active than usual (it is always active with you). This year it becomes even more pronounced as your 12th house of spirituality gets stronger as the year progresses. Your challenge will be to keep both feet on the ground. You might be living in the 'other world' beyond the veil more than in this world.

The year ahead looks prosperous. Your financial planet Mars will spend more than six months (four times his usual transit) in your money house, from June 28 onwards. This should bring increased earnings and earnings opportunities. More on this later.

Uranus moved into your 3rd house last March and will be there for another seven or so years. This signals major changes in your intellectual life and reading tastes. Books and magazines related to science, technology, astronomy and astrology become more appealing. There is a spiritual agenda behind this. This aspect also shows much change and turmoil for students below college level. They can be changing schools (perhaps multiple times), educational plans, etc. There can be shakeups in the school as well. There are upheavals in the neighbourhood you live in – and this will go on for many years.

We will have six eclipses this year – two more than usual. Five of the six will impact on children and children figures in your life, bringing them personal dramas and life-changing events. Many Pisceans are involved in the creative arts, and these eclipses show major changes in the creative life.

Your most important areas of interest this year will be the body and image; finance (from June 28); communication and intellectual interests; friends, groups and group activities; and spirituality (from March 23 to July 1 and from December 18 onwards).

Your paths of greatest fulfilment this year will be friends, groups and group activities (until December 20); spirituality (from December 20 onwards); children, fun and creativity (until May 6); and health and work (after May 6).

Health

(Please note that this is an astrological perspective on health and not a medical one. In days of yore there was no difference, both these perspectives were identical. But now there could be quite a difference. For a medical perspective, please consult your doctor or health practitioner.)

Health looks excellent this year, Pisces. There are no long-term planets in stressful alignment with you, and most are in harmonious aspect. Even those that are not in harmonious aspect are leaving you alone. Thus, if you have any pre-existing conditions they shouldn't be troublesome now and, in general, it is good news on the health front.

Your empty 6th house of health (only short-term planets move through there this year) is another positive indicator. You don't need to focus on health as there is nothing wrong. You can sort of take good health for granted.

Important foot reflexology points for the year ahead
Massage all the foot on a regular basis – the top of the foot as well as the bottom – but pay extra attention to the points highlighted on the chart. When you massage, be aware of 'sore spots' as these need special attention. It's also a good idea to massage the ankles and below them.

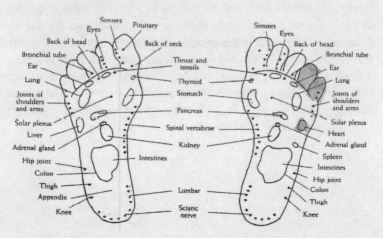

Good though your health is, you can make it even better. Give more attention to the following – the vulnerable areas of your Horoscope (the reflex points are shown in the chart above). Problems, if they happened, would most likely begin here, so keeping them healthy and fit is sound preventive medicine.

- The feet are always important for you Pisces, and foot massage should be a regular part of your health regime. There are inexpensive gadgets about that massage the feet, and some even give whirlpool treatments for the feet. These are good investments for you. Keep the feet warm in winter, and wear shoes that fit well: comfort is preferable to fashion (although if you can have both – comfort and fashion – all the better).
- The heart is also always important to Pisces. The important thing with the heart – as our regular readers know – is to avoid worry and anxiety, the two emotions that stress the heart. Cultivate faith, and let go of worry.

Keep in mind that there will be periods where health and energy are less easy than usual. These periods come from the short-term transits and are temporary and not trends for the year. When they pass, your normally good health and energy return.

Two solar eclipses this year – in June and December – can also impact on health, as the Sun is your health planet. The eclipses bring corrections to the health regime. Often they signal changes of doctors or other health professionals that you see. Sometimes they show dramas in the lives of these people. Sometimes they bring a health scare (but your health is good and these are likely only to be scares).

Your health planet is a fast-moving planet and changes signs and houses each month. Thus there are many short-term health trends that depend on where the Sun is and the aspects he receives. These are best dealt with in the monthly reports.

Home and Family

Your home and family house hasn't been prominent in your chart for some years now and this remains the case for most of the year ahead, with the exception of Venus's unusually long transit from April 3 to August 7. This tends to the status quo. You seem basically content with things as they are and have no pressing need to make changes.

Venus's prolonged stay in your 4th house could show renovations going on at home – and perhaps redecoration of the home. It could also show surgery or near-death kinds of experiences in the lives of family members. A sibling or sibling figure could be staying for a while. You could be installing new communication equipment at home too.

There will also be a lunar eclipse on November 30 that occurs in your 4th house. This can produce dramas in the lives of family members – especially for a parent or parent figure. It often shows a need for repairs to be made in the home as hidden flaws come to light.

There is nothing against a move this year but nothing that especially supports it either. Most likely you will stay where you are.

Both the parents or parent figures in your life are making important financial changes this year. One of them is prospering and focused on finance; the other is having a more spiritual kind of year. The former can have multiple job changes this year – and in future years. Both seem to have a stable home and family year.

Siblings and sibling figures are more freedom-loving and rebellious these days. They are restless. They can travel more and live in different places for long periods of time, but a formal move is not likely.

Children and children figures are having many personal dramas and life-changing experiences – many are quite normal, but change the direction of their life. There is love in their lives this year and perhaps they are considering marriage (if they are of appropriate age). But they should not rush into anything. If they are younger, they have an active social life this year and are making new friends. Those of childbearing age are more fertile this year. The home and family situation tends to the status quo.

Grandchildren (if you have them), or those who play that role in your life, probably shouldn't marry this year. If they are already in a relationship it is getting severely tested. A move could happen later on in the year – but next year might be better. Aunts or uncles could move in the coming year, but it will not be smooth; there are many complications and delays involved.

Renovation and redecoration of the home is likely from April 3 to August 7 – and it's a good time for that. It is also good for buying art objects or other objects of beauty for the home.

Finance and Career

The year ahead is prosperous, as we mentioned earlier. Your money house will be strong for most of 2020: from March 20 to April 19 (a yearly financial peak) and from June 28 onwards. This shows focus and, by the spiritual law, we get what we focus on – good, bad or indifferent.

The Sun in your money house from March 20 to April 19 shows earnings through work – through productive service to others. Mars in the money house from June 28 onwards shows various things. For a start, you will be a lot more inclined to take risks during the second half of the year. You are attracted to 'quick money' – and this has good points and bad. When your intuition is good it can lead to quick money. But if your intuition is off, you can become the victim of all kinds of scammers who prey on this tendency. When intuition is good, financial decisions will be made quickly and with great confidence – and they turn out well. But when intuition is off, you are likely to be too quick in your decision-making. It will be a good idea to sleep on things before making major purchases, investments or important financial decisions.

With Mars as your financial planet, one of your life lessons is to learn financial fearlessness, to develop courage in finance. With you it's not so much about winning or losing, but of overcoming the fear of loss. Even if a financial transaction doesn't work out, if you overcame your fear, you have won. This trend is especially significant after June 28.

It is good to be quick and decisive in financial matters – it saves a lot of time – but your financial planet will go into one of his rare retrograde periods between September 9 and November 14. This will not be a time to be 'quick and decisive'. It will be a time for review, for pulling back a bit, for gaining clarity on financial goals and the current financial situation. If you must make important investments or purchase big ticket items, do it before September 9 or after November 14.

The retrograde of Mars won't stop earnings, but it slows things down a bit. You can avoid unnecessary anguish by doing everything perfectly in finance – taking care of the details. Make sure payments are properly signed and dated, that envelopes are properly addressed, that money transfers from one account to another are correct, etc.

With Mars in your money house for so much of the year you could favour start-up companies. You would have a good feeling for the athletic and military industries. You would probably spend more on the gym, personal trainers or sports equipment too.

Mars will move through five houses of your Horoscope this year before he enters your money house. Thus there are short-term trends in finance that depend on where he is and the kinds of aspects he receives. These will be discussed in the monthly reports.

Career, as we mentioned, is not that prominent this year. This I read as a good thing. You've basically achieved what you set out to achieve last year and now you can focus on other things. Jupiter, your career planet, will be in your 11th house almost all year – thus your technology and networking expertise are important. Your good social connections help the career, and a lot of your socializing is career related. There is foreign travel related to the career happening too.

Your career planet will move into Aquarius, your 12th house, on December 20 and will remain there almost all of next year. So, this will be a time to further your career goals by getting involved in charities or altruistic causes. This will be the case for most of 2021 as well.

Love and Social Life

The year ahead will be an active social year, but not an especially romantic one. It's more about friendships and group activities than about romance. There are a few reasons for this. The Eastern sector of self is, overall, the most dominant sector in your chart this year. While the Western social sector will strengthen as the year progresses, it will never be stronger than the Eastern sector. In addition, your 7th house of love and romance is empty – only short-term planets move through there. Your 1st house of self, by contrast, is powerful all year. Romantically it is a status quo kind of year. I read this as a good thing. You seem content with things as they are and have no need to make major changes. Singles will tend to stay single, those who are married will tend to stay married. Of course, singles will date, but marriage is not really seen here. (There's nothing especially against it, but nothing that supports it either.)

With so many planets in the East (all the long-term planets are there), this is a year for personal independence and personal initiative. It is a year for self-reliance and for having things your way. There is less of a need for others.

Though your 5th house of fun and love affairs is empty (only short-term planets will move through there), five of the six eclipses this year affect this area of life. Thus there can be multiple love affairs and multiple break ups. Or one love affair with multiple break ups and reunions. There are various ways that this can manifest.

Your love planet Mercury is one of the fastest moving – and erratic – of the planets. Sometimes he speeds along through three signs and houses in a given month. Sometimes he moves slowly, staying in one sign. Sometimes he stands still and sometimes he goes backwards. This is how you are in love – very variable, with different needs and attitudes. Because of this, there are many short-term trends in love that depend on where Mercury is at a given time, his rate of motion and the aspects he receives. These will be dealt with in the monthly reports.

Your 11th house of friends, as we mentioned, is the strongest in your Horoscope this year. Thus you are making new and significant friends and these seem to be people of high status and prominence. These are people who can help you careerwise and seem to be involved in your career. Later on in the year, as Saturn, the ruler of your 11th house, moves into Aquarius (between March 23 and July 1, and from December 18 onwards), the social life will still be active but you'll be making more spiritual-type friends.

Self-improvement

Spirituality is genetically built into Pisces. This is so under normal circumstances, but with Neptune in your own sign this is even more pronounced. Add to this the power in your spiritual 12th house this year and the spiritual urges are even stronger.

Pisceans are often described as 'dreamy'. The reason is that for them – and especially now – the invisible world beyond the five senses is more real than the so-called physical world. This is basically good. The invisible world is the world of causes; the physical world is the world of effects. However, Pisceans need to remember that though they are supernatural beings, they are stationed here on earth – in their particular milieu and circumstances. Never lose sight of that. Keep both feet on the ground.

The good news is that this will be easier to do now that Uranus, your spiritual planet, moved into the earthy sign of Taurus in March last year and will stay there for many more years. This favours an 'earth-based' spirituality. You will learn that you need not go to 'other worlds' to contact spirit. It is right here on earth if we look properly. Every rock, every tree, every flower, every animal is the incarnation of a Divine Principle. The Earth itself is the body of a Goddess. This is a good period to explore the earth-based systems such as the First Americans and other indigenous peoples practise and teach. The Divine, through nature, is communicating to us all the time. Did a certain bird or animal cross your path today? Was there a blackbird underneath your car at the supermarket? Did a certain insect buzz around you while you were outside? These all have special meanings and are the way the Divine is communicating. Spirituality these days is not about going off to other worlds but about looking at this physical world properly.

Your spiritual planet will be in your 3rd house for many years, so journaling is a healthy spiritual practice. Keep a diary of your experiences during the day.

With spiritual Neptune, your ruling planet, in your own sign you have been learning the power of spirit over the body. Mind controls the body, but spirit is supposed to control the mind. Thus you are moulding and shaping your body by spiritual means – and this will go on for many more years. The body has appetites and habits, but not a will of its own. Eventually it must obey the dictates of spirit and mind.

With Neptune in your 1st house the body is becoming more refined and spiritualized. (We have written of this in past reports but the trend is still in effect.) So it is best to avoid (or minimize) alcohol and drugs as the body can overreact to them. Also you will feel psychic vibrations in a physical way – right in the body. So it is important not to put too much importance on physical sensations; a bad sensation might be just be a reception of negative, discordant energy. It would be good to keep around positive, uplifting kinds of people – these will come to you in the year ahead.

Month-by-month Forecasts

January

Best Days Overall: 1, 9, 10, 18, 19, 27, 28
Most Stressful Days Overall: 7, 8, 14, 20, 21
Best Days for Love: 5, 6, 13, 14, 15, 18, 19, 25, 26, 27, 28
Best Days for Money: 1, 2, 3, 5, 6, 12, 14, 20, 21, 22, 23, 29, 30, 31
Best Days for Career: 5, 6, 14, 20, 21, 22, 23

A happy and prosperous month ahead, Pisces. Enjoy. Even the lunar eclipse on the 10th will not dim your happiness. It will only bring in some excitement and change. Too much happiness can get boring.

You begin your year with most of the planets in the upper, day side of your Horoscope. It is a period for focusing on your outer activities. Mars will move into your 10th house of career on the 3rd, showing hectic career activity. You have to be more active, more aggressive there. Since Mars is your financial planet, it is a good signal for finance. Mars at the top of your chart is powerful. He is also in the expansive sign of Sagittarius, so earnings will increase. You have the financial favour of bosses, parents and parent figures. Pay rises, official or unofficial, are likely. Your good professional reputation enhances your earnings.

Normally this kind of lunar eclipse on the 10th would be benign for you, impacting more on children and children figures in your life and your creativity. But since this eclipse affects three other planets – Saturn, Pluto and Mercury – it is stronger than usual and affects many areas of life. So take it easy over that period.

The eclipse occurs in your 5th house of children, fun and creativity. So, as we mentioned, the children in your life are affected. They should stay out of harm's way that period. A parent or parent figure has to make important financial changes. The impact on Saturn affects your friends and professional or trade organizations you're involved with. Friends have personal dramas and their relationships are being tested. High-tech equipment will get tested and often needs repair or replacement. The impact on Pluto affects college-level students. There are changes of educational plans and disruptions at school. There are upheavals in your place of worship and in the lives of worship leaders. Avoid foreign travel during this time. The impact on Mercury will test your current relationship and bring dramas to the family and home. Often house repairs are needed.

Your love planet Mercury is 'out of bounds' until the 12th, and so in your romantic life you are searching outside your normal circles. (The grass always looks greener outside your own field.) The eclipse might shake up the love life, but singles will still be dating and going out. Mercury will be in Capricorn until the 16th, which creates more caution in love. You favour older, more established kinds of people. On the 16th Mercury enters Aquarius, your 12th house. Spiritual compatibility becomes very important now. Mercury is powerful in Aquarius – he is 'exalted' there. So your social grace is good. Romantic opportunities happen in spiritual venues – in meditation seminars, spiritual lectures, kirtans and charity events. Venus moves into your own sign on the 13th, further enhancing your social grace.

February

Best Days Overall: 6, 7, 14, 15, 23, 24, 25
Most Stressful Days Overall: 3, 4, 5, 10, 11, 16, 17
Best Days for Love: 6, 7, 8, 10, 11, 14, 15, 16, 17, 23, 24, 25, 26, 27
Best Days for Money: 1, 2, 8, 9, 10, 11, 17, 18, 19, 20, 26, 27, 28, 29
Best Days for Career: 1, 2, 10, 11, 16, 17, 19, 20, 28, 29

Except for the Moon – and that only occasionally – there are *no* planets in the Western, social sector of your chart. Zero. Zip. Nada. This is highly unusual. Further, your 1st house of self is immensely powerful this month. You are in the strongest period of personal independence in your year (and will be next month too). The month ahead is all about you. Your personal initiative, your personal abilities, are what matter now. Other people are important but they don't determine your life or happiness. You are responsible for your own happiness. If changes need to be made, this is the time to make them. (All the planets are moving forward until the 17th, so changes will happen quickly.) This is the time to develop personal initiative. Others might not agree with your moves, but they will come round eventually.

It is a happy and prosperous month. Venus has been in your sign since January 13. So you look good and have an intuitive sense of style. There is much sex appeal to the image. It is a good period to buy clothing or personal accessories. Your love planet Mercury moves into your sign on the 3rd and spends the rest of the month here. Thus love comes to you with little effort on your part. You have love on your terms. If you are in a relationship the beloved is putting your interest ahead of his or her own. When the Sun enters your sign on the 19th you begin a yearly personal pleasure peak. The delights of the senses are open to you.

Your financial planet is still in your 10th house – at the top of your chart – until the 16th, so review our discussion of this last month. Mars in Sagittarius can be speculative and risk taking – money comes easily and is spent easily. But on the 16th, as Mars enters Capricorn, you become more financially conservative. The financial judgement improves. You show more of a long-term approach to wealth and will probably avoid speculations. Friends and social connections are playing a big role in finances – also online activities and the high-tech world. You are probably spending more on technology this period but it can bring you money as well. It seems like a good investment.

Health is excellent this month. If you like you can enhance it even further through ankle and calf massage until the 19th and through foot massage after then. You always benefit from spiritual-type therapies, but even more so after the 19th.

March

Best Days Overall: 4, 5, 12, 13, 22, 23
Most Stressful Days Overall: 2, 3, 8, 9, 14, 15, 29, 30
Best Days for Love: 8, 9, 10, 11, 17, 18, 22, 23, 27, 28
Best Days for Money: 1, 8, 9, 17, 18, 24, 25, 27, 28
Best Days for Career: 1, 8, 9, 14, 15, 17, 18, 27, 28

Another happy and healthy month, Pisces. Enjoy!

Jupiter travels with Pluto all month. This is excellent for college-level (or college-bound) students. There is success in their studies and happy surprises. A foreign trip could materialize too. Your financial planet Mars will also travel with Jupiter from the 15th to the 21st, signalling a nice payday happening. Other happy financial developments are also in the works.

You are still in one of your yearly personal pleasure peaks until the 20th. So it is good to pamper the body a bit (as long as you don't overdo things), and to get it in the shape that you want.

On the 20th the Sun enters your money house and you begin a yearly financial peak. Money comes the old-fashioned way through work and productive service. You can earn through the area of health these days. Your financial planet will be in your 11th house of friends pretty much all month. Thus it is still good to be involved with friends, groups and group activities. Also good (from the financial perspective) to be involved in trade and professional organizations.

Health, as we've said, is excellent. There are no planets (with the exception of the Moon, and that only occasionally) in stressful aspect with you. Your good health shows in your personal appearance and you radiate health and wellness – which is a form of beauty. You can enhance the health still further through foot massage and spiritual-type therapies until the 20th, and through scalp and face massage afterwards. Physical exercise is helpful after that date too. Up to the 20th good health means 'looking good', not just 'no symptoms'. After the 20th good health means good financial health too.

Saturn makes a temporary move into your 12th house on the 23rd. This is really a flirtation with the 12th house, as he will move back into the 11th on July 2, but it is a harbinger of things to come. You will be taking a more scientific and rational attitude to spirituality and your spiritual practice. You will be more inclined to daily, disciplined spiritual practice. Love is wonderful, but you need some science to back it up.

Romance is a bit complicated until the 10th as your love planet is still retrograde. But after then – and especially after the 16th – love is happy. From the 4th to the 16th love and love opportunities happen at spiritual venues. After the 16th love once again seeks you out. The spouse, partner or current love is unusually devoted to you.

April

Best Days Overall: 1, 2, 9, 10, 18, 19, 28, 29
Most Stressful Days Overall: 5, 6, 11, 12, 25, 26
Best Days for Love: 1, 2, 5, 6, 7, 8, 10, 11, 15, 16, 17, 20, 21, 25, 26, 30
Best Days for Money: 6, 7, 8, 14, 15, 16, 20, 21, 22, 24, 25, 26
Best Days for Career: 6, 11, 12, 14, 24

The planetary power has shifted to the lower half – the night side – of your Horoscope. Although there are happy career developments going on, the focus now should be more on the home, family and your emotional wellness. It is time to enhance the psychological infrastructure for future career success. Get things right at home and with the family – get right emotionally – and the career will take care of itself in due course.

Venus moves into your 4th house on the 3rd and will stay there for several months. This is a wonderful time for redecorating the home or buying objects of beauty for the home. There will be more socializing at home and with the family too.

You are still in the midst of a yearly financial peak until the 19th. You are earning from work, the health field, or from a business partnership or joint venture (these opportunities come after the 11th). Your financial planet will spend the month in your spiritual 12th house, enhancing your financial intuition (it is always good, but now it's better than ever). Once again, you are spending on technology, but you can earn from it as well. Online activities are favoured.

Jupiter is still travelling with Pluto all month. This can bring career related travel and other positive career developments. Perhaps you are more involved with foreign countries in the online world as well. You already understand much about the spiritual dimensions of wealth, but this month you go deeper into the subject. It is a month for 'miracle money'. Natural money will come, but miracle money – the money that comes 'out of the blue' – is much more joyful.

Health is excellent this month. There is only one planet, Venus, in stressful alignment with you (although the Moon will make short-term and occasional stressful aspects). You can enhance health further through face and scalp massage and physical exercise until the 19th. After the 19th neck and throat massage will be beneficial.

Venus will go 'out of bounds' on the 3rd, meaning that your intellectual tastes seem outside the mainstream. The spouse, partner or current love is outside his or her usual sphere in finance. Your sexuality is more experimental this period too.

Love is happy. Your love planet Mercury is moving fast this month, your social life is equally fast paced. Until the 11th there's not much you need to do to attract love; it pursues you. After the 11th love awaits you as you pursue your financial goals and with people involved in your finances. Wealth is a great romantic allurement.

May

Best Days Overall: 6, 7, 15, 16, 25, 26
Most Stressful Days Overall: 2, 3, 8, 9, 23, 24, 29, 30
Best Days for Love: 2, 3, 4, 5, 12, 13, 14, 23, 24, 29, 30
Best Days for Money: 3, 4, 5, 12, 14, 15, 18, 19, 22, 25, 26
Best Days for Career: 3, 8, 9, 12, 22

Health needs more watching after the 20th, but there is nothing serious afoot – only a natural period of lower energy. (This is in the nature of things – energy waxes and wanes.) Make sure to get enough rest. Until the 20th health is enhanced through neck and throat massage. After then arm and shoulder massage will be beneficial, as will fresh air and breathing exercises. Good emotional health is very important after the 20th. Work to keep the moods positive and constructive. This is a month for making psychological progress and for psychological-type breakthroughs.

On the 20th you enter the midnight hour of your year (figuratively speaking). The activities of the night dominate. Though outer activity ceases, mighty things are happening inwardly. The body is preparing for the new dawn. And, so it is with you.

The two planets involved with love are in your 4th house this month. Venus, the generic love planet, will be there all month while Mercury, your actual love planet, will be there from the 12th to the 29th. There is more socializing from home and with the family. A romantic evening at home is preferable to a night out on the town. Intellectual compatibility and good communication are important in love (both love planets are in Gemini), but emotional intimacy is also important. One of the dangers with this position is a tendency to live in the past when it comes to love. Perhaps you're trying to re-live happy experiences, or perhaps you're comparing the present to the past. Thus you are not in the 'now'. You don't feel the actual experience of what is happening. The past might have contained happy experiences, but the 'now' is always the best – for it is real.

Often with this position one meets old flames. Sometimes it is the actual old flame and sometimes it is someone who reminds you of him or her, someone who embodies the same qualities. This is for the purpose of healing and resolution. Usually nothing comes of it (although it can). Your love planet Mercury will be 'out of bounds' from the 17th onwards. Thus in love matters you're outside your normal sphere – outside your personal boundaries.

The month ahead looks prosperous. Mars, your financial planet, moves into your own sign on the 13th and spends the month there. This brings windfalls and happy financial opportunity. Money pursues you rather than vice versa. The money people in your life are favourably disposed to you.

June

Best Days Overall: 3, 4, 11, 12, 13, 21, 22, 28, 29
Most Stressful Days Overall: 5, 6, 19, 20, 26, 27, 30
Best Days for Love: 1, 3, 4, 9, 10, 11, 12, 19, 20, 21, 22, 26, 27
Best Days for Money: 3, 4, 8, 11, 12, 14, 15, 18, 21, 22, 27, 30
Best Days for Career: 5, 6, 8, 18, 27, 30

There is a slight shift of power to the Western, social sector of your Horoscope, but the main power is in the East, the sector of self. Mars in your sign almost all month makes the East stronger so the month ahead is still about you. However, it will be good to cultivate your social skills a bit more.

Mars in your sign brings financial windfalls and opportunity. You dress expensively and have a tendency to flaunt your wealth. You take on the image of a money person and people see you this way.

We have two eclipses this month. The first is a lunar eclipse on the 5th. It affects you strongly so reduce your schedule at this time. (In fact you should take it easy until the 21st, but especially around the eclipse period.) This eclipse occurs in your 10th house of career, signalling career changes. There can be shakeups in your company or industry. Government regulations can change the rules of the game. There are personal dramas in the lives of bosses, parents and parent figures. This eclipse affects both Mars and Venus. Thus there are financial disturbances and a need to make financial changes. Cars and communication equipment can behave erratically, and often repairs are needed. It would be a good idea to drive more carefully this period too. Siblings and sibling figures have personal dramas. Neptune, the ruler of your Horoscope, is sideswiped by this eclipse (but not too badly). Thus you need to redefine yourself, your image and your presentation to the world. Every lunar eclipse affects children and children figures and this one is no different. They too have personal dramas and need a good re-evaluation of themselves, their image and how they present themselves to others.

The solar eclipse of the 21st occurs in your 5th house and again impacts on children and children figures (this seems a non-stop process that goes on all year). They are not only forced to keep redefining themselves, but also have to make important financial changes. For you this eclipse brings job changes. This can be where you are or with another firm. There are disturbances at the workplace. The health regime will also change in the coming months.

On the 21st the Sun moves into your 5th house and, once the effects of the eclipse quieten down, life should become more fun. You are in a yearly personal pleasure peak. The focus on the children and children figures in your life is a good thing too – they need your attention.

July

Best Days Overall: 1, 9, 10, 19, 20, 27, 28
Most Stressful Days Overall: 2, 3, 16, 17, 23, 24, 29, 30
Best Days for Love: 1, 6, 7, 8, 9, 10, 16, 17, 19, 20, 23, 24, 25, 26, 27, 28
Best Days for Money: 2, 3, 4, 5, 11, 12, 14, 15, 21, 22, 23, 24, 29, 30, 31
Best Days for Career: 2, 3, 4, 5, 14, 15, 23, 24, 29, 30, 31

Retrograde activity reached a peak in June and is still very strong this month, with at least 40 per cent (from the 12th onwards) and sometimes 50 per cent (until then) of the planets in retrograde motion. With your career planet travelling backwards and with most of the planets below the horizon, you might as well focus on home, family and the children. Only time will resolve career issues; this is a good month for taking a vacation. Your 5th house of fun and creativity is very strong until the 22nd. With so much gridlock in the world, you might as well take some time out.

We have another Lunar Eclipse on the 5th – the third one this year. It occurs in your 11th house and is basically benign for you. Still, it won't hurt to take it easy anyway. It could impact on some area of your actual Natal chart – the one cast especially for you. This eclipse brings dramas in the lives of friends and upheavals in professional or trade organizations you're involved with. Computers and high-tech equipment can behave erratically, and often needs repair, adjustment or replacement. Children and children figures in your life are impacted by the eclipse and should be kept out of harm's way and take it nice and easy. They seem to have some social crisis – a testing of their relationships. Three other planets are impacted by this eclipse, but, happily, not that directly. Thus you too can have a testing of your current love relationship. The beloved can be having a personal drama. A parent or parent figure has some personal crisis and needs to make financial changes. Children and children figures once again need to redefine themselves, how they think of themselves and how they want others to think of them. You could be having a brief financial disturbance – perhaps a sudden expense. A course correction in finance seems in order, but it doesn't appear too severe – more of a friendly tap than a major blow.

Last month, on the 28th, Mars moved into your money house, where he'll remain for the rest of the year. This signals increased earnings, but with much challenge and work involved. Financially things should get easier after the 22nd.

Health is good. You can enhance it further through right diet and abdominal massage until the 22nd and through chest massage after then. Give the heart more attention after the 22nd.

August

Best Days Overall: 5, 6, 15, 16, 23, 24
Most Stressful Days Overall: 13, 14, 19, 20, 25, 26, 27
Best Days for Love: 3, 4, 8, 15, 16, 17, 18, 19, 20, 23, 24, 28, 29
Best Days for Money: 2, 8, 9, 11, 17, 18, 20, 25, 26, 27, 29
Best Days for Career: 2, 11, 20, 25, 26, 27, 29

This is the kind of month where you work hard but also play hard. You manage to do both.

Health is good, yet you seem focused on it. Hopefully this focus is more on a healthy lifestyle and preventative actions. Beware the tendency to magnify little things – minor annoyances – into big issues. Job seekers have good fortune this month, likewise those who employ others. Children and children figures are having a prosperous month – a period of peak earnings.

The focus on health will stand you in good stead for after the 22nd, when health will need more attention. There is nothing serious afoot, just a period of lower energy. This waxing and waning of personal energy is in the natural order of things and nothing to be alarmed about. Until the 22nd enhance the health through massage of the heart reflex point (shown in the yearly report) and chest massage. After the 22nd health is enhanced through abdominal massage. Earth-based therapies, such as mud packs or bathing in waters with a high mineral content – are also beneficial.

On the 23rd the Sun enters your 7th house of love, while Mercury, your love planet, entered this house on the 20th. You are beginning a yearly love and social peak. You've had better peaks in your life, and will have better in the future. This love peak seems lukewarm. The Eastern sector of self is still the dominant sector (by some distance), so you are still very much into yourself and this is not that great for love. Your challenge will be to balance your personal interests with those of others. (You have been more popular in your life.) Love opportunities happen at the workplace and perhaps with co-workers. You're also attracted to health professionals and to people involved in your health. There will be more socializing with the family and from home. Family and family connections are playing a big role in the love life.

Finance still requires more work and there are still challenges to overcome, but it is easier than last month. There are financial disagreements with friends, parents or parent figures that need to be resolved. There is also a tendency to be too quick in your financial decision-making. You need to slow down a bit. Sleep on things before deciding.

The good news financially is that we will have a Grand Trine in the Earth signs, so practical sense should be stronger from the 22nd onwards.

September

Best Days Overall: 1, 2, 3, 11, 12, 20, 21, 29, 30
Most Stressful Days Overall: 9, 10, 16, 17, 22, 23
Best Days for Love: 2, 3, 9, 13, 14, 16, 17, 18, 19, 22, 23, 26, 27
Best Days for Money: 4, 5, 6, 7, 14, 15, 16, 17, 22, 23, 24, 25
Best Days for Career: 6, 7, 16, 17, 22, 23, 24, 25

You remain in a yearly love and social peak until the 22nd. Like last month, the challenge is to balance your personal interests with those of others. The fact that you're not that much in need of others can make love problematic. There is no burning desire for a relationship. Still, this is an active social period (relatively speaking) for the year. It is active romantically and with friendships.

Finance gets more complicated this month. Your financial planet Mars begins to go into retrograde motion on the 9th (this I see as a good thing – you need to slow down a bit in finance) and, after the 22nd, receives very challenging aspects. You will have to work harder to achieve your financial goals. Often, challenging aspects are good for finance. They dispel complacency. You have to pay attention and overcome the challenges. People often prosper under challenging aspects – but they do have to put in more effort than usual.

Retrograde activity once again spikes to a yearly high, matching the level reached earlier in June. From the 9th to the 12th 60 per cent of the planets are retrograde. Moreover, before and after this period the figure is 50 per cent. The pace of life, personally and in the world, slows down.

You can use these planetary retrogrades to your advantage. They give you time. You can review the various departments of your life and see where improvements can be made. Then, when the planets start moving forward again, you can move forward too. (This will happen in November and December.)

Health still needs some attention until the 22nd. Like last month there is nothing serious afoot, just the natural waxing and waning of your personal energy. This is a temporary low period. The important thing is to maintain high energy levels – to rest when tired. Low energy invites opportunistic infections into the system. Enhance the health through abdominal massage until the 22nd. Look up the reflex to the small intestine and massage it regularly. (See the chart in the health section of the yearly report.) Health will improve dramatically after the 22nd and, if you like, you can enhance it further through hip massage and more attention to the kidneys. A herbal kidney cleanse might be a good idea if you feel under the weather.

The spouse, partner or current love is having a banner financial month from the 22nd onwards. He or she will pick up the slack in your finances. This is a good period to make or pay down debt, depending on your need. It is also good for tax planning and, if you're of appropriate age, for estate planning.

October

Best Days Overall: 9, 10, 17, 18, 26, 27
Most Stressful Days Overall: 6, 7, 13, 14, 19, 20
Best Days for Love: 3, 9, 10, 13, 14, 17, 18, 21, 22, 26
Best Days for Money: 1, 2, 4, 5, 11, 12, 13, 14, 19, 20, 21, 23, 28, 29, 30, 31
Best Days for Career: 4, 5, 13, 14, 19, 20, 21, 23, 31

The upper, day side of your Horoscope is now the dominant side. It is daytime in your year. The focus needs to be on your career and outer objectives. Jupiter, your career planet, began to move forward again on September 13, so the timing is fortuitous. Even your home and family planet, Mercury, is above the horizon this month. Moreover, he will begin to go backwards on the 14th. You can let home and family issues sort themselves out now; focus on the career.

Finances are still stressful and confusing this month. Mars, your financial planet, is retrograde all month and, until the 23rd, is receiving stressful aspects. The cosmos is calling you to be more perfect in your financial affairs. To work harder, overcome complacency, and gain more clarity here. Like last month, the spouse, partner or current love – who is having an excellent financial month – should be able to pick up the slack. Finances will improve after the 23rd but still be challenging.

Health is good this month, with only one planet (aside from the Moon) in stressful aspect with you. You respond well to detox regimes all month. Safe sex and sexual moderation are important all month as well.

The retrograde of Mercury on the 14th complicates the love life. Don't make any important love decisions after the 14th. Love seems unusually erotic this month. Sexual magnetism seems the main allurement. Venus moves into your 7th house of love on the 2nd, which indicates some kind of relationship happening. But beware of hyper-perfectionism and destructive criticism. Again, there is a need to balance your personal interest with that of the beloved.

Your 8th house of regeneration is strong until the 23rd and after that the sign of Scorpio (the natural ruler of the 8th house) is powerful. This is a month for decluttering your life on all levels. Take stock of your possessions and get rid of what you don't need or use. Clear the decks. On a deeper level this applies to your emotional and mental patterns as well. If they are not helpful to you they should go in the psychic dustbin. It is a month for purgation on all the different levels. You will feel so much better afterwards. The month ahead is excellent for projects involving personal transformation and re-invention. The purges foster this.

November

> Best Days Overall: 5, 6, 14, 15, 22, 23
> Most Stressful Days Overall: 2, 3, 4, 10, 16, 30
> Best Days for Love: 2, 3, 4, 10, 12, 13, 14, 21, 22, 23
> Best Days for Money: 2, 7, 8, 11, 16, 19, 25, 26
> Best Days for Career: 2, 11, 16, 19

There are a lot of nice things happening in your career this month. First, the upper, day side of your Horoscope is dominant. Secondly, you enter a yearly career peak on the 21st. Thirdly, Jupiter and Pluto are again travelling together. This all adds up to a successful month ahead. The career focus is intense – and this intensity spells success. There is career-related travel, and educational opportunities related to the career. And your good work ethic impresses superiors.

Jupiter travelling with Pluto is a happy aspect for college-level students. They are successful in their studies. Even those who are college-bound but not there yet have success. There is good fortune in legal issues (if you're involved in them).

Finances are starting to improve. On the 14th Mars starts to move forward, so there is forward progress in finance. Gridlock is over. The financial aspects are easier than they were last month too (not easy, but easier). You still need to work hard to attain your financial goals, but if you put the work in, prosperity will happen. Until the 21st you need to resolve some financial conflicts between you, the beloved and a parent or parent figure.

Our fourth and final lunar eclipse of the year occurs on the 30th. This affects you strongly, so take a nice easy, relaxed schedule then. It occurs in your 4th house of home and family bringing dramas at home and with family members. Family members are apt to be more temperamental this period so be more patient with them. A parent or parent figure has a personal crisis. Once again he or she has to make important financial changes. He or she also needs to redefine the self – the image and self-concept. The events of the eclipse force this. Since this eclipse impacts on Neptune, the ruler of your Horoscope, you too are forced to redefine yourself. Thus, in the coming months, there will be changes in the wardrobe, hairstyle and overall appearance.

Health is good this month but needs some attention after the 21st. Since there is only one planet in stressful alignment with you then, there is nothing serious afoot. It is just a period of lower energy. Make sure to rest more. Up until the 21st health can be enhanced through detox regimes. After the 21st give more attention to the liver and thighs – thigh massage will be powerful.

December

Best Days Overall: 2, 3, 11, 12, 19, 20, 21, 29, 30, 31
Most Stressful Days Overall: 1, 7, 8, 13, 14, 27, 28
Best Days for Love: 2, 3, 5, 6, 7, 8, 11, 12, 13, 14, 22, 23, 24
Best Days for Money: 5, 6, 8, 13, 14, 16, 22, 23, 27
Best Days for Career: 8, 13, 14, 16, 27

The cosmic chess board is being rearranged this month and while you might not feel it now, you will certainly feel it next year. A solar eclipse on the 14th is heralding the coming changes. This eclipse will be powerful, so take it nice and easy over that period. Whatever needs to be done should be done, but non-essentials are better being rescheduled. Spend more quiet time at home. Read a book or watch a movie – best of all meditate. Meditation is the best way to get through a strong eclipse.

This eclipse, the second solar eclipse and sixth eclipse of the year, occurs in your 10th house of career, and announces important career changes. Keep in mind that your career planet, Jupiter, will move into your 12th house on the 20th as well, creating important career changes too. So, there are shakeups in your company or industry. There are dramas in the lives of bosses, parents or parent figures. And since this eclipse impacts on Neptune, the ruler of your Horoscope, there are personal dramas as well. Sometimes there is a detox of the body. Once again you have a need to redefine yourself – your image and self-concept. This will result in wardrobe and image changes in the coming months. You will change your 'look', your presentation to others. College-level students have to make important financial changes. One of the parents or parent figures in your life has a social crisis – the current relationship gets tested.

Since you are in a yearly career peak this month, this eclipse is likely to open career doors for you. The career looks very successful.

Health needs attention until the 21st. You can enhance the health through more rest and through hip massage. A herbal liver cleanse might also be a good idea. Health will improve dramatically after the 21st however, and if you would like to enhance it further give more attention to the back, spine and knees. Back and knee massage will be very helpful.

Love is high on the agenda until 21st. Your love planet Mercury is in your 10th career house at the top of your chart. This shows focus and power. You find love and social opportunities as you pursue your career goals and with people involved in your career. You mix with people of importance and prestige at this time, and status is also a romantic turn-on. You might be too quick to fall in love this period – you leap before you look. But this will change after the 21st and you'll become much more cautious.